Lost Innocence

Lost Innocence
The Growth of an Academic's Mind

Roderick McGillis

Rock's Mills Press
Rock's Mills, Ontario • Oakville, Ontario
2025

Published by
Rock's Mills Press
www.rocksmillspress.com

Copyright © 2025 by Roderick McGillis.
All rights reserved. No part of this publication may be reproduced, distributed, or transmitted in any form or by any means, including photocopying, recording, or other electronic or mechanical methods, without the prior written permission of the publisher, except in the case of brief quotations embodied in critical reviews and certain other non-commercial uses permitted by copyright law. For permission requests, contact the publisher at:
customer.service@rocksmillspress.com

For adoption, trade, and bulk orders, contact the publisher at:
customer.service@rocksmillspress.com

Rock's Mills Press (both the name and the styling in Rockwell Bold) is a registered trademark and is used under license.

Library and Archives Canada Cataloguing in Publication data has been applied for.

For Kyla and Kate who will, I hope, remember good times.
For Frances who has accompanied me for most of this journey.
Finally, for my mother and sister, Bessie Helen Ferguson
and Sandra Ann Meyer.

In Memoriam
Jean Perrot (1937–2023)

Contents

Acknowledgements | 9

1. Beginnings—Smiths Falls, Ontario | 13
2. Hitchhiking and Summer Jobs | 45
3. University Years—Bliss It Was in that Time... | 57
4. Summer 1968—Summer of Love One Year Later | 77
5. McMaster University | 80
6. Digression on Illnesses | 86
7. Teaching High School | 90
8. Marriage | 95
9. England for Three Years | 100
10. Return to Canada and Calgary | 126
11. Mexico, Mother, and More | 141
12. An Academic Career | 148
    a. My Mother b. University Life c. Networking
13. Travel in No Particular Order | 178
    a. South Africa b. Russia c. Spain d. Italy
    e. Israel f. Scandinavia g. Australia
    h. New Zealand i. China j. Germany and the Czech Republic
    k. Switzerland l. France m. England and (briefly) Ireland
    n. Mexico o. The American South p. Summation
14. A Way of Life | 244
15. Publications, Children's Literature, and Beyond | 253
16. Accolades | 271
17. Teaching | 277
18. Storytelling | 287
19. Retirement | 292
20. Wrapping Up, or an Endless Ending | 296

Endnote | 297

Acknowledgements

First, I thank David Stover of Rock's Mills Press who was brave enough to accept this book for publication. I realize than not everyone is going to want to read of the peregrinations of an academic. I just hope there is enough of interest here to hold a curious reader, whether an academic or not. I also owe Benjamin Lefebvre a debt for suggesting I contact Rock's Mills Press just when I was contemplating shelving this project. As for academics, I have a long list of them to thank. Here goes: Northrop Frye, Leslie Fiedler, John Baird, Tom Cain, Joseph Sigman, David Knight, Brian Merrilees, Jane Millgate, Graeme Petrie, Ian Fletcher, and D. J. Gordon got me started. Later as colleagues, I note Sandra Beckett, Thomas Van Der Walt, David Rudd, William Raeper, Karen Sands-O'Connor, John Stephens, Clare Bradford, Anita Moss, Björn Sundmark, Karen Coats, Anna Jackson, Jan Susina, George Bodmer, Joel Chaston, Jill May, Jon Stott, Cristina Perez Valverde, Maria Nikolajeva, James Holt McGavran, Jr., Kenneth Kidd, Perry Nodelman, Richard Flynn, U. C. Knoepflmacher, Shaobo Xie, Michael Sharp. Special notice goes to Colin Manlove, Stephen Prickett, and Jack Zipes. Colleagues who became dear friends: Jean Perrot, Kerry Mallan, Dieter Petzold, David Kent, John Docherty, Victor Ramraj, Anne Hiebert Alton, Om Dwivedi, John Pennington, and Nancy Ellen Batty. I also note the publisher Robert Trexler. Not all of these people remain with us, but none are forgotten. Two writer friends have inspired me, Keath Fraser and Laurent Chabin; the latter especially has encouraged me over the years and translated my two forays into fiction. I would be remiss if I did not mention Laurence Sterne and George MacDonald, the writers who initiated my work when I was a graduate student, first at McMaster University and then at Reading University.

The list of academics whose work has influenced me is too large to set out here. Names will appear throughout this book.

My working life was mostly at the University of Calgary, although I did spend time at a few other institutions as Visiting Professor: University of Puerto Rico, University of Winnipeg, Queensland University of Technology, Roehampton University, and Hollins University. Thanks to all these places and those who hosted me. Students from Calgary I remember fondly are John

Kerr, Stefan Smith, Erina Harris, Jake Kennedy, Catherine McLauglin, Mavis Reimer. Special notice goes to William Hageman and Brigitte Clarke.

In retirement, I have found people who have encouraged me to keep going. These include Don Mabie and Wendy Toogood, John Boivin, Bob Toews, and Claire Paradis of the Nakusp Public Library.

As ever, Kyla and Kate have been good friends and inspiration. Most importantly, I have had the continued and continuing support of Frances Batycki, without whom I would never have travelled so far. Let's hope that we have a few more trails to travel together.

A final note: a few names along the way here I have changed for the sake of diplomacy. This is not a tell-all book, but you can never be too careful.

Even after years of journaling or jotting down passing thoughts, the act of sharing your first-person stories with the world can feel like a kind of perversion, like sweating all over someone's couch or coughing into the clam dip at a cocktail party. On the wrong day, even popular writers' rallying cries—such as Anne Lamott's *Bird by Bird* or Natalie Goldberg's *Writing Down the Bones*—feel like gorgeously embossed invitations to spread your germs far and wide.
—Heather Havrilesky, "True Stories,"
Bookforum, September/October/November 2015

Some things are best not remembered.

Memory is a hobgoblin, a practical joker and a shape-shifter.

Beware, beware, the stirrings of this mercurial creature.
Perhaps weave a circle round it thrice.

Your past begins the day you were born and to disregard it is cheating yourself of who you really are.
—Bob Dylan

Let's adapt M Baudelaire:
Mémoire, ce monstre délicat,
—Hypocrite lecteur,—mon semblable,—mon frère!

CHAPTER ONE

Beginnings: Smiths Falls, Ontario

88 Russell Street East, 528-J—the address and phone number of my childhood home in Smiths Falls, Ontario. I can understand, I think, why the address stays in my memory, but not why I retain the phone number. Indeed, numbers do not stay with me easily. I have no recollection, for that matter, of the several phone numbers or addresses that I have had since leaving the Russell Street house for good in 1966. Perhaps living 19 years plus two more summers in that house riveted these numbers in my brain. I can't recall when our phone service changed from a party line with an operator to direct-dial, but I suspect this was in the late 1950s. The years in this house I have largely forgotten or repressed, although I have no doubt they were formative, crucial to the person or persons I now am. I am now old enough for that long-term memory, so long folded away in some inaccessible cranial cell, to slither into consciousness slowly but surely enough for me to attempt something of a reconstruction of the past. The past is another country, fantasy-filled for future fashioning. Memory is miasma, someone once said, but the air is not all bad. The disease memory causes may be the disease of conceit, or it may be the dis-ease that unearths a satisfying sense of life and its stubborn proclivities.

But why do I have the audacity to embark on such an attempt? Is this a solipsistic exercise? Who in the world would be interested in reading about my past, my growing up, my experiences in both the closed and the wide worlds? Frankly, I have no idea. A life's a life, for all that. A life worth living is a life worth sharing. When I was quite young, I was convinced that my life was miserable, as miserable as any life could be. No one had the misery I had. Before too long, I learned that this innocent ennui was no less real for being untrue. My life had its miserable moments, perhaps many of these, but really, golly gee, I had it pretty good. Whatever force pervades this sphere and doles out experience after experience to this person and that, I received preferable treatment. I mean, life is beautiful, eh. It has been a good ride. For the most part, I've stood in tall cotton, wandered through a fat city, lived the good life, and eaten high off the hog. Spice has sprinkled my days. The sting that inevitably comes cannot cancel days and nights in the enchanted forest. The dream of midsummer has stayed for a few more seasons.

And so I go back to that Russell Street house. My first memory, if this is in fact a memory and not some concoction of my youthful anger misplaced only because innocent, sees me waking in the night and hearing harsh voices, the voices of my mother and father as they hurl invectives at each other. And through the darkened doorway of my bedroom, I see blood on my mother's face. Years later, when I was sixteen, my mother asked me to take a photograph of her bruised and swollen face after another one of these domestic nightmares. My father found and destroyed that photograph, but I had secreted the negative and when my father died in 1999, I had that negative processed. I had not seen my father since November 1969, but I had the vision of my first memory and the imprint of that photograph with me through the years to remind me just why I remember so little from those first nineteen years, and just why I did not go to my father's funeral.

Memory intrigues me both for its hit-and-miss recapture of the past and for its intricate connection with fiction. What we remember, or what I remember at least, strikes me as a nice combination of that which actually happened and that which we—or I, at least—imagine happened. How to separate memory from fantasy is not so much a problem as a needless concern. A needless concern is nevertheless a concern, and so my point here is simply a warning: reader—mon semblable,—mon frère!—beware. The writer never fully knows the truthfulness of what he or she writes. This never fully knowing performs the beauty of writing. Not only do we discover our life in the writing of it, but we also create this life in the writing of it. Life writing is a term literary people use for a certain form of autobiographical writing; it means fashioning a life by writing that life. I hasten to add that writing, what I am doing right now as I tap the keys and see the words appear on the computer screen, is not necessarily tied to letters on a sheet of paper or a computer screen. We can write our lives in many ways. Another way for me to say this is to note that we have many choices when it comes to performing our lives. We come into being through performance of one kind or another. Our lives consist of a myriad of connected performances. We are judged by how well we have performed in any given part. We can judge ourselves by performing a review of performance.

My early performances were moody, recalcitrant, whiny, and downright unpleasant. Apparently, I was prone to tantrums, or so I am given to understand. Who knows? I came along about three years after my sister, and in those days boys were often welcomed more warmly than girls. My welcome was warm, as far as I can tell, although I have an anecdote that tempers my sense of warmth. As long as I can remember, I have had a crooked nose. My nasal septum is not straight; it shifts to the right slightly. Apparently, when I was still in a perambulator, I came out of that perambulator and onto the hard surface of the Russell Street pavement. In short, I fell and landed on my proboscis. That I would tumble from a perambulator says something of my physical development as well as my resistance to confinement, I guess. Anyhow, my mother was always someone who preferred homeopathic remedies to nature's knocks, and so she did not take me to see old Doctor Walker; she just let my bloodied and bent nose heal as nature intended it to heal and in nature's good time. Ever since I have had a crooked nose. I'm not complaining, but I do worry when I think of having to undergo an operation and of the discomfort I will feel when they force that tube down my constricted right nostril. Anyhow, I have no memory of this mishap. This is the stuff of family legend, and family legend folds neatly into the remembrance of things past.

Another family legend has the four of us fishing near a weir not far from town on the road to Jasper. I must have been about four or maybe five. The land met the water just below the weir where the water was three or four feet deep, deep enough to cause trouble for anyone, such as myself, who could not swim. Somehow, I managed to tumble into the water right near the weir; my mother screamed and tossed her fishing rod aside; the hook on the end of her line nicely flew across the space between its starting point and my sister, entering my sister's lower lip; my sister cried; my mother ran to the shore; by the time she arrived at the shore, I had awkwardly but successfully swum to shore and climbed out of the water. I like to think this memory carries accurately from the past, and my sister has a scar on her lower lip that testifies to the event. She also carries a small scar on the side of her nose, caused by a shovel Roy Hollingsworth applied unpleasantly to her face during one of the backyard squabbles she often had. But these are memories better suited to others. For me, the memory of this incident marks my learning to swim.

And really, I have precious memories and few of things past. I do remember my first baseball glove. I was playing ball from a young age, and I dearly wanted a trapper, the glove first basemen wore. I pestered my mother asking and asking her for a trapper so I could play ball and not look like a duffer without a glove. She tried to tell me that she could not afford to buy a glove. They were too expensive for her modest budget. But I kept asking. And then one day my mother returned home from somewhere, and she had a broad smile on her face. She proudly announced that she had a baseball mitt for me; she had found one in a park. Apparently, it was just lying there on the ground waiting for her to pick it up and bring it home to me. Then she held out the object for me to take. What I saw was a somewhat battered pillow-like catcher's glove, the leather cracked and worn. It was round and stiff with padding. It was useless for any position other than catcher, and I was never going to be a catcher. I suspected someone had abandoned it in the park because of its ungainly uselessness. I fear that my reaction disappointed my mother. As so often in my childhood, I was an ungrateful son. I ought to have been sent to live east of Eden. Have I mentioned tantrums? Anyway, I did play catch on the street in front of our house, and for a while I used this fat mitt. Eventually, I saved enough money from my paper routes to purchase a fancy glove, not a trapper, but an all-purpose glove that served me well for several years. I suspect most of us have random memories such as this one.

As for my mother, she was, I fear, continuously disappointed by my actions. I remember how intensely I wanted a cowboy hat, a hat like Roy Rogers wore or even one like Hoot Gibson wore. I wanted a cowboy hat more than anything. Of course, I also wanted the holsters and pistols and other paraphernalia I saw the cowboys wear in the movies. But mostly I wanted a hat. My mother repeated many times that she could not afford such an expensive item. Then one summer, I can't remember exactly how old I was, we were up at the Swayne's cottage when my Uncle Chuck and Aunt Doris (Doris was my mother's only sister) arrived back from a trip to Mexico. This was noteworthy because members of our family did not travel to such exotic places, and so the return of Uncle Chuck and Aunt Doris was something everyone looked forward to. This was an event. They came home and drove to the Swayne's cottage to surprise us. Before I continue, I ought to let you know that my mother and Teresa Swayne were friends. They had met when they were both giving birth to sons, myself and David Swayne. Throughout my childhood Teresa and my mother were in a competition to see which one had the more impressive and successful son. They always traded our report card results to see whether David did better than I did or vice versa. Most often, David came up tops. Anyway, we were at the Swayne's cottage on Otter Lake when Uncle Chuck and Aunt Doris came back from Mexico. Of course, they brought us presents from their trip, and Aunt Doris was most proud of the present she and Chuck had brought for me. Doris knew how much I wanted a cowboy hat. And so she had purchased for me a gaudy and colourful Mexican sombrero complete with tassels dangling around the broad brim.

Tassels? What self-respecting cowboy wore a hat with tassels?

And besides, Mexicans were more often than not the bad guys in the movies. The Cisco Kid was an exception to the rule that Mexicans were greasers. And his sidekick, Pancho, was a duffer. I took one look at that hat and shrank inwards. Aunt Doris placed the hat on my head. While the crowd was looking at me, admiring my new hat, I reached up, removed the hat from my head, and began methodically pulling the tassels off the brim one by one. My audience greeted this action with puzzlement and no little consternation. My mother's puzzlement quickly became anger. She was livid. She promptly grabbed me by the arm and marched me over to the bunkhouse. Inside she told me just how rude and ungrateful I had been. Then she gave me what we used to call a licking. I rarely received corporal punishment when I was young, but this time I did. And sadly, I cannot end this story by saying I later bought a cowboy hat with my paper-route money. I knew my mother would not appreciate seeing me in a cowboy hat after this incident.

Before I list some random memories, I should say that, yes, I did have paper routes, two of them. In the early morning, I rose at 5:30 in order to pick up my copies of the *Globe and Mail* to deliver around town. This was a route that took me all over the place, and just for twenty-two papers. It was hardly worth the effort, and I did not keep the route for too long. The other route, however, was cash rich. After school I went down to Brinkman's grocery store to pick up my copies of the *Ottawa Journal* (no longer in existence) to deliver. I had some seventy to eighty customers, and they were all in a five- or six-block radius from where I lived. Many of the customers knew me, and at Christmas I received a bounty in tips. With the money from my paper routes, I bought the baseball glove, and I also bought a three-speed bicycle. And I socked much of what I earned in a bank account. My mother was already tutoring me to get ready to pay for my own education. What I do not remember is precisely when I began to deliver papers, but I was most likely around ten years old. By the summer when I was fourteen, turning fifteen, I was working full time at the Rideau Ferry. But this comes later.

Here is a collection of random memories: the delivery of bread and milk in horse-drawn carts, the milkman's name Walt Holiday, the delivery of ice blocks carried into the house in huge tongs and placed in the icebox, the rattling of coal as it tumbled into the coal bin in our basement, the burlap wall covering in the dining room and the sound of its removal just before the transformation of this room through the application of paint, the large burn hole in the sofa, courtesy of my father, covered discreetly with a blanket, the dish cupboard in the kitchen in which the glass was broken, again courtesy of my father, the sight and sound of donuts in hot grease, the bouncing of the wringer washing machine as it slowly moved across the kitchen floor in a slow rumba much to my mother's consternation, the frozen long johns and socks my mother wrestled into the house from the clothesline in winter, the snapped clothesline in the backyard winter after winter, the two nails bent across each other on the woodshed door to receive a bolt and serve as a lock, the pillow folded over the iron bedstead I used as a saddle in my pretend cowboy games, the blur of recognition when I saw my father and sister and Doctor Walker after a night of breathing coal dust, the struggle against unconsciousness the morning the dentist, accompanied by Doctor Walker, removed my teeth as I lay recumbent on the kitchen table, the taste of castor oil taken from a table spoon on Sunday mornings, the gathering around the radio in the evening to listen to *Gangbusters* or *The Lone Ranger* or some other drama, the taste of cascara bark taken whenever my parents thought this was necessary, the taste of sulfur and molasses, the taste of turpentine and sugar, the feel of castor oil on the palate. These tastes are the tastes of home remedies meant to kill worms, ward off germs, and keep us regular. I can, of course, dredge up more of such random bits of time, but these serve to indicate the distance we have traveled from that time to this time of cell phones, home computers, flat-screen televisions, and an array of technological wonders to serve us. Instead of providing more such small detail, I shall take one of these for extended consideration.

This is the story of the backyard clothesline. I have told this story elsewhere, but it seems suitable in this place because that clothesline is a metonymy for time itself, for memory, for the manner in which this narrative unfolds and for the manner in which we live our lives. At the back of our house was a woodshed, and attached to the outside back wall of the woodshed was a stoop. In the middle of this stoop a pole emerged from below the floor between five and six feet into the air, and attached near the top of this pole was a clothesline roller. The clothesline went clear the length of the backyard to another pole with another clothesline roller attached. This pole was just a few feet from the Perkins's side steps, which took anyone who wanted to visit into the Perkins's kitchen. Anyhow our clothesline spent a lot of time dragging the ground because each winter when my mother put hot, wet long johns, socks on metal stretchers, bed sheets, and other freshly washed items of clothing and bedding on the line, the combined weight of all this soon-to-be-frozen finery inevitably was too much for the line and it gave way dropping its load of washing to the snow-covered ground. By the time my mother discovered what had happened, the clothes were usually frozen, and I can still see her carrying pairs of frozen red long johns into the kitchen as if they were mannequins, headless wafer-thin bodies with arms and legs stiffly akimbo; this sight variously struck me as funny or frightening, but it always struck my mother as one of the many burdens she had to shoulder because of my father's failure to keep the property in order.

To get the clothes ready for this winter airing she had to wash them in what was even then a washing machine just one remove from metal tub and wash board; she had an old clunky wringer washer and as regular as the clothesline breaking were the howls of pain when the fleshly part of my mother's upper inner arm was gathered into the wringer. The machine itself danced about the kitchen floor while it swung the clothes to and fro, usually leaving a river in its traces. My mother always washed the kitchen floor when she used the washing machine.

One winter, after my mother had voiced many and vigorous complaints about the downed clothesline, my father decided he would fix it, fix it once and forever. Never would the recalcitrant clothesline come to earth again. Now I should tell you that my father was not the handiest man in town. When I came home from Cub Scouts with orders from Akela (who was in reality Mr. Knapp, Donny Knapp's father) to build a birdhouse for a competition to be judged by the Ladies Auxiliary, my father quickly took over and I knew my trial had begun. When complete, my birdhouse tilted distinctly like one of those old abandoned farm buildings that dot the southern Ontario landscape, and its entrance hole was rough, even jagged, so that any bird—I suspect a wren or even a hummingbird—must leave its feathers at the door when entering. I don't think I can take any credit for that birdhouse; even the paint job, such as it was, came from a brush in my father's not so steady hand. You see, when he worked, my father needed fortification, the kind that comes in a twenty-six-ounce bottle. We rarely saw the bottle, but the results of my father nipping from it were all too evident. Perhaps to him the birdhouse was perfectly symmetrical. To my small, unpracticed eye the birdhouse listed so much I wanted to hide it rather than take it to Cubs. But take it I did, and placed it among the other birdhouses that shone in painterly glory. All these others were examples of the carpenter's art: perfect and smooth, a veritable suburbia of tract houses fit for the finest birds. Red, green, white, yellow, orange: the bright primary colours set off beautifully the well-proportioned, many windowed aviary mansions. I was, to say the least, humiliated. So you'll never know the confusion I experienced when after the first, second, and third prizes had been awarded one of the ladies announced a special prize. (I still think of this as the booby prize.) Yes, my birdhouse was honoured because it was the only birdhouse of the lot that looked as if the child had actually built it himself. I showed my father the silver spoon with the wolf's head on it that I won thanks to his efforts, but I never did tell him why his birdhouse received its special honour.

Once my father recreated our bathroom, replacing the old raised toilet with a fancy new one level with the floor, moving both it and the sink away from the window, installing a new bathtub without legs, putting splendid pink and grey tiles halfway up the walls, and laying shiny charcoal linoleum on the floor. My father worked hard on this project; he also cursed hard and made life a misery for the rest of us in the house. The sounds that shot from behind that closed bathroom door were guaranteed to bemuse the curious and to put a quietness on the knowing. Night times were the worst, for it was as if the demon work had my father in thrall. He insisted on staying at his hammering, and sawing, and gluing, and plumbing, and cursing, and imbibing long into the dark hours of night. After nine weeks of work during which the McGillis family often paraded next door to the McCoons to use their bathroom, and during which we stayed out of my father's way as assiduously as we could, he emerged triumphant, the sweat upon his brow certainly gained not in vain. The new pink and grey bathroom shone as testimony to my father's hard work and ingenuity. This was his fifteen minutes of fame.

Back to the clothesline.

To survey the clothesline situation my father went through the woodshed and out onto the back stoop. Of course, the stoop was wearing its usual coat of winter ice fashioned from much stomping of feet and no application of shovel. My father discovered that the wire had snapped for the umpteenth time. The cold was just too much for the length of line, and father decided that not only would he have to take a short length of clothesline wire and reattach the snapped line together, but that he would also be wise to loosen the line somehow, to give it more slack. That way, when the cold drew the line tighter it wouldn't put too much strain upon it. To accomplish his end, he thought he would simply push the clothesline pole forward a little, tilt it a few degrees. When he tried pushing the pole, nothing happened because the hole through which it pierced the stoop was too tight to allow any tilt. Undaunted, my father stomped back into the woodshed and fetched an axe. The first swing of the axe, intended to enlarge the hole in the stoop floor, merely succeeded in jarring my father's shoulders and loosening several of his teeth. He also had to descend into the snow of the back yard to retrieve the axe head that had flown off with his powerful swing.

I suspect it was my father's rather loud utterance rather than the noise of the axe that brought Orville Hollingsworth and Homer Weir to their respective backyards to survey the goings on at their neighbour's. Orville just watched; Homer offered assistance. "Are you all right, Rod? Can I help?" "Yes, I'm fine, and no, assistance is not necessary." The line only needed a little slack and this was easy business, my father confidently asserted. After all, hadn't he remodeled the most impressive bathroom on Russell Street?

A second swing of the axe broke through the floor of the stoop. The axe disappeared followed by my father. He got a larger hole than he had planned on. It seems several planks that had been in need of replacing would now have to be replaced. Homer asked again: "Rod, are you all right?" My father did not deign to reply. He climbed out of the hole and proceeded to push on the pole, but still he could not budge it. Homer once again offered to help. My father refused to accept. He had the bright idea that if he climbed onto the roof of the woodshed he could put his two booted feet against the pole and shove with all the terrific force of his whole body. He got the stepladder and climbed onto the shed roof. He placed his feet against the pole, which was some eighteen inches or so from the roof. Trying to get his hands planted firmly behind him for a good shove was difficult because of the ice and snow on the roof. Anyhow, he got ready. Then he heaved all his weight forward down his legs and into those feet against the pole. His slippery boots slid one to each side of the pole and his prostrate body shot into air. He didn't stay airborne for long.

His groin hit the pole and his body tilted downward, and then he landed on the broken stoop headfirst. The sound of impact was rather unpleasant. Orville looked a little bewildered; Homer asked my father if he was all right. He got no answer. My father would not come to until the next day, and even then, he just stared into space and mumbled things about his pink and grey bathroom. Old Dr. Walker said he would come round in time, and that we should just keep talking to him about familiar things. We propped him up in the living room in front of the monstrous TV with doors that he had insisted on buying—the first TV on the block, he never tired of reminding us. People from the neighbourhood were eager to help, and I can still remember Bella French sitting for hours with my father showing him photographs of her husband Harvey as he lay in his coffin in her front parlour. "He looked so natural," she would say. "Pink," my father would reply. Just when we began to worry that Bella would take up permanent residence in our living room, my father snapped out of his pink funk.

All he said about the accident was that winter was no time to be fixing things outside. By spring it was clear that he had no will to return to the scene of his ignominy. The back stoop might never have been fixed had I not gone to grade nine that winter. You see, I was somehow forgotten in the school roster at the beginning of my grade nine year; the result was that I ended up in 9D, a non-academic group who were hopeless in English and Science and History and Math, but who were skilled in the ways of the lathe and saw. During the year several of the boys in the class worked out a deal with me: I did their homework and they did my projects in wood and metal shop. By spring this arrangement worked so well that I was on pretty good terms with the boys of 9D. So good, in fact, that I suggested they could show their appreciation for my unflagging work on their behalf after school hours by fixing the back stoop at my house. So: one Saturday morning in early May my mother was surprised to see four big fellows—Billy Grey, Earl Dwire, Art Lee, and Pedro MacLeod—enter our yard with planks, hammers, saws, nails, and other paraphernalia. When she saw what they were up to, she even allowed them to smoke. That was the first and last time that I fixed anything in the Russell Street house. I think it was also the last time my father ever fixed anything in the Russell Street house.

The house was a two-story brick structure with a rough basement. Unfinished is an understatement as a descriptor for the basement. The stone floor was uneven, the room dark and musty with the acrid scent of coal dust in the air. The dust came from the coal bin that occupied about a quarter of the space. The furnace filled the center of the room and the other couple of walls had rough shelving. The stairs led up to a narrow pantry that served as a coatroom, as well as a repository for canned foods and other stuff. Also stored where the pantry became stairs were two or three shotguns. I used to play in this small pantry, clicking the shotgun hammers and donning my father's winter caps and heavy plaid shirts that hung from hooks near the guns. The memory of those guns delivers to my mind's eye a particular winter weekend sometime in the mid-1950s.

I find myself with my father, uncle, and a collection of cousins at grandfather's cottage, a place raised on the edge of Rideau Lake's primeval slime, now frozen for the winter. For some insane reason we carry shotguns, family heirlooms used every fall for the annual duck-hunting safaris undertaken by my father and his brothers, John and Stan. Now we have these obscene shooters for some primitive ritual that will prove we are a family, a gaggle of laughter prompted by explosions of cannon thunder aimed at a Sears catalogue. What brings us here I can't remember: beer has helped and no doubt stronger spirits as well. But how and why we have come no longer matter. The bleary-eyed men hustle the giggle of children to the lake's edge for the shoot-out. We gather on the ice in front of the cottage facing the shore and the camera that appears as part of my mental picture. There we are: two young girls, ages eight and ten, two young boys, myself and my cousin, both of us thirteen, my father, wearing a beery smile sure to stay until our relatives depart, and my Uncle Charles, simple and unaware of the hatred lifting us into a photograph that will be forgotten before any of us sees it. Someone else takes the picture, the most fortunate of the party since he or she has dropped out of this personal history.

God, how miserable I am. Wearing one of those loosely hanging heavy wool sweaters with a zipper down the front that were the fashion at the time, I look as if I were a captive forced into some mysterious and horrid ritual that arouses all my fear and anguish. The sweater hangs on my lean frame making me look longer and leaner than I am, a beanpole. Gangling and hunched, I lean on the twelve-gauge shotgun as if it were a staff; I could be nothing more than rags and bones. What did I feel? Nothing more than fear. Of all the faces in this picture only mine refuses the festivity of the occasion. The others surrender. And there is my father, the master of the troupe, Prospero with a gun loaded with rye. We shoot the Sears catalogue, watch its torn and tattered pages fly like scared and scattered birds, and then go into the cottage to warm ourselves. I suppose we lit the stove and had a bite to eat. Maybe we played euchre or just told stories that made laughter warm the air. I always refused to laugh, as that photograph keeps reminding me.

Now that some sixty years and more have passed, can I remember what really happened that day? Certainly, we didn't expect to find anything irrevocable on that cold windy shore watching pages of a fat Sears catalogue flutter in bits until they landed on the snow. This was not ritual killing; no bloodletting; no smearing of hands in the warm life-blood of some Ontario animal. No bear. Yet some ritual was at work. That picture insists. It contains a romance. At the time, it was some kind of hell, the smoke from the rifles serving as the noxious fumes of brimstone, and the smiles and cheer of my relatives as punishment for my fear. The snow-covered land and lake strike white against the black of trees and farther shore underlining the simple conflicts. And on that far shore was a camp for physically handicapped children, a place that reminded me others were less fortunate.

That cottage was many things: California for the summer, but primitive in its slip of weeds and slime, a gathering place for family, a drinking port for the men of the family, a camp for autumn hunters, exotic territory for kids to explore, an ice rink in winter. The waterfront moved with water snakes, frogs, turtles, and minnows; it was more swamp than open water. In the overgrown meadow behind the cottage lived simpler versions of the creatures we fear: garter snakes and green frogs. The frogs living in the grass disgusted me with their cowardice: they pissed on your hand whenever you managed to snatch one from among the tall grass. The big croakers of the lily pads would never reveal their fear this way. Their song rolled the evening into night to be followed by the dark choir of crickets that would sing us to sleep. Outside in the dark, all manner of wonderful things would take place while we imagined ourselves safe as long as we didn't allow a hand or foot to stray over the edge of the bed.

I say "we," but I can only speak for myself, and even then, not with certainty. The few pictures that remain from my childhood and adolescence remind me of times, moods, people, places, and perhaps relationships. But how do I relate to them now? Something must remain of that time, or do I recreate my past each time I think of it? The past can only exist in photographs and in language. The photographs don't alter, but the language does. The reconstruction of my past is only as permanent as my language; that is to say, it keeps changing. Anyway, why try to reconstruct the past? I am writing over sixty years later and two thousand miles from the Rideau waterway. The sun shines and my life is here, suitably where the sun goes down. Whatever puberty did to me cannot be rectified now. Only the pictures remain, and memories that remind me I have a past. A past that waits for my dotage in order to re-emerge gloriously as something that no one ever experienced although many may have wished they had. Still some things won't recede; that picture, for example. It shines, its glint cold like the winter it archives. But as we have just seen, that winter in its turn recalls summers of snakes and frogs.

I find myself in a marsh with my father duck hunting on a late October morning sometime sixty-five years ago, my hate no different than that evident in the photograph. I hate the cold, the wet, the uncomfortable crouch, the quiet, the guns, the company:

there are two of us. I even hate the decoys we have placed strategically among the reeds. One duck flaps blithely overhead, confident of our incompetence. My gun blasts, innocuously; my father snaps a few curses; the duck quacks once or twice and leaves us cold and silent, as the smoke from my gun drifts on the breeze. What can words do? A few curses accomplish a settlement. We leave for the cottage and then home, my father sullen all the way. This was my only hunting trip, an experience by all family measures a failure, but in retrospect a crowning victory.

Words barely make it above curses in our house. We live an argument, but one that never recognizes itself. Without the consciousness of itself, it can only breed pestilence. I remember a cluttered house badly needing a thorough cleaning. That tacky feeling touches me from the sofa and chairs of our living room, complimented by the distinctive smell of dust, beer, body odour, and a collectivity of food clinging to stove and fridge in the kitchen. I suppose cigarette smoke helped. It permeated everything. And the lugubrious burlap wall covering that lined the dining room insisted on capturing and holding each disparate and cacophonous smell. My mother tried valiantly to keep order in this chaos, but she had to work eight-hour shifts five days a week at the hospital and on days off she tended to the infirm in our neighbourhood. My sister and I learned early to fend for ourselves.

All that really matters is the fact that both the milkman and the breadman, now extinct species both, came on their rounds in horse-drawn buggies, leaving the streets decorated with wasted oats and probably wasted apples and carrots proudly offered by eager children like my sister and me. We secretly yearned for animal contact. Only once did we have a pet, a puppy my father and a neighbour castrated in the woodshed, and shortened its life beyond memory. Some houses had visits from an ice truck from which were drawn huge blocks of frozen water hauled by the iceman with great tongs; this feat seemed the height of accomplishment to me who so desired to manipulate these great iron grapplers. These things matter; they are part of a pesky past that won't disappear. A neighbour's boy falling from a tree and losing a mouthful of protruding teeth is comedy of the highest order, while tragedy lurks in the case of the little boy whose early life consists of spying on his bigger brother in hopes of catching him smoking. This boy wants more than anything to be an actor; he becomes a male nurse and later a representative of a pharmaceutical company.

I wait at home for my father who has tickets for a hockey game in Montreal, tickets that I procured by writing to the team's general manager, Frank Selke. I am, I must guess, around twelve. This is to be my first trip to Montreal to see my favourite hockey team. Father is away somewhere, not at work, I think. Time passes and I wait, feeling the usual fear accumulate, this time accompanied by the disappointment that only youth can feel. How many trips do I take to the kitchen to check the clock? The time agonizes; it fails me. Why prolong this? After the last moment had gone forever, he arrives. We rush and somehow make a train. Again, a photograph is my memory: on a train triumphantly holding a Montreal Forum program. This is Freud defeated. This is an imaginative moment. All things conspire against this being memory; it is a permanent moment. It is what justifies our pasts. It informs our futures. This is history as it should be, a nightmare redeemed. We went to that hockey game and experienced victory: Montreal 7, Boston 3. In an interesting twist, I often remember this trip with my mother, not my father, for it was she who provided me with the safe environment. Memory and desire sometimes fold together like some borromean knot.

Speaking of nightmares, I had one, a recurring dream during these early years. I find description difficult. Whatever it was that my mind conjured in sleep, I am not certain. But whatever it was came oppressively close. The dream itself pressed so close to my inner eye that it seemed to press intensely, to make itself felt along the body. This dream, so opaque now, so unfocused, and so unclear except in the touch that it left behind nicely represents memory itself. My memories of childhood are unfocused, unclear, unfinished, and largely, I suspect, unconscious. I sometimes wonder if repression works this way for everyone. Or does memory work differently over time? I mean, do we remember more things the more time stretches and we move into arthritic age? If we do, then this chronicle should wait for a more auspicious time, once arthritis has curled fingers to the point of uselessness. Can't wait. Instead of waiting, I merely reconstruct, force memory to work in overdrive. It is as if I looked back into that dream and insisted the contours become clear whether they will or not. And the house helps.

Yes, the house helps. I remember the banister that lines the opening to the stairs in the short upstairs hall. Entering the front door of the house, you saw a hall running the length of the house into the kitchen. On the right, a few steps inside the house, was a stairway leading to the second floor. At the top of the stairs, a few feet straight across the landing, was the bathroom. To the left of the bathroom was my father's bedroom, a cavernous place that always seemed dark and haunted. This was a room fit for the gothic. The odour emanating from it was strong with fermented grains. The bed was never made. Under the mattress were magazines with salacious covers. You can tell I entered that room because I know about the magazines. I also went in to check the dresser top where my father stashed a pile of coins, especially a lot of 1951 commemorative nickels with the Peace Tower on the back instead of the familiar beaver. I used to pilfer these every so often. Remember, you could buy an ice cream cone for a nickel back in those days, and that same nickel could give you a full bag of penny candy: black balls, jujubes, suckers, green mint leaves, caramel squares, and so on. Anyway, if you turned at the top of the stairs and headed down the small hallway, the banister was on your left. On the right was a bedroom in the middle of the short corridor. In the early days, this was my mother's room, but later it became mine when she traded with me for reasons I no longer remember; perhaps she wanted to put more distance between herself and my father; perhaps she thought I deserved a larger room because my sister had a large room. I don't know. Next was the corner room, the largest bedroom, and the one occupied by my sister. Then at the end of the hall was a small bedroom that looked over the porch to the street and across the road to the parachute factory. This was where I slept until sometime in the mid-fifties when I changed rooms with my mother. The bed in this room had a metal head-piece and foot-piece. I used to place a pillow over this foot-piece, fashion crude stirrups with the belt from my housecoat, use a belt for reins, and pretend I was riding a horse. I was emulating the movie cowboys I admired: Eddie Dean, Roy Rogers, Hopalong Cassidy, Bob Steele, and Lash LaRue.

Since I mention cowboys, I might as well note that my family went to the Canadian National Exhibition (CNE) in Toronto in 1954 to see Roy Rogers. The performance was billed as the Roy Rogers Circus, and it included Dale Evans, Trigger, and Pat Brady and his jeep Nellybelle. I have clear memory of Roy putting Trigger through his paces, of Nellybelle backfiring as Pat Brady drove it by the bleachers, and of Roy and Dale riding by the bleachers at the end, and waving to the crowd. This was one of only two trips I remember with my family. The other was to northern New York State to visit what they called the North Pole and another tourist place called Frontier Park. The trip took us through the Adirondack Mountains. The only other travels I recall from my childhood were journeys to my maternal grandparents in Peterborough, Ontario, and also a couple of trips to visit my mother's sister and her family in Tillsonburg, Ontario. It is strange the things memory chooses to record. On one of those trips to Peterborough, on the return home, we stopped for gasoline at Perth, about a dozen miles from home, and someone, my sister probably, dropped a small box containing water and a goldfish onto the macadam where it spilled and the small gleaming fish flipped and flopped in what I assume were its death throes. This is just a sample of the crises every child experiences.

We lived on Russell Street East, the second house from the end on the north side. One house to the east and Russell Street came to a T-intersection with Victoria Street. On the south side of Russell Street was the Parachute Factory, a small two-story brick building. Across Victorian Street and running the length of the two blocks north and south was a ditch filled in summer with tall grass in which young bodies could hide. We could also hide under the freight shed that was just over the tracks. Our town came with lots of trains, the steam kind until I was around ten or eleven years old. Not far from where we lived were an icehouse, a stockyard, and a round house. More about the trains later. Just to the north on Victoria Street was the metal box factory, Beach Industries. When I was young, my friends and I explored the factory yard, and we would find bits and pieces of metal to carry away in our pockets. Most useful were the round smooth slugs we used in pop machines or candy machines. These small pieces of silver metal were the size of a quarter and they would sometimes fool the dispensing machines. We rummaged through the waste metal in the factory yard until someone would appear to chase us away. Then one morning I woke early to the sound of unusual activity downstairs in our house and to an acrid smell in the air. Out the bathroom window, on the second floor at the back of our house, a spectacular sight waited. Behind the Perkins house on Victoria Street, the metal box factory was ablaze. Smoke and streaks of fire rose into the early morning air. The activity below in our house was the coming and going of firemen who took a few minutes from their work to have a cup of coffee prepared by my mother still in her nightgown. Our house and adjacent houses were dowsed with water to protect them from sparks. The fear was that the whole block would fall to the incendiary beast. Firemen stomped in and out of our kitchen with their great boots, bulky coats, and back-winged hats. I was entranced. This was a great adventure right here in my house, the bastion against an encroaching disaster just yards away from our back yard. The fire raged through the morning to midday, and then rested. The factory was in ruins. In the days and weeks that followed the factory eventually rose from the rubble, but when it did it was enclosed. No longer did we have a yard with the bits and pieces of metal drawing us to cross the line. Irrevocable change was the message. Some things do pass away not to return.

Visiting that block and what was my home years later, I was struck with the size of the place. It was, after all, a universe when I was young; it was a world unto itself, a place of adventure, exploration, discovery, retreat, travel, play, and even work. But seeing it after many years, I was struck by how much it had shrunk. It was barely more than a playhouse and a play area. How such a grand blaze could have occurred in this place is beyond me. It looked no bigger than the palace that Gulliver saved from fire. Childhood and its places are truly Lilliputian. We were little people playing hide and seek of a summer's evening: the kids on the block, Sharon and Bobby Nolan, the two Noble boys from Victoria Street, Roy Hollingsworth, and at various times the two Weir boys down from Ottawa or the Clark girls from across the street. I recall hiding beneath the stoop behind the Weir house, hiding and waiting and hearing the voices from the front of the houses and watching the sun as it dropped out of sight behind the roofs to the west of us. I sometimes stayed in my concealment until it was truly dark. No one seemed to miss me. The invisible boy crouched beneath a backyard stoop. Sometimes I went across the road to the freight sheds where I could crawl underneath the sheds and be invisible among the dust and posts of this wooden structure. This was the place where we later came to smoke cigarettes and then eat oranges to disguise the odour. This was the place I would later imagine as a hiding spot for my father. We were in those days young and easy under the streetlights. We scampered and played all the livelong day.

We lived on a block of characters, people like old Mr. VanMeer, who always seemed to carry himself like a walking scarecrow, like an aged and bent Ray Bolger from MGM's *The Wizard of Oz*. Across the road and to the west of the Parachute Factory was the home of Harvey and Bella French. Bella was a harridan, often chasing us from the side of the Parachute Factory where we played ball. Next to the French house was the home of Mr. and

Mrs. Bates and their son Donny; they kept a horse in a stable behind the house. Then came the Clark's, the Cook's, and finally Mrs. McGregor's. That was the south side of the street. Across from Mrs. McGregor, on the northwest corner, was the Nolan's house. Then VanMeer's, Doyle's, McCoon's, Weir's, our place, and lastly the Hollingsworth's house. That was the block. Twelve homes plus the small brick Parachute Factory. The houses varied. Seven were two-story brick homes with tiny verandas, and five were made of wood. The wooden houses had more elaborate verandas than the brick houses had. Behind the houses on the north were small yards, and most occupants divided their small yard into a garden and a lawn. Everyone had a small garage. The houses on the south side had an assortment of arrangements for backyards. The Bates had a corral for the horse. The French's had only a scrap of rough land. As for the rest of the houses, their backyards remained something of a mystery to me. We did not go there for some reason. And speaking of mystery, I ought to mention the Cook's house because it was a double house, two houses attached. Who lived in the second of these houses I do not remember, although I would have delivered a newspaper to this place. Tricks of memory. We remember some things and not others. The Cooks I remember because the whole extended family—mother, father, two children, and two grandparents—suffered from diabetes. In my memory, this family are grey, as if they inhabited an old photograph. We saw this family going for an evening walk most days in the year. But I have no recollection of who may have lived next to them.

The block was at the eastern extremity of town. Next to us was the rail yard. The town boasted two rail lines, the Canadian Pacific Railway (CPR) and the Canadian National Railway (CNR). The one by us was the CPR. You had to travel to the western edge of town to find the CNR line. But the CPR was the important company in town. Its network of buildings and tracks was extensive. Smiths Falls was an important center for the railway, a version of Crewe, only in Ontario. It had a stockyard, an icehouse, an extensive line of freight sheds, a roundhouse where engines were serviced, and an impressive station with baggage room, waiting room, and café. We lived just across from the freight sheds, and in my early years, before the advent of diesel engines, I listened at night to the huff and chug of the steam trains as they waited for their load of freight. In later years, when I was in my first three years of university, I worked in those freight sheds in the summers. Actually, I worked what they called the swing shift. For six days and nights a week, I worked various jobs, driving delivery truck on Thursdays, in the billing office on Mondays, moving goods from boxcar to freight shed and from freight shed to boxcar on Tuesdays, attaching containers to flatbeds another night, and so on. I recall knocking the same eavestrough from the same corner of the same house three times on Thursdays when I drove the big one-ton truck. I also crushed a lady's flowerbed more than once while backing the truck into her driveway. In the freight sheds moving goods, I got along with the older men, although they continuously told me not to work as fast as I did because they always had to look busy when an inspector dropped by. I never did get the hang of this; I felt like a malingerer if I did not work as hard as I could. I liked getting a job done and then resting for a bit.

Once something happened on a night shift that gave me pause. A young man named Ricky worked the night shift, driving a forklift and moving heavy goods about the platform and onto the big truck trailers. I remember chatting with him at our break, and he had recounted a time when he and his father went to a fortuneteller. The fortuneteller did a conjuring and told Ricky's father that he would die in his fifties of a heart attack. She told Ricky that he would die in his twenties in a car accident. Ricky's father did die in his fifties of a heart attack, and so did his father before him. A weak heart seemed to run in the family. As for Ricky, well, he did not die in a car accident, but he did drive his forklift off the platform and into the back of an eighteen-wheeler one night and crushed his chest. He died at twenty-seven. I have made a point of never consulting a fortuneteller.

What else is worth recounting from these early days? Memory is such a scattered thing; it works in an alchemical manner, transforming the past, sometimes into gold, sometimes into ether. And speaking of ether, I remember having my teeth or at least my molars removed while lying on our arborite kitchen table. Why the dentist came to my home to carry out this operation is beyond my memory, but I clearly recollect the small basket thing with chloroform descending onto my mouth and nose and I think I can still feel the squirming resistance I attempted before the fumes overcame me. And speaking of fumes, I return to the coal dust that just about finished my sister and me. The olfactory sense is supposed to be effective in activating the memory, but truth to tell I have few memories associated with smell. Our house did have a distinctive odour, although I am hard pressed to describe this. Cigarettes obviously had something to do with the way the house smelled. Cooking odours, body odours, laundry, coal in the basement, alcohol, dust, and I don't know what all contributed to the musty atmosphere in 88 Russell Street.

When does memory begin to work? I seem to have a first memory, one I recounted at the outset of this memoir; I am not sure if this is something that actually happened or not. Similarly, I have this memory of my first day of school. I went to kindergarten at Elgin School, and two memories stay with me from this first year of education. That first day, I think my mother accompanied me to school, as did the mothers of the other kindergarten children. I do not know if Pedro McCloud was my age or if he was in my class at school, but my memory has him in that kindergarten class; on the first day he is crying and crying until his mother peels a banana and gives it to him. I like to think this is true. I also remember the rhythm band because my experience in this band begins my lifelong feeling of incompetence and diminishment. I wanted desperately to play the drums, although I would have settled for the cymbals or even the sticks that you clacked together, anything that made a loud noise and that you could pound or smash or generally expend energy playing. When it came time to dole out the instruments, however, my teacher handed me a triangle with a small finger of metal to strike it with. The sound was a gentle "ping" no matter how hard you hit the triangle. I was mortified.

Memories of elementary school are scarce and scattered. I spent two years—kindergarten and grade one—at Elgin School. I have vague memories of the schoolyard and the monkey bars, and of skating there in winter when they created a rink in the open space east of the school building. I also remember an incident after I had apparently struck a young girl schoolmate at recess. I think her name was Gail. Gail ran to Miss Lesard, the grade one teacher, and complained about my aggression. Miss Lesard called all the kids to her and told us to form a circle. Then she took Gail with her to the centre and told me to come forward and apologize. After my feeble apology, Miss Lesard told everyone that hitting girls was not nice, that girls were "precious jewels" and deserved to be treated with gentleness and care. I place "precious jewels" in quotation marks because I distinctly remember Miss Lesard using these words. Some things cling to memory and those two words obviously made an impact upon me. Mostly, however, my elementary school years run together. I moved on to Central School for grade two and stayed there until grade eight, after which I went to high school. I recall a succession of female teachers until grade eight when the teacher was a male, Mr. Peebles. Having a male teacher was something of a revelation, although he did not make me any less of a troublemaker. I recall a comment he made on one of my report cards: "Roddie needs to take his work more seriously." Perhaps had he not called me Roddie, I might have worked harder than I did. Of the female teachers, I remember only one with any degree of clarity: Miss Cameron. Miss Cameron seemed old to me, exceedingly old, and she had one sunken cheek, as if she had had an accident. She was wire thin, and husky voiced. She scared most of us, and if she gave us detention, we knew we were going to have to do some work from her "little brown book." The little brown book contained exercises in arithmetic that would haunt our imaginations. The exercises were variations of "multiply 4 by 24 ten times." This meant that you multiplied 4 by 24 to get 96. Then you had to multiply 96 by 4 to get 384, and then 384 by 4 to get 1536, and so on until you had multiplied ten times. Sometimes we had to do division instead of multiplication, or addition and subtraction. We dreaded the threat of the little brown book.

Central School was an impressive, if small, stone building adjacent to the town library. The school grounds hosted the town's only air raid siren, a device meant to give warning if an enemy—well, the Russians—launched a missile attack or, more likely, dropped an atomic bomb. I suppose our town feared such an attack because of its relative proximity to the nation's capital, Ottawa. In any case, we had periodic practices when the siren blared and we were instructed how to cower beneath our school desks. The fear that such an exercise instilled manifested itself whenever military jets flew across the town, something that happened all too often. I am not sure why these jets sped over town, but I can guess that their flybys had something to do with geography. To the south of town maybe one hundred miles away was Trenton, home of a military airbase; to the north, maybe a similar distance, was Petawawa, another airbase. In any case, whenever the jets flew over town, I experienced the paradox of fear laced with a romantic sense of adventure. Those jets remain clearly etched in memory. They connect with a memory of my arrival in Toronto in October 1964, just two years after the Cuban missile crisis; I recall some of the returning members of the house in which I lived narrating their stories of packing to leave for home in October 1962 because they thought the bombs were about to fall.

Another memory of Central School playground has to do with two annual fall fairs, one organized by the Lions Club and the other organized by the Rotary Club. Not much differentiated these fairs. They occupied the small schoolgrounds with rides such as the merry-go-round, the swinging chairs, and the Ferris wheel. Barkers challenged people to try their luck at ring toss or throwing baseballs at wooden milk bottles or hitting a small bell by swinging a heavy mallet. Probably my most vivid memory of the fairs was the cotton candy. We could only experience such sweet delight at the fair and since both fairs took place within a week or so of each other in late August or early September, we had to wait a year before we could taste this decadent delight again. I was not much interested in the rides, but the crowds and the games and the barkers who hailed us to come see their mysteries fascinated me. That schoolyard was not large, yet the fair seemed to occupy the entire town.

Anyhow, I moved on to high school where another succession of female teachers greeted me. These were mostly elderly spinsters: Miss Orr and Miss Code were the two I remember most, although Mrs. Lloyd was the teacher we tormented more than any other. Miss Orr was short and round and enthusiastic; we, in the unkindness of youth, referred to her as "Piggy Orr." She taught English, and I can recall her grasping the yardstick, brandishing it like a sword, leaving the room to talk to us from the hall, and then bursting back into the room reciting appropriate words from *Macbeth* as she swung the yardstick from side to side, causing those in the front row to lower their heads. Miss Orr was well known in town for driving about with her sister Hilda; she was so short that she had to peer through the steering wheel to see out the windshield; she also had to have wooden blocks on the pedals so she could reach the accelerator, the clutch, and the brake. Miss Code taught Latin. Her brother, Art, also taught at the school. He was married and had a family, but Miss Code lived with and cared for her aged mother. As for Mrs. Lloyd, she was younger and pretty, the wife of a local doctor known in the community for his ill-advised use of pharmaceuticals. We liked Mrs. Lloyd, but this did not keep us from causing her anxiety. I suspect our behaviour in her class was a form of pubescent flirtation. Her classroom was on the second floor and I recall once we took a desk and balanced it on the windowsill. When she came in the room, she saw the desk teetering in the open window and began fretting about what to do. Truth to tell, we did terrible things to the teachers who did not elicit our fear. For example, we once took the intestine from a rabbit we had in zoology class and stretched it out on the ledge of the blackboard. Mr. Weir, our teacher, went frantic when he discovered what we had done.

We also had to take part in cadets during the high school years. The first year I had to do this was in grade nine. I embraced the experience as if Sergeant Stryker was our leader. Not only did we march up and down the football field, but we also had rather mild war games in the bushes that surrounded the school grounds. Running through the trees carrying a heavy rifle and hollering to beat the band had its satisfactions. But the experience quickly palled, and by second year I was hiding out in the washroom trying to avoid conscription. Of course, I was not alone and of course we were discovered. My only option was to seek an officer's position and so by my last year I was a lieutenant with my own troop. Somewhere I have a photo of the big parade on the final day of cadets. I am out front of my troop with my head turned to the right and my right hand raised in salute; behind me is the troop, their feet resembling a game of pick-up sticks, completely out of step. I was so happy with them.

Speaking of marching, I also had a brief stint with the Orange Young Britain's Marching Band. The Orangemen had their meeting place just around the corner from us on Victorian Street, and I had several calls to join. Truth to tell, I was always a reluctant joiner. I had short spells in both Cub Scouts and Scouts, but I never did enjoy either group. Anyhow, the young man who would later become my brother-in-law convinced me to give the band a try. I did not play an instrument (no triangle in a marching band), but they assured me this was not a handicap for membership in the band. I could be one of the honour guard. Behind the band leader, the magnificent fellow with the staff he twirled and tossed to the great admiration of the audience, came the colours, the honour guard, a group of four fellows, two of whom carried flags and two of whom carried swords raised in some kind of mystic salute. I have a photograph from our local newspaper, the *Record News*, showing me front and centre with uniform and tall hat carrying my sword erect and looking serious, if not ferocious. My stay with the band was not long, and about my only memory is of a bus trip to Almonte during which members of the band sang out in chorus "pee parade" over and over until the bus stopped and most of us trooped out onto the side of the highway.

What else might I recount from those days in high school? I did join the drama club and performed as a character called Trigger Pomeroy in a drama festival in Kingston. I also wrote for the school newspaper, and I have a collection of columns that now make me smile. I was the sports reporter and my columns appeared in a special section of the *Record News*, along with other school news. I crafted a prose laced with familiar clichés I picked up from reading the sports pages of the *Ottawa Journal* and from the *Hockey News*. I was a sport's enthusiast throughout my childhood, playing most games adequately, but not exceptionally. I was tall for my age, and so in grade nine I tried out for the junior basketball team at high school. The coach asked me which hand I shot with, and I did not know. Either one worked for me. Impressed with this display of ambidexterity, the coach told me to come out to the senior team practices. I did. That year, I rode the bench on the senior team. Five years later, in grade thirteen, I was still riding the bench of the senior team. I was a whiz in practice, but once an audience began gawking, I became self-conscious, all thumbs, awkward, and downright terrible.

This self-consciousness also interfered with my play in the sport I was actually quite good at: baseball. I began as a pitcher in Little League, but when I was around fourteen or fifteen, I entered Pony League ball and became a short stop. I had a good glove hand and an infielder's arm. I could throw a strike to first base from anywhere in the infield. I also held myself like Don McKenny, a local boy who had made it to the National Hockey League, and who came home every summer to play in the local softball league. He was also good at this game, and he had a distinctive way of carrying himself on the field. I copied this.

In short, I was a pretty good short stop, although I could not hit worth a damn. Our team, sponsored by the Canadian Legion, was noteworthy because we rarely lost. In fact, we won so often and so handily that we began to find ourselves mentioned in the press throughout the area. I must have been sixteen or seventeen when a man appeared saying he was from the Boston Red Sox organization, and he was going to watch a few games to see how we played. We had an exceptionally fine pitcher and a first-rate infield. After the man from Boston had been in town a while, he called a group of us into the dugout after a game. He talked about Rochester and Triple League baseball, and he said he wanted to speak with six players from our team. I was one of these six. He asked what I thought of playing some serious ball. I was at the time when high school was nearing the end and I had to think of what to do next. Baseball was never my passion; I had always wanted to be a hockey player. But the prospect of going to America to play ball had its attractions. I said that I could not hit very well and that I always made a mistake when a game was on the line. I was fine as long as we were winning, but once things got tense, I was always the one who made the foolish play or booted the ball. And, as I said, I could not hit worth a damn. The man from Boston suggested that good coaching could improve my hitting and discussions with team psychologists could work out the other problem. He said to think about it and he would call in a couple of weeks.

In those weeks, I talked with my mother about what the man had said. As always, my mother was accommodating. I could go and play ball if I wanted, but I should remember that Don McKenny had a brother, Glen, who went off to play hockey just as his brother had. Glen's story, however, did not have the same narrative arc. He did not make it far in professional hockey; he was soon back in town telling tales in Knotty Lee's beverage room and selling used cars for Ustel's Motors. I should, my mother said, think of this before I made any decision; Glen's story, she said, was the more familiar one for young persons who went off to become professional sportsmen. She added that if I went to Rochester, then I would not get a university education. I have no memory of whether or not that man ever called back.

The prospect of going to Rochester was the first of two possible detours from the educational path my mother had set for me. The second came courtesy of my youthful adventures hitch hiking in southern Ontario. Throughout my teen years, when I wasn't playing ball in the summer, I hitchhiked to visit and work with my cousin who lived in Tillsonburg (and later in St. Thomas, south of London). The two of us got along well, and we decided that when we completed high school, we would hitchhike out west. I had not taken long to decide playing baseball was not for me. I spent considerably longer thinking about a life out west in the woods doing I was not sure what, except I was sure that I wanted a life free of what Dave and I thought of as the rat race. And so in the early summer when my last year of high school ended, I received a phone call from my cousin. He was ready to head west. I held the phone from my ear and told my mother that the trip west was about to take place. She said fine, but if I chose to travel and not get a job close to home, I would not receive any financial help from her for university. That did it. I decided to stay put, work for the CPR, and go to the University of Toronto in the fall.

And finally, what about people from those school days? I remember names from the time in Smiths Falls: Donny Knapp, Stephen Ing, Bernard Easforth, Molly Ann Ketchum, the Baxter girls Lynne and Lois, Cheryl McIntyre (my first date), Doug Shearer, Susan Nesbit, Cathy Dulmage, Chris Burnett, Pedro McLeod, Art Lee, Arlon Popkey, Donnie Cooper, David Bothwell, Owen Pardy, Dick and Jimmy Perkins, Johnny Code, Dougie Noble (his brother's name now forgotten), Johnny Bean, Wayne Rombo, David Swayne. To most of these I can put faces. Many other names and faces are gone, even the last name of Elsie, my girlfriend in the last year of high school. The same is true of the people I knew in university. Names: Bob Fewster, Paul Baker, John Brough, Larry Lawrence, Larry Beaton, Ward Passey, Walter Lemon, Wally Brown, Ben Pritchard, John Bywater. I have forgotten so many.

And I have no contact with any from the early days, and perhaps just one or two from those days in Toronto. People come and people go on the slow drift onward. The names serve but to load memory and to pass for a kind of poetry.

CHAPTER TWO
Hitchhiking and Summer Jobs

I started hitch hiking when I was about fourteen when I had to get to work at the Rideau Ferry, some ten miles from town. A bit later I traveled this way to visit my cousin. Dave lived over three hundred miles from us in southern Ontario, the other side of Toronto. I cannot remember exactly when the hitchhiking began, but I know the two of us went back and forth to each other's house several times. I recall once returning by myself from Dave's in the late summer. I was wearing a new sailing jacket I had purchased with money I had earned painting a house. Just outside Toronto on Highway 401, a car stopped and offered me a ride all the way to Kingston. The driver said he had to stop in Bowmanville, and if I did not mind waiting, he would take me the rest of the way to Kingston. I hopped in. As we drove along, we chatted about this and that, until he noticed my new jacket. He admired it and this made me feel good. Asking what make it was, he reached over and touched it near the bottom of the jacket at my groin area. Instantly I reached up and took the collar, saying, "The fucking label is up here, buddy." I was young, but big for my age and in fairly good shape. The driver was small. He pulled his hand away and said "No problem." I said I wanted out. The ride came to an end.

Reflecting on this experience later, I suggested to my cousin Dave (or perhaps he suggested to me) that we should create a guide to hitchhiking. We had a list of rules.

1. Do not wear a hat so that drivers can see your face.
2. Do not stand on a curve.
3. Do not stand on a hill.
4. Do not stand in an underpass.
5. Do not sit down while you are seeking a ride.
6. Do not carry much luggage.

7. Do not travel with an animal.
8. Do not walk far; the point is to catch a ride.
9. Do not take a ride if the car stops in front of you.
10. Do not look as if you had spent three or four nights in the ditch.

Number 9 I ought to have remembered when I took the ride I mention above. If the driver stops in front of you, this means that he (or she) does not care what you look like, whether you are scruffy or well-groomed, and did not evaluate you before stopping. If this was the case, then the driver's motive for picking you up might be suspect. We based our rules on the assumption that both those seeking a ride and those who might pick up those seeking a ride wanted the experience to be safe. Safety first.

And mostly we were safe. Over the years, I hitchhiked a lot both in Canada and in Europe. Once my cousin and I were hitching from Smiths Falls to Tillsonburg and we got a ride in the back of a pick-up truck. You could legally occupy that space back then. We fell asleep and woke up somewhere in the middle of Toronto, a city we did not know. Toronto seemed enormous. Years later, hitching in France, I was picked up by a young couple somewhere not far from Paris. I was traveling with my partner and we were heading to Amiens. The young couple was on their way to Evreux. We got talking, and we mentioned that we had been in Reims. They asked if we had visited the champagne cellars and we said no. When we reached Evreux, they asked if we would like to accompany them to their flat for something to eat. We accepted this generous offer. While we were nibbling on a baguette and cheese, the young man gestured to me indicating I should peek in his fridge. I did. The fridge was replete with bottles of champagne. It turned out that these two had worked in a champagne cellar and they had the wares to prove it. They opened a new package of champagne glasses and popped open a bottle. I do not know how much we drank, but I do know we were in no condition to continue hitchhiking. The young man kindly took us to the bus station where we bought tickets for Amiens. While waiting for the bus, I grew more and more uncomfortable. A very large man with fishing gear noticed my discomfort and he gave me to understand that I should follow him. He led me down a street to a large metal screen that provided privacy. This was the public loo, for men.

Hitchhiking gave me many experiences. After graduating from university, I hitchhiked across Canada. Going west, we were two, Lois and myself, and we had fifty dollars between us. Arriving in Banff, we found ourselves in dire straits. My cousin, the same cousin with whom I was to have gone four years earlier, was living in Banff. He lent us a tent, which we erected after dark on Tunnel Mountain and then took down at dawn so we would not have to pay camping fees. We had no money by this time. One day, while we were crossing the bridge over the Bow River, a woman stopped us. She had noticed my sweatshirt with the words "Annesley Hall" across the chest. Annesley Hall is a women's residence at Victoria College, University of Toronto, and the woman knew this. She was a dean at Mount Royal College in Calgary and she sensed that we were in penury. We passed the time of day and she said she thought we could use some help. She then said that she would feed us our evening meal if, afterwards, we would play bridge with her and her husband. We did this for several days, before we left for Vancouver with twenty bucks that my cousin Dave lent me.

We arrived in Vancouver around two in the morning. Never having been there before, we had no idea how to proceed after we were left on the freeway. As we waited for a ride into the city, a Volkswagen Beetle passed us with two people in it. A short time later, this same Beetle returned with only the driver. He stopped and told us to hop in, he would take us to a place where we could get a bed for two dollars. In we got, and off we went. The driver began to drive through the downtown streets pointing out this building and that building, thoroughly disorienting me. Then he pulled up in front of a building on a side street. There, he said, we could get a room for two dollars. Out we got, and as I approached the door, I saw a dark stairway inside. Instinct told me not to take those stairs. The man in the car was gesticulating to indicate we should go in. I suggested we hotfoot it up the street, and this we did. The man in the car jumped out and started after us, hollering. Another man appeared following us. As they got close, urging us to come back, I said no thanks, but they persisted until I swung a large duffle bag I was carrying and knocked the one fellow back. We ran. A short distance brought us to a well-lighted street where a taxicab sat at the corner. We went to the taxi and got in, asking the driver to take us to the train station. I assumed that in Vancouver the train station would be open all night. My assumption proved wrong. We got to the station, exited the cab, paid the fare, and turned to see the place in darkness. Across the street, a flashing neon sign announced the Ajax Hotel; at least this is what I remember. Perhaps its name was Archer. I find no evidence of such a hotel—either Ajax or Archer—now. Anyway, we went across the street to the hotel (whatever its name was), saw a few men slumbering in the lobby, and tried the door. It was locked, but the man at the desk saw us and came over to let us in. No, his name was not Miles! Nor was it Norman! We got a room for a few dollars and there we spent the night.

On this same trip, I got a summer job. After a couple of days in Vancouver, we hitchhiked back to Banff where my cousin got both of us jobs at the Cave and Basin. My job was commissionaire. I looked after the parking lot. Another fellow working there was from Australia. This was Byron. He had a fine sense of humour, and he also fashioned pendants and rings from found bones. He told me that he arranged for a local store, The Quest, to sell his work, but that this work was stolen, but never sold. He gave me a ring. Passing by The Quest one day, I went in and saw Byron's work. I asked about it and the salesperson said they rarely sold any, but that once in a while a pendant or a ring would go missing. Strange.

Anyhow, I worked at the Cave and Basin until mid-August when, one day, I saw my companion leave from her shift with some fellow I had never seen before. They were holding hands. I was distraught and left for Ontario a day or so later with a couple of hundred bucks in my pocket. I hitchhiked as far as Winnipeg. There I met with a university friend and the two of us hitched over to Sudbury where I spent a few days sleeping on the floor of a stranger's apartment. I dried out and proceeded to Ottawa where my sister lived. The story does not end here. The friend with whom I had hitchhiked to Vancouver, played bridge with the Mount Royal College dean, and planned a long life together, phoned to say that she was back at her home in Smiths Falls and she wanted me to come there. Her parents were away on holiday. By this time, with the help of my mother, I had acquired a 1962 Volkswagen Beetle. It was pale green. Mom had helped me buy this so I could have transportation when I went back to university in Hamilton in the fall. I had been accepted into the M.A. program at McMaster University. I drove myself to Smiths Falls and stayed with my friend, Lois. We decided that she would come with me to Hamilton unless she was offered the job in Vancouver that she had sought earlier in the summer. The day before we were to leave for Hamilton, she received a phone call and a job offer in Vancouver. The next day I drove her to the Ottawa airport and watched as she climbed aboard a plane and flew out of my life. I have never seen her since.

I went on to McMaster and my hitchhiking days were just about, if not quite, over.

As for summer jobs, I had several over the years. My first summer job came when I was fourteen (I turned fifteen in late July of that summer). I went to work at a small general store, post office, and gas station at the Rideau Ferry, a resort place about ten miles from where I lived. That first summer I worked for a woman named Mrs. McCallum. She was a widow and she needed help keeping her place of business going. I was a fast learner and soon I was doing just about everything at the store. When the next summer, the summer I turned sixteen, arrived, Mrs. McCallum had sold the store to a family; their names I have forgotten, although the man's first name was Ernie. Ernie indicated that he would like me to return for the summer to help him learn how to run the place. When Mrs. McCallum heard that I was returning, she lamented that had she known I was willing to return she would not have sold the place. In any case, I did return. By the latter part of the summer, I was driving myself to and from work; I got my driver's license a couple of weeks after turning sixteen. The work was mostly forgettable, although I do remember splashing myself with gasoline while filling up a vehicle. In those days, the hoses just kept on flowing when the tank was full, unless you released the handle when you heard the gasoline begin to gurgle in the pipe. I failed to do this and received a flood of gas as a result. The gasoline dried quite quickly, but my employer wanted to know why I smelled like fuel. I just thought that it was a good thing I did not smoke at the time or that the owner of the vehicle did not decide to light up in my vicinity.

The family had, I think, three children, but I remember only one child clearly. Her name was Molly and she was a Downs syndrome child. She and I got along well and I think the both of us looked forward to lunch when we had a bit of time to kibitz. I recall her hearty laughter at some silliness I would perform.

After the two summers at the store, I began hitchhiking in earnest (I had hitched rides to work for the past couple of summers), and went to southern Ontario to find work with my cousin Dave. The first year I did this, I arrived to find my cousin was already working on a tobacco farm and the farmer had all the help he needed early in the season. So, I walked the concession roads south of St. Thomas stopping at farms to see if they needed help. One morning I arrived at a farm around 8:00 a.m.; the farm family was just finishing breakfast. The farmer said he could use help with the hay baling, and so after they had finished their breakfast and cleared things away, I followed the father and son out to where they had a tractor with a baler attached. Behind the baler was a small platform with a tray and a lever. I was to stand on the platform and as each bale came from the baler, I was to snag it with a hook and place it on the tray. As I recall, the tray could carry six bales piled in a triangular shape forming a small pyramid.

I had never done this work before and as the morning wore on, I grew weary; those bales seemed heavy to me. What was worse than the weariness was the blister that formed between my right thumb and forefinger. This blister soon burst and before long the wound was festering and deepening. It oozed. I said nothing. We stopped for lunch and while we were seated around the kitchen table the farmer noticed my wound, which did look nasty. I swear you could see the white of bone. I thought perhaps the farmer would find another task for me after lunch, but as we headed back to the tractor, he merely offered me a pair of gloves. So on with the baling. By late afternoon I was spent. The farmer could see this and he suggested I drive the tractor to end the workday. We finished and I headed for the highway to hitch a ride back to town. My right hand was oozing and painful and ugly looking.

When I got to my cousin's place, the family was seated round the dining room table after having finished the evening meal. I walked in desiring sympathy for my suffering right hand. All eyes turned to me as I came through the doorway holding my hand out so everyone could see how badly I was hurt. I stopped. Waiting. Then a burst of laughter filled the room. To this day, I am not entirely sure what was so funny, but I guess some absurdity existed in my pathetic condition. My uncle suggested I go and clean the wound and then come and have something to eat. I think I learned something from this experience, but exactly what, I am not sure.

This was the family with whom I spent a couple of summers. After my hay-baling adventure, I found a job working near London, Ontario. The job was landscaping the median and overpasses on Highway 401. This meant laying sod and, on the overpasses, digging holes with a huge augur, fixing poles into the holes, laying wire mesh that was hooked onto the poles, and then placing sod on top. The wire held the sod in place on the slopes. The foreman, for some reason, called me Topper, not because he was a film buff, but because he and his sidekick, Shorty, had worked in the bush felling trees and he said I looked like someone who could scamper up trees to take down the tops. He did not know that my fear of heights meant that a topper I would never be. In fact, my cousin and I had a brief stint as house painters, and the house we painted was a grand old Ontario house of two tall stories plus an attic. We had to climb ladders to paint the upper portion of the place. Once up there, I could work, if somewhat unsteadily. But then a couple of girls would walk by down below and begin to chat with us. My cousin scampered down the ladder and flirted. It took me some time to get myself ordered with brush and paint can and then gingerly to climb down the ladder. By the time I got to the street, the conversation had ended and the girls were on their way. I had to turn around and climb the ladder again.

One of the girls liked me. This was Penny Lane. No, really, that was her name. She told me that on Sundays she had a difficult time paying attention at church because every time the pastor said God, she thought he said Rod. She also said she wished the local Woolworth store sold little dolls that looked like me and she would buy the store out of its stock. I suspect we have all had similar youthful crushes. My relationship with Penny, such as it was, lasted only a short time and mostly it occurred at a long distance. But it did wonders for my self-confidence!

As I was saying, the foreman on the highway crew called me Topper. The job involved long days, beginning at six, but it was not particularly difficult. The pay was terrific, especially for a sixteen-year-old. The pay was so good that my cousin, Dave, left his job on the tobacco farm and came to work on the highway. We left home at 5:30 a.m., getting a lift from a couple of other fellows who worked with us. That's when I heard this joke: there goes a train. Where, I don't see one? Well, it just passed and there are its tracks. At a particular time and in a particular place and with particular people, this unfunny joke elicited laughter. It was funny the first time I heard it. Working construction was fun because the crew was fun. I can remember the foreman, whose name I no longer remember, choosing someone every mid-morning to go for coffee and snacks. We would all place our order, hand over our money, and then the foreman would tell the fellow making the run to take his time going, but to hurry back. I enjoyed the camaraderie.

When the highway job ended, it was time for the tobacco harvest and both Dave and I got jobs on a farm priming (picking) tobacco. Priming was notoriously a difficult job, a job that caused many a person to quake and falter. If I remember correctly, we had a crew of five or six primers. The job began early, at 6:00 a.m., when the plants were still covered with dew. A mature tobacco plant stands five or six feet tall, and the leaves ripen from the bottom. This means that the primer begins picking from the bottom of the plant. The large leaves flap in your face and the morning dew drips down from your brow. It is easy to ingest some of this dew. Then there is the boat, a horse-drawn wooden contraption into which we place the picked leaves. Pick an armful and then deposit these in the boat. The horse that pulls the boat does not respect the civilities of human society, and he or she or it poops, pisses, and farts with impunity. If you happen to be behind the boat when the horse accomplishes one of these feats, then the smell is overpowering or your boots slosh in urinated mud. In short, the morning dew coupled with the odour of ordure could turn a person's stomach. We had a fellow working with us who wore a white T-shirt and an Ed Norton pork-pie hat. He was always complaining, and once I heard him retching and then moaning, "When do we get to the end of this row?" A disembodied voice rose from another row saying: "Don't worry, buddy, there's another one waiting right beside it." People retched and groaned, and most days we heard accounts of nightly dreams in which the dreamer found himself surrounded by gigantic tobacco leaves in a maze he could not navigate. I did not have these or any other dreams, as far as I know.

I might also note that the farmer told us that tobacco plants ripen from the ground up, and we were only to pick ripe leaves. I mention this because when you are bent beneath a large tobacco plant staring at the leaves to pick it is not uncommon (in my experience anyway) to see a leaf above a yellow one that appears green and ready for picking. The first and only time I picked a yellow leaf in order to pick a green one above it, I received such a lecture that I never did this again.

At the end of the day, before we headed home, we had to hang the kiln where the leaves are cured. This involved taking the bundles of tobacco leaves that the tyers had prepared and transporting them inside the kiln where they would be hung to dry. The kilns were quite high, and with my love of heights I kept myself close to the ground as we passed along the bundles. My cousin, however, nimbly climbed to the top of the kiln and was the principal hanger. I might add that as the harvest went on, we lost most of the crew, replaced them, lost another two and so on. By the end of the harvest only two primers remained from the beginning of the season, my cousin and myself. And the only reason I was still there was that I did not want my cousin to think me a sissy.

Yes, a sissy. I was never the manly type, and my father fretted that I was less than what he considered a normal male. I never did disabuse him of his fear; for myself, I was confident in who and what I was. I seemed always to know where I was going and why. As for sexuality, this too never seemed confusing to me. I am not sure if this is the place to tell a story about my final summer in Toronto, but here goes. That summer (1967), I stayed in an apartment with three other fellows from Gate House, the place where I had lived during term while attending Victoria College. I decided I could take less money this one summer because I was nearly finished my undergraduate education. I found work driving a dry cleaning delivery truck. This was one of those jobs in which you punch in and punch out, and it paid only around sixty dollars a week. Anyway, I tell this story because it has to do with sexuality. One morning, after a night of partying in the apartment, I woke to find one of my roommates doing something to my anatomy that, to say the least, caught me by surprise. I jumped out of bed and punched this fellow hard enough that he fell to the floor and began crying. Next thing I knew, I was beside him telling him everything was all right, but that he would have to find someone else for a friend of this kind. In short, I have never found myself sexually attracted to males, although homosocial relations have proved important to me. I like male camaraderie.

The summer jobs I had were tough, but I knew the money I was saving would allow me to leave my small town and leave behind the kind of life I saw around me and did not admire. I still wanted a life free from the nine-to-five routine.

The last summer job before high school ended was at the grain elevators in Port Stanley, Ontario, not far from St. Thomas where my cousin, Dave, and his family lived. The two of us worked twelve-hour shifts, from 8:00 p.m. to 8:00 a.m. We would arrive home around 8:45 in the morning after a night's work, wash up, have something to eat, and get a few hours' sleep. In the early afternoon, we would return to Port Stanley to lie on the beach and flirt with the girls. Port Stanley at that time had a boardwalk at the beach, complete with an outdoor roller dome. My cousin and I prided ourselves on being fit, tanned and buff, as they say. We thought we were swingers. We would hang out at the beach until around five when we went back home to get ready for the night shift. The work was not particularly difficult. Mostly it involved emptying freight cars of grain or soybeans, testing the truckloads or freight car loads for moisture, and shoveling the silos clear when their contents were loaded onto boats.

I will mention one more job I held briefly, just before I began to work for the CPR. My mother left my father and moved to Ottawa in 1964. I graduated from high school that same year, and my sister married and was living in a basement suite on Florence Street in Ottawa. I did not want to stay in Smiths Falls with my father, and so I went to stay with my sister and look for a job in Ottawa. What I found was a job as janitor at a small apartment building. I was to empty trash, polish floors, and generally look after the upkeep of the building. After only about ten days on the job, my boss came and instructed me to go to a specific apartment and clean it up. The tenants had left after a loud party the evening before. When I opened the door and stepped inside, I saw a horrendous mess, blood on the walls, broken glass throughout, and rubbish strewn higgledy-piggledy. I was disgusted. I took a bucket and simply began tossing water onto the walls. My boss entered and saw my angry performance, and promptly fired me. Off I went, back to Smiths Falls and the CPR, and to this day my disgust with the things people do has not diminished.

CHAPTER THREE

University Years: Bliss It Was in that Time

In the fall of 1964, I left my hometown. Oh, I did come back to work for the CPR the following two summers, but when I left for Toronto, my mother also left home and moved to Ottawa. This was the end of our family living in proximity: my sister and mother were now living in Ottawa, I was in Toronto, and my father remained in the Russell Street house for the next several years. To tell the truth, I am not sure when he left. The things of mine remaining in the house, memorabilia from my school days and my collection of hockey cards, must have left with him. I did not see them again. My final days in that house were in late summer of 1966.

I remember arriving at 89 Charles Street, Burwash Hall, Gate House, the University of Toronto, where I lived for the next four academic years. The memory of how I got there is not clear, but the hollow feeling as if the world had emptied of everything familiar was intense. I was not confident. After all, I had not distinguished myself in high school. By the time I was in grade thirteen (Ontario schools had an extra year of high school), expectations for myself and for several of my classmates were high. Our class was to graduate four or five Ontario Scholars, that is graduates with averages of 80 percent or higher. As it turned out, we did not have one Ontario Scholar. We were a disappointment to the school. In fact, I received 50 percent in English Composition and barely 70 percent in English Literature. I did, however, win the History Prize for our school. Perversely, I decided that what I wanted to study in university was English. Why did I choose English? Looking back, I understand the mystery of human choice. Throughout my childhood and adolescence, I was not a reader. I had an Uncle Bill who regularly gave me books at Christmas, classics such as *Gulliver's Travels*, *Kidnapped*, *Tom Sawyer*, and

Huckleberry Finn. But I did not spend much time reading these. Instead, I read, and read avidly, comic books, those cheap and to the conventional adult unsavoury sensation narratives, sort of the chapbooks or penny dreadfuls of my childhood. These were the days before Marvel. My reading consisted of DC, Dell, Charlton, and Classics Comics. I remember Blackhawk, Wonder Woman, Tarzan, Superman, Batman, Merlin the Magician, Jonah Hex, and Six-Gun Western; more precious were the EC Comics I managed to acquire, *Tales From the Crypt* and *Vault of Horror*. I also remember meeting Gulliver, Odysseus, Long John Silver, and other characters from the literary past in the Classics Comics rather than in the books given to me by Uncle Bill. I received comics from my Uncle Lloyd, read them, and then traded them with my friends. I might also note that my mother read fairy tales to my sister and me when we were quite young, and these stories, especially "The Fisherman and His Wife," "The Bremen Town Musicians," and "The Wind and the Sun," stayed with me in a vivid way over the years. But I was not an avid reader.

I date my coming out as a reader to my final year in high school. That year, we read two works in English that proved to be formative: *Wuthering Heights* and *Hamlet*. The first grabbed me emotionally—"I am Heathcliff." I have never read this book since that school year (1963–4), but its power remains clear to me. Even more important was the second book. *Hamlet* is an adolescent's dream. The family romance, the youthful dithering, and the intensity of emotion resonated, but not as intensely as the language itself. Words, words, words. Quietus, bodkin, contumely, fardels, occulted guilt, breaks my pate across—the language burns with a gemlike flame, and I loved it. I still do.

> O, that this too too solid flesh would melt
> Thaw and resolve itself into a dew!
> Or that the Everlasting had not fix'd
> His canon 'gainst self-slaughter! O God! God!
> How weary, stale, flat and unprofitable,

> Seem to me all the uses of this world!
> Fie on't! ah fie! 'tis an unweeded garden,
> That grows to seed; things rank and gross in nature
> Possess it merely.

How could a young person not be moved by such words, such sentiments, such turmoil? I wanted more of this.

I am not certain if it was at this time or a year later when I had arrived in Toronto, but I began to make a list of words that were new to me. I kept this list for most of my undergraduate years, and I still have the yellowed paper. The list is notable for what it says about what I did not know back then, and also about my passion for language, for speaking with grace. Here is a sample:

Tantamount – equivalent

Sycophant – flatterer

Efficacious – sure to produce (efficacious means)

Eclectic – selecting doctrines pleasing from every school

Virago – turbulent woman

Peculate – embezzle

Gelid – icy, cold

Effrontery – shameless audacity

Splenetic – ill tempered, peevish

Sententious – compact, terse, short & pithy

Atavistic – recurring after years

Hyperdulia – the worship offered to the Virgin Mary by Roman Catholics

Emoluments – profits from an office (salary)

Lucubration – meditation, literary work (I did not note the overblown aspect)

Sedulous – diligent

And so on, for several pages. As I review this list, I am struck by how many words I ought to have known, but did not. What I see here is both a young person desperately trying to improve himself and someone genuinely enthusiastic about language itself. I liked the way words felt in the mouth and along the blood.

I applied to Victoria College, selecting the Honours English program. How I got accepted, I will never know, but they advised me to take a "double history option." This I did. When I arrived in Toronto around the end of September 1964, I was the proverbial young innocent experiencing the big city for the first time. I felt rather lost.

I did, however, have an uncle who taught high school in Toronto, Uncle Bill, he who had gifted me books during my childhood. I called him because I did not know what else to do. He was my father's youngest brother, and notable in the family for bringing pretty young men home to Smiths Falls in the summers. Bill said he would be right down, and he was. He arrived with a smile, and promptly said he was taking me over to the Park Plaza to buy a suit. A suit? The two of us walked the two or three blocks over to the Park Plaza Hotel and entered a men's shop located in the building. The place looked very posh to me, and did little to make me feel more self-confident. The person in the shop measured me for a suit and said I could return in a week to pick it up. Uncle Bill paid for it. I still have that suit, that bespoke suit, hanging in my closet.

Bill left and I went back to my room in residence fearing I would find my roommate to be some hulking hail fellow well met who would dominate my life for the next seven months or so. In my room I found evidence that my roommate had arrived. I saw a suitcase and a couple of shirts on one bed. The shirts looked as if they belonged to someone too young to be in university. They appeared to be child's wear. Later that day, I met the owner of these small shirts. This was Sandy Hutala. Sandy was, if anything, more nervous than I was. Like me, he was experiencing the big city for the first time. I soon found myself looking out for Sandy. I say "soon," because late that first afternoon we were asked to attend a meeting in the Common Room to meet the other new members of the house. That year Gate House had seven first-year undergraduates, known as freshmen or frosh, among its twenty-seven residents. Around four in the afternoon we met the other members of the house, an assortment of young men of varying sizes and personalities. Sandy was clearly uncomfortable. He was soon to become even more uncomfortable. Before the short meeting was over, I found myself voted freshman rep; in other words, I was to be the leader of this group of seven. We were not, however, magnificent.

That night, around 2:00 a.m., I heard a loud pounding on the door followed by someone entering the room and rousting Sandy and me from our beds. Noise was loud throughout the house. We were ordered to get up and put on our winter coats and boots, plus gloves and of course our freshman beanies. These beanies we were supposed to wear all the time throughout the first week of term, Frosh Week. Once we had on our winter gear, we were herded down to the basement and into the furnace room. It was hot. The older fellows, who were in shorts and T-shirts, acted like drill sergeants, hollering at us to do various exercises. It was hot and getting hotter. I cannot remember specific details of that first night, but I can remember the feeling of bewilderment mixed with a bit of fear. And it was hot, very hot.

Thus began Frosh Week, and my university career. The first week was a succession of trials, an initiation into the life of the house. I am not certain I can recall all the tasks we were required to perform, but some remain fixed in memory. One morning we were rousted with reveille at about six. Orders were to leave our pajamas on and come down to the Common Room. After we had gathered, each of the seven of us received a subway token, and then we were marched over to the Museum station where we caught the southbound train to Union Station. At the Station we were taken to the left-luggage place where a large and heavy trunk was waiting for us to pick up. This trunk we were to carry back to Gate House on foot. Our route took us north on College Street, and by the time we were trudging up College Street in our pajamas the morning was alive with people coming to work. I am not sure what this humiliation was supposed to achieve. But we made the best of things, and found reasons to laugh.

Another night we were gathered together in the Common Room at midnight. This was scavenger hunt night; we were handed a slip of paper on which were listed the things we had to find and bring back to the house; we would not be allowed in without all the items on the list. I cannot remember all the things, but what I can remember are the following: a Bible from a specific church (I cannot recall which church), a pair of women's panties, Ronnie Hawkins's signature, and the wrought iron sign from in front of the Colonnade, a large building on Bloor Street, not far from our House on Charles Street. I had the duty of assigning people to the items on the list. I chose a clergyman's son for the task of securing the Bible, and he accomplished his task without undue difficulty. Two other fellows were to get the panties, and they simply went to the women's residence and threw pebbles at some windows until someone opened a window and helped the fellows with their problem. I chose a fellow named Hugh to get Ronnie Hawkins's signature; Hugh had no idea who Ronnie Hawkins was, but we directed him to a place down Yonge Street near Dundas called Le Coq D'Or. Later that night, Hugh returned with a bar coaster on the back of which was scribbled a name, mostly undecipherable. This signature, Hugh claimed, was Ronnie Hawkins's. Hugh had entered Le Coq D'Or, walked over to the bar and stood beside what he described as a large fat man with a beard who was leaning on the bar with a large glass of beer in front of him. Hugh said, "excuse me" to this person, and he replied, "What can I do for you, kid?" Hugh explained that he was seeking Ronnie Hawkins's autograph. "What do you want that for?" was the large bearded man's retort. Hugh explained, and the big man reached out, took a bar coaster and turned it over, asked the bartender for a pen, and then scribbled something on the coaster. He handed the coaster to Hugh and said, "There you go, kid. Good luck from The Hawk." Whether Hugh had actually met with the man himself or not, we will never know. But that bar coaster with the scribble on the back got him back into Gate House.

For myself, I chose the wrought iron sign. Since I knew this would be at least a three-person job, I took a couple of other fellows with me. That sign was sure to be heavy. What the three of us did not know is that our senior housemates had alerted the police that the sign would be stolen this night; kindly enough, they had also explained why, that this was part of the initiation at Victoria College. By the time we got to the front of the Colonnade it was about 1:00 a.m. and the street was fairly quiet. But we did see a police cruiser driving slowly past. We thought we had to act quickly in case the cruiser returned; the driver of the car had looked at us intently as we loitered near the sign. So we picked up the sign and started to run toward the alley that would take us back of the Colonnade, through a gate and onto the grounds of Victoria College. But the damned sign weighed a ton. We were making slow progress when suddenly two policemen appeared at the Bloor Street end of the alley; they were shouting at us, telling us to halt and put our hands up. We were terrified, and in a panic we dropped the sign breaking one of its legs and bolted down the alley and over the fence and across the grass to Charles Street and into the confines of Burwash Hall. When we got to Gate House, we tried to go in, but the seniors waiting for us refused entry because we did not have what we were supposed to have. We were nonplussed and not a little scared. We waited for a while in the cold night air, and then we trudged back to the Colonnade. Assuming the sign had been taken back to the street, we looked there. No sign. So we checked the alley, and there, where we had dropped it, was the wounded sign. We hauled it back to Gate House and displayed it proudly in the Common Room, using a few books to prop it up where the missing leg had been. In the morning we were told to take it back where we first found it. We never did receive a reprimand for breaking one of its legs.

Such activities filled the first week of my university career. I remember one punishment for violating Frosh Week etiquette: cleaning the steps of the old Victoria College building with a glass of water and a toothbrush.

I might recall here a few adventures of my undergraduate years. November of my first year saw me in the hospital. It happened this way. One night while I was trying to sleep in my dorm room, I felt a pain in my stomach or abdomen. I thought perhaps I was experiencing extreme dyspepsia, and so I took an Alka-Seltzer. This made me retch, and it did not relieve the discomfort. I took another one, and retched some more. Then I thought that if I went out for a run, maybe this would help. Quietly, so I would not wake my roommate, I dressed and went out. It was probably about four in the morning by now, maybe later. I ran about campus for a while. But the pain persisted. Finally, around six in the morning, I went to the campus clinic. Someone there quickly checked me, and then suggested that I go over to Emergency at Toronto General Hospital for a thorough check. Over I went, and before you can say Jack Robinson, I found myself on a gurney, someone jabbing me with a needle, and someone else handing me a consent form for an operation. The next thing I knew, I was waking up and feeling groggy in what appeared to be a basement holding area. Several beds lined the walls, and across from me an elderly man moaned and groaned. Nurses came regularly to remove a pillow from between his legs. I received an injection that made me swoon and wish no one would talk to me. Before long, they had me standing and taking a few steps. My appendix had been removed.

I remained in the hospital for several days. No one knew where I was until the second day, and on the third day my mother arrived. Within a week, I was discharged and returned to Gate House. By now it was getting close to the Christmas break. Freshmen in the house had the responsibility of providing the house with a Christmas tree, and one late evening we trooped out to find a tree. Despite the fact that it was not long since I had had the operation, I went along, climbed a fence, and participated in the purloining of a tree.

University life was stimulating, although many of the classes were less than riveting. I mean the life one leads while attending university; this was stimulating. Just being on campus, having a butter tart, and reading a book in the cafeteria in Hart House is something I look back on with great pleasure. As for classes, I skipped as many as I attended, and this truancy nearly cost me my degree in my fourth year. That year I took a course in modern poetry and drama. The first half on modern poetry provided me with my second opportunity to take a class from Northrop Frye, a formative person in my education, and someone whose work I admire as much as I admire anyone's. I never missed a class by Frye; I also remember attending his public lectures on Shakespeare, the Alexander lectures delivered in Convocation Hall because the scheduled room in Hart House was too small for the huge audience. For me, Frye was all in all. The second semester was devoted to modern drama, and the instructor was a young fellow named Lee Patterson; I remember he wore cowboy boots. Anyway, his lectures did not find purchase after the scintillating first semester lectures by Frye, and I stopped attending. When classes were over in April and examinations pending, I received a phone call from Professor Patterson. He asked me if I was aware that I was not going to pass his course because I had not fulfilled the requirement of giving a class presentation. I gulped. He suggested I come to see him in his office. I did. He gave me a lecture on responsibility and academic life, and after he concluded this lesson, he said I could write a paper and get it to him forthwith and he would take this in lieu of the class presentation. I wrote the paper and scraped by in the course. Professor Patterson later left Toronto for Johns Hopkins, finally ending his teaching career at Yale. I owe him a debt.

Thinking of nearly failing my fourth year, I can also recount the misadventure with my friend Lois. Lois was from my hometown; she was the person I would later hitchhike west with. She turned up at Victoria College a year after I began my studies there, and before long we were involved in a torrid relationship. Lois suffered youthful angst more than most; perhaps she was depressive, I don't really know. But she needed support, even when support meant having me climb through her basement window to avoid being seen by her landlady. To be fair, to avoid the evil eye of my house don, she climbed down the rope that served as a fire escape from my second-floor tower room in my fourth year in Gate House. In that same year, Lois moved across the street from where I lived, into a large brick house. Her room was on the second floor and her landlord did not allow male visitors. On the night before my final examination in Canadian Literature, Lois called and said she wanted me to come over. Her landlord was out, and I had no trouble entering this off-limits place. The next morning, however, things had changed. Her landlord obviously knew something was up because he had ensconced himself on a chair right by the front door, my only exit. Examinations began at nine and Lois had an examination that morning. She left, but pleaded with me not to get caught because if I did get caught, she would be evicted right in the middle of the examination period. I waited and fretted. I kept peeking over the banister to see if the landlord had left his vigil. Time crept on. At about a quarter to nine the phone rang and Mr. Landlord left his perch. I took the opportunity to scamper down the stairs and out the front door. I hotfooted it over to the Benson Building where the doors were just about to close. I made it.

Those were heady days. I recall an examination in my third year, the exam in Restoration and Eighteenth-Century Literature. Students were seated, doors closed, papers distributed, and the instruction to begin delivered. Suddenly there was a kerfuffle. And then people were on their feet and the invigilators were calling for order. One student, emulating Gulliver I guess, had climbed on top of his desk and urinated on the examination paper. The room was cleared and students were informed that they should check bulletin boards for the time a rescheduled exam would take place. Times have changed. Those were the times when at convocation a student would tear his parchment in two to protest something or other. Those were the days of sit-ins and protests against everything from unjust university administrations to the war in Vietnam. We were entering the era of Stonewall and Kent State. It was not possible to ignore interesting times, and I recall the fervour with which many of us welcomed the hope for peace and love. Bliss it was in that time to be alive and to be young was very heaven. We were on the merry-go-round of history, once again experiencing a moment when all things seemed possible despite the crushing realities of war and poverty and injustice and bigotry. We thought we could have the world we wanted; we were mistaken.

On a somewhat less fraught note, I report that I remained active during my time in Toronto, learning to play squash and coaching an intramural basketball team. Squash became a lifelong passion. I also made friends with one of my professors; this was Brian Merrilees, a young French professor who had come to Toronto from New Zealand. I invited him to become attached to Gate House; I no longer remember what title he held, but he came to House meetings and was photographed with the rest of the House in the annual photo session. I used to play catch with Brian on the Common, and he invited me (and Lois at times) to his house. I recall how fond he was of the Procol Harum's song, "A Whiter Shade of Pale." The things we remember. When I left Toronto, I lost touch with Brian. Years later, once Facebook had changed social relationships, I reconnected with him, but not long after this reconnection, Brian's daughter wrote to tell me that he had passed away.

I return to the beginning of classes. I was enrolled in a program called English Language and Literature with a double history option. This meant that I took mostly English and History classes, with French and a one-hour a week option. My first-year courses were Chaucer, American Literature, Restoration and Eighteenth-century Drama, Greek and Roman History, Medieval History, French Romantic Literature, French Language, and a one-hour-a-week Anthropology course. That's eight courses, and I was just getting started. Things got more hectic year to year. And by the way, I distinguished myself with a third-class overall grade that first year, receiving PWH (Pass Without Honours) in two courses and BL (Below the Line) in one course. I squeaked through. Things did not improve greatly over the next three years, and I graduated with a second-class grade (B) and stood thirty-fourth out of approximately seventy students in my program. In other words, I had a mediocre undergraduate career, so mediocre in fact that Toronto would not have me as a graduate student. I did, however, have a couple of instructors who believed I could, given the opportunity, improve. I refer to John Baird and David Knight, two of my Victoria College instructors. Both had eccentricities. Well, Baird had more of a challenge than an eccentricity; he stuttered. His stutter was extreme and I often thought he must have suffered greatly to perform in class. I remember one magical occasion when he managed to speak clearly and precisely without a hint of a stutter; this was the day when he read "The Aged Aged Man," the White Knight's song from *Through the Looking Glass*. Oh, callooh, callay, the frabjous joy of speech liberated by another famous stutterer. Professor Baird taught me the literature of the late eighteenth and early nineteenth centuries, and he was reading Lewis Carroll's poem because it is a parody of a well-known poem by William Wordsworth. I might add that this class was my first introduction to the Romantic poets and I was not impressed with them. For the most part I found these classes tedious; I say for the most part because Professor Baird did introduce me to William Blake and the introduction was an immediate fit. I found Blake's voice compelling. He spoke truth to power as they now say; he championed the human imagination as well as the human body. His was and is a voice for liberty, equality, and humanity.

As for David Knight, he was a true eccentric. I recall the first time he came into class. He was wearing a flowing academic gown, flowing because of the velocity of his entrance, and he was carrying several large rolled pieces of paper. He came to the front of class, flopped the rolls of paper onto the desk, looked at us with fierce eyes, and said: "God help you poor souls. You are about to be ridden down by a hobbyhorse." I had no idea what to think. In any case, these two agreed to provide reference letters for me when it came time to apply to graduate school. Taking a cue from Baird and Knight, I have always admired the student who was curious, smart, but not yet mature in his or her thinking. The easy A student who crossed every "t" and dotted every "i" did not particularly interest me.

I might note the few other instructors that stick in memory. First Miss Cox. In my first year I took a course in American Literature; the instructor was Miss Cox. I can only think she was attempting to mirror Emily Dickinson. Miss Cox was svelte and severe, with a notably stiff beehive hairdo. She was pretty, but oh so distant. In class, she sat behind the front desk with an open book before her on the desk. From this book she read, without much in the way of inflection. I was quickly bored, despite Miss Cox's strange allure. I skipped class. Just before Christmas break, I thought I ought to return to class to see where we were on the syllabus. When I walked in to the room, I chortled sotto voce; only one other student was present. Back in October there were some 25 students in this class. Apparently, I was not the only one who found Miss Cox boring. I remember reflecting on how Miss Cox must feel entering the classroom and finding it almost empty. She, however, carried on in the same manner as she had when I first sat in her classroom. She sat stiffly in front of the two students occupying desks and spoke in monotone as she read from an open book. What a surprise, then, when sometime in the middle of the second term I happened to cross paths with Miss Cox on a nearby street, and she smiled and nodded as we passed. Despite the stultifying classes, I remember Miss Cox fondly.

I should also mention Dennis Lee, who taught Shakespeare in my second year. He is the only instructor I ever had who wept in class. He was teaching *Henry IV*, Part 2, and we were at the place in which Mistress Quickly is pleading with Doll Tearsheet to come and be kind to Falstaff who is about to leave for court. It is clear that Mistress Quickly has affection for Falstaff and would like to please him, no pleasure him, but she thinks he wants the more dramatic Doll. This is how I recall the situation. Mr. Lee was reading the scene and growing visibly more emotional, when suddenly he jumped from his seat at the front of the class and bolted down the aisle between desks and out the back door. Students just sat in silence for several minutes before it became clear that Professor Lee was not returning. Later in 1968, Dennis Lee left Victoria College to help set up the infamous Rochdale College, an experiment in alternative education run by the students. There was no tuition and students and teachers lived together. The experiment lasted until 1975 when Rochdale was closed because of financial failure. From there Dennis Lee went on to become Canada's best-known children's poet, publishing such best sellers as *Alligator Pie* and *Nicholas Knock and Other People*, both appearing in 1974.

Other instructors of note include J. R. de J. Jackson who completed two Ph.D.s on S. T. Coleridge (he did the second one because he said he did not know enough after completing the first one), Kathleen Coburn, a noted Coleridge scholar, George Grube, a famous classicist, Peter Hughes, John Robson, and Jane Millgate. Ah, Jane Millgate. She was my Honours Project supervisor in my fourth year, an extended essay on Henry James, and I had a crush on her. Her husband was Michael Millgate, the noted Faulkner scholar and biographer. I recall spending an evening at their house listening to high talk, and hearing Faulkner speak on a record for the first time. Some years later, at a conference at Dalhousie University, I met Jane Millgate again. She was handing out conference packages at the registration table. I approached her and remarked that she had been my supervisor "many years ago." Missing not a beat, she promptly replied: "Oh, not so many years ago, I am sure." I suspect she had no memory of me. As for the rest of my undergraduate instructors, I can see faces and recall lecturing styles, but the names have left me.

I insert one short anecdote simply because I remember the occasion. I was giving a presentation in class on the eighteenth-century poet James Thomson. The particular text was "Winter" from Thomson's *Seasons* (1730), and I noted in passing that Thomson knew little about ornithology because he had a robin hopping about in winter. I was trying to be clever. My instructor, Peter Hughes, laughed and condescendingly informed me that in England the robin was a winter bird, and it differed from the thrush-like feathered creature we know in Canada. Perhaps this short tale explains my reluctance to speak out in class. Oh, and years later I met the English robin, and a sweet small friendly fellow it is.

I should mention names of academics who influenced me through their work, although I never knew them or studied with them. Along with Frye, I read and admired Leslie Fiedler, Geoffrey Hartman, Harold Bloom (although I have a conflicted relationship with him), Frank Kermode, Lionel Trilling, Morse Peckham, and M. H. Abrams. Two books formative in my education were Northrop Frye's *Fearful Symmetry* and Leslie Fielder's *Love and Death in the American Novel*. I read both of these books as I would read a novel; for me, they were page-turners, as well as eye-openers. The first was my introduction to Frye's writing as well as my first in-depth meeting with William Blake, the writer who speaks as convincingly to me as any other writer. Frye writes clearly, with wit and erudition, and he made his subject both understandable and compelling. Frye and Blake are worthy companions, visionaries both. I admire their uncompromising commitment to their work, to art, and to its civilizing capacity. As for Fiedler, he too writes without obfuscation; he too has a comprehensive vision; he too embraces both literature and the reader. Frye and Fielder taught me, among other things, to cross the border and close the gap, to avoid discriminating between high and low, to see cultural production democratically. I understood through these books that the enterprise I had embarked upon was politically egalitarian, non-discriminatory, tolerant, inclusive, creative, and above all critical. More recently, I have admired the work of Slavoj Žižek, and for similar reasons. Žižek writes with equal verve about Hegel and Lacan, Hitchcock and Ford, philosophy and Hollywood. His mind ranges over the cultural and political scene with quick wit and deft understanding. I could add here another scholar, James Kincaid, who writes with wit and verve. These are writers critical of what they examine. They are radical in the true sense of returning to origins and rendering a thorough explanation of the fundamental nature of what they discuss. For me, they are also radical in the political sense of calling for reform. They perform the marriage of art to the polity.

I might take a moment to reflect on the word "critical" here. A few years ago, Stanley Fish wrote several pieces in the *New York Times* arguing that the classroom was not the place for politics. In one piece, he wrote: "I would never deny that there are some college and university teachers who mistake the classroom lectern for a political platform and thereby substitute indoctrination for instruction. But, I argue, this need not happen—it is not an inevitable consequence either of our fallible natures or of certain subject matters—and when it does happen, it should be labeled as wrong and regarded as a reason for discipline by the school's administration" (June 8, 2008). Later, Fish expanded on his arguments in *Save the World on Your Own Time*. He sees professing in the classroom as passing on the skills to read and interpret a body of material. If this material happens to be political history, then the professor has the duty to explain and describe this history, without partisanship. In the case of literature, politics is an unnecessary intrusion and diversion, unless one is reading an overtly political work, say something by George Orwell or Robert Penn Warren's *All the King's Men*. Or Milton's *Areopagitica*. Even here, the professor's duty is to clarify and explain, not to promote. My teacher, Northrop Frye, also eschews, ostensibly, political indoctrination. And okay, I can understand Fish's and Frye's objection to the classroom as recruitment office, and I can agree that the study of English should not be an interpellation into left-wing or right-wing politics. The classroom should attempt to locate itself outside the desire of the Industrial State Apparatus. On the other hand, the classroom, like anywhere else, is not an ideology-free zone. No such zone exists. Here I touch on territory claimed by Frederic Jameson (see *The Political Unconscious*, for example). We cannot help but bring politics into the classroom. We do so right from the get-go when we construct a syllabus. Why do we select this book and not that one? Formerly, the answer rested on aesthetic views, but as Frye correctly (to my mind) argues, aesthetics is a mug's game. We prevaricate when we say that our syllabi contain the best that has been thought and said; we choose the books we teach for reasons other than aesthetic excellence. This should be clear in these days of postcolonial studies and LGBTQ+ Studies and other cause-related studies. True, we may behave as if we teach politically loaded work simply to inform and not to proselytize, but in truth we cannot present such work neutrally. Let's take race for example. To study the history of literature by and about Black people inevitably turns us towards an anti-racial viewpoint, unless we are proponents of some kind of racial purity. Ridding ourselves of a political point of view (I take matters of race, gender, as well as attitudes to class and economic status as political) is well-nigh impossible if we are actively engaged in thinking about the human condition. We gravitate to certain writers for reasons other than their formal beauties, although their formal beauty may be an expression of their political position.

The literary stock market (see Frye's *Anatomy of Criticism*) runs bullish and then bearish on the same writers. Shelley is for early modernists such as Eliot and Leavis a youthful passion to be left behind with childish things, and then Shelley, for later critics such as Bloom and Abrams, is one of the great mythopoeic poets ever to have graced anthologies of good literature. Such assessments are always subjective, and they rest largely on unspoken political foundations. We like writers who speak to our sense of the way things are or ought to be. As Fish rightly points out, readers coalesce into communities, and communities share assumptions and values. This does not mean that we teach only those works we admire; it means that when we construct a syllabus, we do so for reasons that have ideological implications. We might select a work of fiction that represents ideas and values we do not share, precisely so that we can critique these values as expressed in this particular work. We do the same with works that represent ideas and values we do share. The classroom is, or should be, a space for deliberation, negotiation, explanation, and healthy debate. Debate is healthy when we put our cards on the table, when we make it clear just where our sympathies lie and why. This is not indoctrination; it is awakening. The challenge is: think. Of course, most of us, including Fish, I dare say, would like to see our vision of the world replicated in those we teach, but this does not mean we demand such replication. To demand such would surely call "for discipline by the school's administration." We do not call for everyone to parrot our vision, but we do call for informed critique. Critical thinking, so much a buzz concept over the years, means understanding just how implicated each of us is in ideology, and it means struggling to surface our own ideological assumptions openly. The classroom is, as the cliché states, a place for open dialogue. In the classroom competing voices and competing idiolects share the space and strive to be understood. The challenge is to bring differences in sound and sense to some kind of understanding, to forge a language that grasps the essential slipperiness of language and its desire for control. The question is, as Humpty Dumpty says, "which is to be master," you or the words you use. The trick in English class is to understand the other's language and to master your own.

William Blake: "Opinion is one Thing. Principle another. No Man can change his Principles Every Man changes his opinions. He who supposes that his Principles are to be changed is a Dissembler who Disguises his Principles & call that change." The classroom is a place where opinions change regularly, and also a place where principles are open, clear, and unchanging as stone. Principles do reflect politics, even though politics are often without principle. This is the kind of thinking I began to undertake as a student in Toronto. I may have changed opinions many times over the years, but my principles remain as they were at the outset. As someone once sang, "I'm liberal, but to a degree/I want ev'rybody to be free."

In other words, I began an education in politics. Books that were important to me include Norman O. Brown, *Life Against Death* (1959), Paul Goodman, *Growing Up Absurd* (1960), Herbert Marcuse, *One-Dimensional Man* (1964), John Kenneth Galbraith, *The New Industrial State* (1967), and a bit later Theodore Rozak, *The Making of a Counter Culture* (1969), and Charles A. Reich, *The Greening of America* (1970). These writers presented a coherent criticism of capitalism, wage inequality, exploitation, diminishment of difference and dissent, and general malaise of modernity. My thinking, such as it is, developed from this range of writers who all, in their own way, called for a radical return to pleasure and generosity and individual freedom that found itself under siege in a society more and more controlled by the corporate imperative. From these writers, I came to the conclusion that western societies have opulence to spare. The west is rich to the point of obscenity; the obscenity lies in the fact that the vast majority of this wealth belongs to the very few. It does nothing other than perpetuate and accumulate more wealth. Wealth upon wealth arises, to adapt a line from Alexander Pope. An equitable and proportional tax system could support such measures as a guaranteed annual income, free tuition for a first degree, universal health care, food and shelter for all, protection of natural resources and the environment, as well as upkeep of the country's infrastructure, in short a life with dignity and security for everyone. Some fifty and more years later, the story these books tell has not altered greatly. If anything, the situation is worse and the hope of that so-called sixties generation with its call for peace and love is dashed on the rocks of corporate greed.

Reading was no doubt formative for me at that time. However, I often think that much of my education during those four years in Toronto took place on the streets, often at night, and in the museums and cinemas nearby. I lived just down the street from the New Yorker Cinema, an art house the like of which you rarely see these days. The New Yorker introduced me to the cinema of the French New Wave, especially Godard, and to the likes of Kurosawa, Bunuel, Bergman, Visconti, Fellini, Ozu, Antonioni, Mizogouchi, and de Sica. I had grown up with Hollywood cinema, especially westerns, but here was a whole new world. It was a revelation. Indeed, university life itself was a revelation. The eagerness with which I took in new ideas and discovered the powerful political messages in art was intense. I was a drifter in a strange but compelling new world, a world I would never leave. During these undergraduate years, I explored opera, fine art, cinema, popular music, classical music, and of course literature.

CHAPTER FOUR

Summer 1968: Summer of Love One Year Later

1968 was an auspicious year. The Vietnam War increased in intensity with both the Tet Offensive and the My Lai Massacre, both Martin Luther King, Jr. and Robert Kennedy were assassinated, Pierre Trudeau became prime minister of Canada, students took to the streets in France, the Democratic Convention in Chicago fostered anti-war riots and resulted in the trials of the Chicago Seven. In other words, this was a tumultuous year. I graduated in late spring and decided to hitch hike across Canada with Lois Baxter, who wanted to seek employment in Vancouver. Between us we had about fifty dollars when we headed out on Highway 400, traveling north to pick up the Trans-Canada Highway. I am no longer certain, but I think it took us only five days to reach Banff, Alberta. I recall that a strange man picked us up outside of Sudbury and took us to Sault Ste. Marie. He offered to take us all the way across the country, but we were suspicious of this person's motive and chose to stay in Sault Ste. Marie with a friend of mine from university. This was Ben Pritchard. He took us to a cottage not far from the city where we also met two other fellows I had known in university: John Brough and Larry Beaton.

From Sault Ste. Marie we were lucky to find a ride all the way to Winnipeg where we once again stopped overnight, this time at a cousin's place. Next morning, we were back on the road when a car stopped and the driver offered us a ride all the way to Calgary. This was Gerry Moore, a shoe salesman from Edmonton. Gerry stopped in Swift Current, Saskatchewan, and stayed overnight. He knew we did not have much money and he generously paid for a motel room for us. The next morning, he drove us to Calgary, but not before he bought us breakfast in Swift Current. As we approached the motel restaurant, Gerry pointed out a sign in the window: "Whites Only." "We're going someplace else," he said. That was it. I reflected that the sign made reference to First Nations people. Gerry made a great impression on me; I no longer remember anything of his conversation, but he made such an impression that I recreated him as Dinty Moore in my novel, *Les Pieds Devant*. Meeting people like Gerry Moore made hitchhiking rewarding. On the other hand, the man who drove us from Sudbury to Sault Ste. Marie made hitchhiking dangerous or at least unsettling. I used this person for the character of my villain in that same novel.

Anyhow, we made it to Calgary in early evening when the sun was lowering over the Rockies. It was a crepuscular time. It was magic. We said goodbye to Gerry and hitched a ride to Banff, where I planned on crashing at my cousin Dave's place; he lived above the Lux Theatre on Wolf Street. We arrived well after dark, but found a welcome reception at Dave's. He told us that we could sleep on the floor one night, but that we should go to the Tunnel Mountain Campground if we wanted to stay longer. His landlord did not appreciate guests in this flat. To help us out, Dave lent us a small pup tent that we would put up at dusk when the park wardens had left for the night, and then take down in the early morning before the day really began. This way we avoided the nightly fee for staying at the campground. During the day, we explored Banff and the surrounding area. One day we were crossing the bridge heading toward park headquarters when an older woman stopped us. She had noticed the sweatshirt I was wearing. It had the words "Annesley Hall" in bold letters on the chest. Annesley Hall was the oldest female residence on the Victoria College campus, and the sweatshirt was Lois's. This was the woman—a dean at Mount Royal College—who fed us for the next several days, and in return we played bridge with her and her husband after dinner. Luckily, both Lois and I knew how to play bridge; I had taken the game seriously while I was an undergraduate, and I continued to take it seriously for several more years. By the mid-1970s I ceased to play this game, and I have not played since.

After a week and a bit in Banff, Lois was anxious to get on to Vancouver to seek her job. I borrowed twenty bucks from Dave and we headed back to the highway. We made it to Vancouver, but in the middle of the night, well after midnight. I recounted this story earlier. We stayed the night in the Ajax Hotel. I cannot recall now how much the room cost, but I do recall placing a pearl-handled knife I had (now long gone) under the pillow as if this somehow made us safer than we otherwise would have been.

To be honest, I do not remember how long we were in Vancouver or where we stayed after that first night. Twenty dollars did not stretch too far. But Lois did contact the place where she wanted to work. They told her that they would be in touch at the end of the summer. She left information on how they could reach her at the beginning of September, and we left, headed back to the road, and thumbed our way back to Banff. Once in Banff, we again received help from my cousin Dave. He managed to find us jobs at the Cave and Basin, Lois inside and me outside looking after the parking lot. I assisted people parking and provided information regarding the Cave and its history and the surrounding environment. I became friendly with Byron. He cleaned around the place. He was also an artisan who made rings and pendants from bone he found in the forests. I earlier told about his wares and The Quest store. Looking back, I remember Byron as a Romantic figure, well worthy of his name.

In any case, I worked at the Cave and Basin until late August, when, as I outlined above, I went back to Ontario. The romance that took place that summer came to an end, and I made my way to Hamilton in September, found a place to stay, and began the M.A. program in English at McMaster University.

CHAPTER FIVE
McMaster University

I enrolled in three courses in Fall 1968: James and Faulkner, Edmund Spenser, and the Eighteenth-Century Novel. The year unfolded unremarkably, except for a couple of things. First, I recall the course on James and Faulkner for its intensity and for relieving me of my innocence perhaps not for the first, and certainly not the last, time. We were six students, four males and two females. Of the four males, three had been McMaster undergraduates; the fourth, me, came over from Toronto. The two females had come from England. Our instructor was J. D. Brasch, a scholar of little publication but much braggadocio. He also cultivated orchids. We wrote two-page papers for each class, two pages, no more, no less. Brasch would not mark a paper than spilled over onto a third page. He marked these papers with a check, a plus sign, or a minus sign. Over the year, the six of us became close and we regularly compared pluses, minuses, and checks. We were all doing about the same when we arrived at year's end in April 1969. Once classes had ended, late on a Friday afternoon, each of us received a note from Brasch that contained a quotation from Walt Whitman and an invitation to visit Brasch in his office. We each had an assigned day and time. When I went to his office, he sat me down and began asking me about a large poster of John Wayne that I had in my office. We talked about John Wayne, western movies, and I don't know what else. The chat was genial and lasted between one and two hours. Later I learned that this was a final examination; I received A for the course. So did the other three males, one of whom would later turn up at the university I worked in for nearly forty years and become Vice President Academic there.

The two women were not so lucky. Each spent ten minutes or less with Brasch. When they received their grade for the course, both received a failing grade. This meant that they were out of the program. Once the six of us had compared our grades, we were outraged. It turned out that Brasch had, during the year, asked each of the women to travel with him to Buffalo, ostensibly to visit the art gallery there. Each of them had declined the invitation. We urged the two women to go to Brasch and appeal their grades. They did. Apparently, he told them that he did not like English people, he did not like these two women, and he would deny saying these things if they made this conversation public. The two women were in despair. Some of us rallied the other graduate students; we had a meeting and decided to appeal en masse and in writing to the department head. We got signatures from all graduate students but two, one of whom was the fellow who had been in the James and Faulkner course and who later became VP Academic at the university where I taught. The petition went to the department head, who conferred with other members of the department and with the dean, or so we were given to believe, and the department decided in its wisdom to uphold the instructor's grades and to consider the matter closed. As I said, I lost innocence. I had thought of the university as a place of fairness, equality, and justice. I was to learn otherwise again and again.

During the year, I became close to one of the two women who fared so unluckily in Brasch's course. By the end of the second term, we were living together in an apartment in Dundas, not far from campus. The academic gods smiled on my fortunes. I had graduated from the University of Toronto with an undistinguished record and managed to get into McMaster largely on the strength of letters of recommendation from David Knight and John Baird, both of whom had connections with McMaster. Once in the M.A. program I continued in undistinguished achievement. Not far into the fall session, all new students to the program had to write a comprehensive examination. I wrote this and failed. I did, however, have a second chance to pass the thing in the spring. Also, all new students had to take a one-hour-a-week course in bibliography. I started this course, but found it tedious. I soon began to miss the class. In fact, I missed the class so much that I never did do the assignments. How I managed to get by without completing this course is a mystery to me, but I did. Once spring arrived and our courses ended, I had collected firsts (A) in all three of my courses. The time had arrived for me to rewrite the comprehensive examination. I did this in April. About a week after I wrote the exam, I was called to a meeting with Tom Cain, the coordinator of the examination, and, by chance, the instructor of the Spenser course in which I had received an A. Professor Cain sat behind his desk with a stern look on his face. He showed me my examination paper and said it was terrible. He talked with me for a while; I cannot recall what passed between us. Finally, he grabbed a pencil, scribbled "68" on the paper, shook his head, and told me to get out of his office. I left feeling ambivalent about what had transpired; sixty-eight was a minimal pass. I was through to the next stage—the writing of a hundred-page thesis.

For my thesis, I chose to write on Laurence Sterne, the eighteenth-century novelist of two strange and what we would dub today experimental or avant-garde novels, the cock-and-bull stories of Tristram Shandy and Parson Yorick: *The Life and Opinions of Tristram Shandy, Gentleman* (1757–1769) and *The Sentimental Journey Through France and Italy* (1768). My supervisor was the instructor of the eighteenth-century course I had taken, Graham Petrie. Professor Petrie was one of the most reticent and unassertive persons I have known. He asked me to see him once a week to report on my progress. I did this, but more often than not I had no progress to report. I would say this. He would sit opposite me and stare. He rarely blinked. He just looked at me and waited. I squirmed and waited. These meetings were an ordeal for me, and most likely for Graham as well. He was not a mean or unpleasant person, but he did have the social skills of a tea tray. In any case, I managed to research and write my M.A. thesis on Laurence Sterne and complete the requirements for graduation by the end of the summer. I felt at the time that I knew everything there was to know about *Tristram Shandy*. Years later, I reread the novel in order to teach it; I was flummoxed by much of it. Then, not too long ago, I came across my M.A. thesis on the internet. Reading a bit of it, I am embarrassed at the quality of the writing. I have, I hope, improved since then.

As for Graham Petrie, he had a successful career, even turning to fiction writing later. I last saw him while I was studying for my Ph.D. in England. I often spent the days wandering the streets of London, peering in bookstore windows or looking for blue plaques on buildings or exploring churches or galleries. One day, I was staring at a book display in a bookstore window on Charing Cross Road. The store was the venerable Zwemmer's; it is no longer there. In fact, I was contemplating going in to purchase a book I was staring at, a book on the French New Wave filmmaker François Truffaut by none other than Graham Petrie. I turned from the window and standing inches from me was the author of the book, Professor Petrie himself. As usual, he stared. We had a few uneasy words, and he departed. That was the last time I saw him, but he was a role model, someone I looked up to. His foray into film studies and fiction struck me as creative and nicely unconventional. He was an academic to emulate.

By the end of the summer 1969, my partner had returned to England and I had accepted a teaching job in Port Hope, Ontario. Back in June, I had seen an advertisement for a teaching job at Port Hope High School. This was a late ad and I suspected the school was anxious to find someone. I applied and received an invitation for an interview. I drove down to Port Hope and met the principal and head of English for my interview. I remember that the first question they asked was, "Why do you want to be a high school teacher?" I also remember that my answer was: "I don't." Of course, the two interviewers looked askance. I went on to explain that I did not envisage myself teaching high school for the rest of my life, but that teaching was a vocation I certainly did want to pursue. My hope was, I said, to work for a few years, save money, and then go back to school. My interest in my subject was such that I wanted to pursue an academic career. From this distance, I do not remember the precise argument I conjured, but they were suitably impressed and offered me a job teaching grades ten and twelve. I had no training in pedagogy.

I completed my thesis in time to turn up for work in Port Hope in the first week of September. I found a place to stay in a nearby town, Cobourg. My teaching life had begun. Actually, my teaching life had begun the previous academic year when I took up a teaching fellowship at McMaster. The money I received effectively paid for my M.A. year. I taught a first-year tutorial for the survey course that served most students starting out in English, the standard course that used *The Norton Anthology of English Literature* in two volumes. I have little or no memory of this experience, except for the student who appealed a grade I had assigned on one of the essays. I recall this because Alvin Lee, my teaching supervisor, supported my grading and in doing so gave me confidence that I could grade fairly and thoroughly.

Anther experience I recall from my time in Hamilton was softball. Our graduates had a team, a very poor team. On third base we had a pregnant woman. Our outfield had players from England who had never played ball before, although they had played cricket. In short, we had a team that regularly lost and lost embarrassingly; scores of 18–1 or 23–4 were common. For a while we laughed the losses off, but eventually we began to feel that melancholy that takes fun away. That summer Neil Armstrong landed on the moon, providing testimony to what humans can achieve. We, however, did not manage to achieve a mark in the win column. Fun became a struggle. In these later days I see grad school too has become struggling fun, a slog that must leave us asking, why are we doing this?

As far as grad school is concerned, I did not ask that question. I enjoyed the experience, despite the comprehensive examinations and the loss of innocence. Most important were Spenser and Faulkner and Sterne and the other writers that filled my days. Reading literature was my métier, a calling, a desire realized as nearly as desire might be. As far as I knew, nothing could be more important than the reading of, thinking about, and writing about literature. Literature informed life. Literature reminded us of what was important in life. Literature opened vistas of tolerance and understanding. Literature was important precisely because it was not life. Literature imagined the best and the worst of what life was. Literature was democracy at its best. In the world of books anything was possible. Literature offered hope for a broken humanity. I still hold close the desire that all this is true, knowing just how woefully inadequate such a view remains. Literature has not saved the planet and it is unlikely to do so as we go forward. Still and always, what literature and art promote is possibility and a world without possibility is empty and lost. The creation of worlds that do not exist is a necessary component of a world that has peace and tranquility and good will, even as it has strife and upheaval and greed.

CHAPTER SIX

Digression on Illnesses

Finally, in the fall of that year in Hamilton, I drove over one gloomy day to Toronto to visit my Uncle Bill in the hospital. Uncle Bill is the person who bought me that suit when I arrived in Toronto four years earlier. He was my father's gay brother, and I had a terrible argument with him one time on the street in Smiths Falls. The argument was about my father's alcoholism. I had no interest in hearing my father's brother defend my father. In any case, Bill was a good person and he taught me something deeply moving when I visited him in the hospital. I had no idea he was so ill. He had cancer. When I saw him, he was just a stick man, all bone with a veneer of skin. He was so thin that he had to use a rubber ring to lie on because his tailbone was raw and painful. He was, however, friendly and welcoming when I entered his room. We talked for a short time, and then he asked if I would do him a favour. I said I would, and he asked if I would take him for a walk. He was bird light as I assisted him from the bed and then up and down the corridor. The walk was not far, but he was breathless when I helped him back onto that rubber ring in his bed. His hospital gown did not cover much, and Bill remarked that you had to leave your dignity behind when you entered hospital. As I was driving back to Hamilton, I realized that I had not done him a favour; he could barely walk or even stand. The truth was that he had done me a favour, giving me a sense that I was doing something useful for him. He had great courage and much generosity. And he certainly had not left his dignity behind.

Twice more I attended people during their final days as they succumbed to cancer. After Bill, the next person whom I visited in hospital was Jennie Friesen. During my first few years in Calgary, I met her husband, Abe Friesen. My partner, Suzanne, was working at a high school in the city, and she met Jennie Friesen as a colleague. But not long after these two met, Jennie entered hospital with late-stage cancer. I would go to the hospital and sit with her husband, Abe. At the time, Abe was a high school teacher of chemistry. We had little in common, and we had never met before. I would sit with him, more often than not in silence. The days passed, as they must, and Jennie finally passed away. Not long after, Abe resigned from his teaching job and departed for Mexico. After perhaps six months, I received a letter from Abe in which he told me how grateful he was for my support during his difficult time. To be honest, I had not thought much about it; we help out when we can. This was my mother's way. Anyway, when Abe returned to Calgary a year or so later, he became a friend.

I knew Abe for many years. He was a squash partner, and, much to my frustration, what he would call a business partner. Instead of returning to teaching, Abe became a real estate agent. And he went into this profession with gusto. In the early 1980s, he came up with a scheme to gather some fourteen friends and pool resources and build an apartment building. In short, he did this and he convinced me to get involved. For several years this project proved to be a great help in reducing my annual taxes; however, as time went on and the economic situation changed, I began to feel this investment something of an albatross. I was never sure about Abe's financial wheeling and dealing. And also as time went on, I saw less and less of Abe. He became associated with something called the Calgary Centre for Positive Living, and he was eager to haul me aboard this spiritual vessel. I recall one time he drove me home from somewhere in his large shiny Cadillac. He pulled up in front of the house I was living in and began to talk about spiritual matters, informing me that every cell in our bodies was connected to every cell in the universe. And so on and so on. I tried to end the conversation agreeably, but he just went on ignoring my claims of lack of interest. Later Frances (my partner then and now), reported that she was watching from our kitchen window what was transpiring in the large Cadillac; she could see me growing more agitated until finally I began beating my fists on the dashboard. Abe remained calm. He was nothing, if not persistent. He was a friend.

The other person I attended through her final illness was Barbara McQuaid. Barbara was a secretary in my department at the university, and a good person. Many of my colleagues made fun of Barbara because she was what they thought of as dim. I knew her as a well-meaning good person. She and her young daughter had come west from Belleville, Ontario, after her husband died. She told me that she attributed his death to their winning of the Irish Sweepstakes. They had won a considerable amount of money, enough that Barbara's husband quit his job, and they purchased what Barbara called their "dream home." It was not long after they moved in that Barbara became aware that her husband had turned to drink. She said she knew this when she heard him go to the fridge and begin swallowing something. She looked to see him swigging from a bottle of vodka, and he remarked, "Just like milk." He drank himself into the grave, and from that time Barbara hated lotteries of any kind. The point is, I liked Barbara and sometimes visited her in her home. Frances and I went to see her one winter when it must have been between thirty and forty degrees below zero.

Barbara suffered from a tumour on her head, and she ended spending quite a few days in the hospital. I would go and spend time with her most days, although on most occasions I don't think she knew I was there. She had an enormous swelling on the side of her head. It was painful to see, and must have been excruciating to experience. Barbara had great courage.

Her days in the hospital are memorable for another reason. One day, three of us were visiting: Frances, Kyla, and me. I don't know why Kate was not with us. Anyway, Kyla suddenly went white and began to waver. Frances took her to the washroom, and when they came back Kyla's life had passed into another phase. The coincidence of life entering its fertile stage and life ending did not pass unnoticed. Not long after this, Barbara passed away.

That was then. Now I have entered that time when passings occur more frequently than they once did. Not long ago, my longtime friend Victor Ramraj died. My sister has begun to show signs of dementia, and my brother-in-law is infirm (since I wrote this, he has passed away). Both Frances and I have had serious health concerns, me for the first time that I can remember. Having mentioned health and mortality, I hasten to add that we continue cycling and walking and kayaking and generally keeping active. Life goes on until all of a sudden it no longer happens. As far as I know, there is not really more that one can say about moving through time. We collect pieces of time until time is no longer.

CHAPTER SEVEN

Teaching High School

I began teaching in the fall of 1969. My assignment involved teaching the top three grade ten classes and the bottom two grade twelve classes. In those days, students were divided into academic streams and vocational streams, and the classes designated with letters. For example, Grade 10A, 10B, and 10C were the academic classes, whereas Grade 10D and 10E were the vocational classes. I taught the first three grade ten classes. I also taught 12E, a class of some forty females whose vocation was typing, and 12F, a small class of twelve "difficult" students, students who were misfits; the administration considered these students unmanageable. For the most part, I got on well with all the grades. I say for the most part, because truth to tell my relationship with the young women in 12E was what I might term uneasy. They chatted loudly through class while I tried to holler above the racket. The fact that I taught in a mobile classroom way back behind the school helped. No matter what noise we created, we did not bother other classes. As for the 12F class, I enjoyed these students. They were energetic and anti-authoritarian; we understood each other, or so I thought. The grade ten classes were not a challenge.

I had no teacher training other than my experience conducting a tutorial at McMaster. I found, however, that I had no trouble with the material. I could, and sometimes did, play bridge all night, get up from the bridge table and go to school and teach. I never felt that I did not have things to pass on to the students; I never felt that the students challenged my knowledge. And this was the problem. I wanted a challenge. I wanted to find my thinking moved, contradicted, countered. Because I did not find such challenge, I decided by Christmas that I did not wish to continue teaching high school, and I began to apply to schools in England to continue my studies at the Ph.D. level. I chose English universities because I knew I could not manage the North American system with its various written examinations. I just could not write examinations successfully. I applied to many universities in England, but I had only two positive responses, one from Keele where I had applied to do work on Henry James, and one from Reading where I had applied to work on Romanticisms from Mozart to William S. Burroughs. The latter application is perhaps the first indication of my tendency to wander over the artistic map. In this application, I had mentioned in passing the Scottish writer George MacDonald. While at McMaster I had heard about MacDonald from one of the professors, Joseph Sigman, and one weekend in early fall 1969 I drove from Cobourg to Toronto to see the film *2001: A Space Odyssey*. While waiting for the film to begin, I started reading MacDonald's *Lilith*, in the Ballantine edition with a short preface by Lin Carter. This is as much as I knew of George MacDonald. The response I received from Reading University was from Professor D. J. Gordon. He pointed out that I could not write the "history of the world," but that Dr. Fletcher had read my proposal and remarked that if I were willing to concentrate on George MacDonald, then he would be willing to serve as my supervisor on the Ph.D. project. I accepted this proposal and was set to go to England in the late summer of 1970.

I did not tell the people at Port Hope High School because I did not see any need to tell them. By the time I had sorted out my plans for the Ph.D., it was clear that I would not be invited back to teach in the fall of 1970. Near the end of my first term at the high school, we had to submit grades for our classes. I submitted mine and a few days later I got a call from the head of department. Would I please come to see him? I did. He told me to change my grades so they accorded with the Bell curve. I said that I would not do this. We had a discussion during which he pointed out that the students would never know that I had altered grades to conform to some schema. I said that I would know. To convince me, he gave me an example, Charles Wickett, a chubby kid from my Grade 10A class, and said that Charles would not mind if his grade of 58 was lowered to 55. I said that we should call Charles in and ask him which grade he preferred, 58 or 55. And so it went. Finally, I said that he or anyone else in authority could change the grades if they wanted to, but I would not do this. Later, sometime around mid-February, the school held a public meeting to discuss the planned switch from the present way of channeling students into academic and non-academic streams to a cafeteria-style system in which students could choose what classes they wanted, as long as they took the subjects necessary for matriculation in their chosen career paths. During the meeting, support for the change was pretty much universal. I stood up and pointed out that the new system would raise the student/teacher ratio and serve the interests of the government more than it would serve the interests of the students. The administration at the school did not receive my remarks kindly. And so, as I anticipated, I was not offered a renewal of contract for the next year.

Before I left Port Hope High School something took place that moved me deeply and secured my sense of the importance of teaching. The school held a final teachers' meeting before everything broke up for the summer. At this meeting gifts were passed out to those who were leaving for other teaching jobs or those retiring or those just leaving the profession. I did not receive one of these gifts of parting. The meeting was just about over when a knock came to the door. Someone, I do not remember who, answered the knock, opened the door, and revealed a group of my grade ten students, headed by Charles Wickett. (I am not making this up!) They had come to leave a gift for me. They came in and presented me with their gift, a huge poster of Bob Dylan taken from the photograph on the cover of his *Blonde on Blonde* album. No doubt you will hear more about Bob Dylan as I ramble on, but for now you just need to know that I had taught several Bob Dylan songs during the year to all my classes. Regularly I had played his songs just for the benefit of the students' sense of the present moment. This was the time of protests and resistance to convention and counterculture and non-conformity and tuning in and turning on and dropping out and new industrial states and guaranteed annual incomes and the coming of leisure and so on. I had brought all of this to the classroom, and Dylan had been very much a part of this. "Masters of War," "The Lonesome Death of Hattie Carroll," "The Ballad of Hollis Brown," "Gates of Eden," "My Back Pages," "Desolation Row," "Ballad in Plain D," "Chimes of Freedom," these were my teaching aids. I had been in a round portable classroom mixing up the medicine, one hand waving free, urging the students to be younger than they had been when they entered my classroom. We met on edges and maybe we looked into the abyss. In any case, I learned that teaching could be deeply satisfying; I also learned that the impediment to teaching was the administrative bureaucracy. So much wasted time on curricula change and fretting over methods and fearing to alienate a youth that was puzzled by a world caught in the desire for constant easeful death. Youth was already alienated. Alienation is the condition of youth.

As for Mr. Dylan, I first heard him in the fall of 1963 when my friend Donnie Knapp came to school with the news that he had joined the Columbia Record Club, and that he had received a record by some guy who wrote some good songs, but who couldn't sing worth a damn. When pressed, Donnie said one song was about "going down the road, with a suitcase in my hand, bling bling bling." He reiterated that the guy—he could not recall his name—just could not sing and that he (Donnie) was going to return the record to Columbia. For reasons I can no longer remember, I asked Donnie if I could listen to the record before he sent it back. Donnie just lived around the corner from me on Winifred Street, and so I went to his place after school and listened to "The Freewheelin' Bob Dylan." I was eighteen years old. I was not a child, but when I heard those songs, I felt as if I had been hearing them all my relatively short life. That was the year I began to read. That was my last year in high school. That was when I began write what you read here. If you had asked me back then what I thought of that singer who could not sing, I would have said that Donnie Knapp was half right—the songs were great—but that his evaluation of the singing was way off in the circle of hell devoted to tin ears. That voice struck me as a voice for the ages; what I could not say back then was that Dylan "had the blood of the land" in his voice; that is the best description of his voice that I have heard.

Despite Mr. Dylan, I was a callow youth, avowing this and disavowing that, "fearing not that I'd become my enemy in the instant that I preach." What I write here are my back pages, and I wish I could say that I was so much older then and that I am younger than that now. I understand what the lyrics mean, and yes, I think they are acute. On the other hand, the years do not, my friend, bring us closer to the wisdom of the child, the innocence that burns with a hard gemlike flame and that allows us an intuitive grasp of life's precious gestures. The outreach of youth has its innocence, but as always innocence is a small slip away from ignorance. As for age, this brings nothing more or less than decline. Would it were otherwise. On the other hand, I am no less committed to the values I held back then.

I ought to mention one more thing. In November 1969, while teaching in the portable classroom at Port Hope High School, I saw my father for the last time. I was teaching the small group of students in Grade 12F, the supposedly difficult students, when the door opened and my father appeared silhouetted by the light outside. Needless to say, I was dumbfounded. I hastily made my way across the room and ushered my father outside, shutting the door behind me. I no longer remember what we said, although my father was just passing through town and decided to drop by and see his son. I do remember that when I said my goodbyes and re-entered the classroom, the students were curious to know whether that was an inspector come to check on me. My father would have liked this; he was always hoping to be someone of importance. My mother often referred to him as Big Dome, a character from the Little Iodine comics. I never saw Big Dome again.

CHAPTER EIGHT

Marriage

I left Port Hope High School, as I left university, as I left the town in which I grew up, quietly and without fanfare. The story of my life—leavings without fanfare. But I also left with a partner. Remember those two young women who had taken the course in James and Faulkner with me and three other young men? One of these young women was Suzanne. She was the person with whom I shared an apartment in Dundas while I finished my M.A. thesis. Anyhow, she had gone back to England, but she had not gone from my life. In December 1969, after school closed for the holidays, I flew to England to get married. This was my first trip abroad and I was an innocent. I landed at Heathrow, picked up my suitcase, and looked for transportation into London and Euston Station where I would get a train north to Wellington in Shropshire. I found myself in a line waiting for a bus. When it arrived, the bus had a small caravan attached to the rear; this was the luggage place. I deposited my suitcase in this caravan and stepped back to the line, but before I could react, the doors of the bus closed and the vehicle departed in a whiff of black smoke. I was a pathetic stranger in a strange land. Without thinking, I went to the line for taxis and waited, wondering if I would ever see my suitcase again. Finally, I was on the front line and a cab stopped. I climbed in. The glass partition between front seat and back slid open and a cheerful young man asked me where I wanted to go. I said Euston Station. Off we went. Instead of closing the glass panel, the driver asked me where I was from. In a flurry of excitement, fueled by jet lag and anxiety, I told him where I was from, why I was in England, and what had happened to my baggage. The driver tried to calm me down by saying that my suitcase would undoubtedly be waiting for me at the train station. Then he asked me if I knew about English money—pounds, shillings, and pence (this was before England went decimal in their currency). Of course, I said no. He proceeded to give me a lesson, showing me sixpence pieces (tanners), thruppences, a crown (five shillings), a ten bob note (half of a pound), and so on. I was thoroughly confused. But I was also enraptured. It was dark and drizzly as we rode through the streets of London, and I was pleased to have found a friend. When we arrived at Euston Station, I told the driver (I wish I could remember his name) that I did not know how much I owed him. He looked at my wallet and took some money from it, saying this was good. Then he accompanied me into the station to show me where the luggage carousel was located. When we got to this carousel, we saw one bag slowly making its rounds. My suitcase. I recovered this and said so long to the taxi driver. He left. Before I had time to make it to the ticket kiosk, he was back. He asked if he could take my picture. I agreed, smiled, and said goodbye once again. I later learned that he had taken a ten bob note from me for taxi fare, about a dollar and a half in Canadian money. In other words, he was a friend. This was my introduction to England.

I made my way to a small village called Coalport on the Severn River, just about a mile downriver from Ironbridge, the birthplace of the industrial revolution. Suzanne's parents lived in a brick house on the hillside overlooking the Severn, and only a short distance from a second iron bridge, a sort of companion bridge to the more famous one a mile upriver. In the nearby parish church called Sutton Maddock, we were married.

I have few words to offer on this occasion. I do, however, have fond memories of Suzanne's parents, Molly and Bill Higginson. Molly especially is someone I grew to respect. She grew up only a short distance from where she lived with Bill in Coalport, and she did not travel more than two miles from her home until she came to visit her daughter in Canada. In other words, she lived a sheltered and what I might call a simple life, her interests largely local and familial. She worked as a charlady for a family named Ridley that lived nearby. She was conservative in her views. And so when her only child had marital difficulties and divorced some thirteen years after that wedding in 1969, you might think that she would take the natural partisan position and abandon the person who hurt her daughter. This did not happen. Molly remained warm and friendly, sending a letter and Christmas card every year until she died at just over ninety years of age. We might learn a lot from a person such as Molly Higginson. Clearly, she knew about forgiveness, she knew about human foibles and weaknesses, she knew how to separate goodness from the rubble of human interaction, and she knew all this without having the schooling we tout so highly. Quite simply, she was a good human being who understood that being human ought to mean being tolerant and generous to those who make mistakes. Not all mistakes are either willful or unkind.

Bill too was a good person. As I indicate elsewhere, he made a cabinet for me when I was a graduate student in Reading. He also made bookcases for my study in Calgary. He was a master craftsman and I still have those bookcases. He was a gentle, kind person.

Before leaving this family, I want to mention Ken and Norma. Norma was a cousin of Suzanne's, and she and Ken lived in a council house not far from the parish church. One time, when we were living in Reading, Norma came to visit, and she was agitated because of an experience she claimed to have had in the council house. What follows is the story she told, as she told it. Take it for what it's worth. She said that for some time she had the sense that someone else was in the house with her, Ken, and their two children. She had kept this feeling to herself because she knew Ken would just think she was being silly. He took no truck with such irrationalities. Then one night she woke with the distinct feeling that someone else was in the room. She looked up from where she lay and saw standing at the foot of the bed a woman wearing a black dress. This woman had white hair and she appeared to be weeping. She also gestured to Norma, but then she just evaporated. First, she was there, palpably; then she was not there. The room was cold. Norma looked over to see if Ken was awake, and he was. She said he lay there with eyes wide open. Now Ken was a no-nonsense fellow who made fun of any notion of spirits or ghosts. But there he was with eyes wide open, looking just as if he had seen a ghost. Norma asked him if had seen the weeping woman at the end of the bed, and he said no. This is what convinced her that the experience was real. Ken said he had not seen any person in the room, but that he woke with the distinct feeling that someone was there. Norma told him what she had seen, and to her surprise he believed her. He never did see this woman, but Norma saw her on several occasions.

Neither Ken nor Norma knew what to do. But as the days passed, their two children began to ask if someone was in the house. They came home from school one day and said they knew someone else was in the house. They checked all the rooms and even went out to the back garden. They insisted someone was there. At this point, Norma thought they had to do something or the kids would suffer. She went to the local vicar and told him what they were experiencing. He took her seriously and said he would check into the situation. Not long after, he came to see Norma and Ken and told them that prior to their living in this house, an elderly couple had lived in it for quite a long time. They had arranged for the two of them to be buried in the local churchyard. The woman died and was duly interred in the nearby Sutton Maddock churchyard cemetery. The husband then moved down to Sussex to stay with his daughter and her family. He died there and was buried there. The vicar surmised that what Norma had seen was the lady coming back to the house to look for her husband. He said they should have an exorcism and see what transpired. And so they had a quiet ritual in the house, burning some candles and saying a few prayers in which the vicar assured the woman that her husband was well. After this, Norma said, she did not see the woman again and Ken and the children stopped feeling as if there was someone else in the house. There you have it. Believe it or not, as Ripley said.

After a few days' honeymoon in England, Suzanne and I headed back to Canada and I resumed work at the high school to finish the year's teaching. Then in the summer of 1970, we made a bus journey across Canada. This trip took us to Vancouver Island, as far north as Courtenay. After this trip, we headed to England where I was to begin my Ph.D. at Reading University.

CHAPTER NINE
England for Three Years

We arrived in England at the end of August 1970. Before locating in Reading, we went for a trip to the Lake Country with two people we knew from McMaster, Suzanne's friend Terry and her beau, Phil. Phil had a rickety old automobile that was so rickety that we had, at times, to jump out and put a large stone behind a back wheel while Phil coaxed the thing up steep inclines. This was a memorable trip. I have often said that the English Lake country is the most beautiful country I have seen. On that trip we visited Grasmere and Rydal Mount, two places closely associated with Wordsworth, and Keswick where Coleridge and Southey lived, and Cockermouth, birthplace of Wordsworth. My education in the English Romantics had begun in earnest. Years later I returned to the Lakes and visited Brantwood, Ruskin's home and also Hill Top where Beatrix Potter lived. On the same trip, I explored Hawkshead where a young Wordsworth went to school.

On the trip with Terry and Phil, we visited Haworth and the Yorkshire moors, home of the Brontë family, and we walked across the moor to Top Withens, supposedly the inspiration for the home of the Earnshaws in *Wuthering Heights*. On the return trek, I saw an uncanny sight—a figure in flowing black dress floating across the moor. On closer inspection, this ghostly apparition resolved into a nun who was on the same walk as we were. The flowing dress was her black habit, and her wimple gave her appearance that ghostly glow. Sometimes life imitates art.

Three more places on this trip come to mind. One is Beverley, location of the beautiful minster; the visit to Beverley Minster began my exploration of gothic ecclesiastical buildings. A second place is the city of Hull, a northern port city, strong and dreary. Finally, a word about a short stay in Bradford. Here we stayed with relatives of Phil. The lady of the house was lame, but she managed to get around the house nimbly enough. She also made her own wine. Suzanne and I were to sleep outside in a caravan, but before bed the family had a rousing get-together and I imbibed more of the homemade elixir than I should have. At one point we were listening to records and grooving to that mid-sixties supergroup, Cream, when I found myself standing in the centre of the sitting room with my arm around Phil. I remember thinking, "But I don't even like this guy." I was on my way to a night not to remember. I understand that when we went out to the caravan, I was whooping and hollering to beat the band. The family was worried that neighbours would call the bobbies. Anyhow, I have seen neither Phil nor Terry since that trip to England's north country.

After finding a flat in Reading and getting settled, I made my way to the university in Whiteknights Park. First, I met the professor (UK universities in those days had one professor); this was D. J. Gordon, a Renaissance specialist who had worked on Ben Jonson and Inigo Jones. I was ushered into his office at ten one morning. He offered me sherry and commented that "I was the young man from Toronto." Toronto meant something then; Hamilton and McMaster did not. As for the sherry, this was a portent of things to come. Professor Gordon died some years later after he was beaten one night in a pub. Apparently, he had picked the wrong young man to seduce. The morning I met him, he chatted for a while and then plunked an open book on my lap, instructing me to read. I began to read aloud, and he interrupted saying I should just read silently. So, I began to read. Shortly, he snatched the book from my hands, placed it in front of him, glanced at a page, turned the page, a second or three later he turned the page again, repeated this a couple of times and then clapped the book closed. "If you cannot read this quickly, young man, you will find difficulty doing the Ph.D." I was dismissed. I was crushed. Professor Gordon waved me away, saying I should get in touch with Dr. Fletcher as soon as possible.

I went right down the hall and knocked on Fletcher's door. "Come in," he said, and I entered a spacious book-lined office. I could not see anyone. "Down here," I heard and located a kneeling man at the base of one bookshelf. This man, Dr. Ian Fletcher, unbent, rose and stood before me, tall and slightly stooped, with a balding head. His trousers were loose and his jacket was wrinkled. An awkwardly gangly person, he was holding a book. This he put down on his desk and wiped his nose with his sleeve. We spoke for a few minutes, when he suddenly went over to a cupboard, opened the doors, and extracted two fat volumes that he promptly plopped onto his desk. These, he told me, were his Ph.D. thesis, some thousand pages. When I had written an amount to balance these volumes on a scale, I would be done my Ph.D. thesis, he said. That effectively closed our first meeting. I left the university that morning stunned. I knew no one except Suzanne; she found a job teaching at a nearby secondary school. As for me, I wandered the streets of Reading, finding my way to the river (the Thames) where I threw bread to the swans. I also found the local library that offered noon-hour concerts most days. The library was not far from Reading Jail where Oscar Wilde had spent his incarceration. And near the jail were the ruins of Reading Abbey where a plaque hung with the words of "Sumer Is Icumin In," a medieval song associated with the abbey because the earliest manuscript was found there. In other words, my education had begun here, as it had begun way back in Toronto, on the streets and byways of the city in which I lived.

Sometime during that first year, I also began regular treks to London; Paddington Station was a short thirty-minute train ride from Reading. My trips into the city were, ostensibly, to spend the days at the British Museum Reading Room researching my thesis. I did go to the Reading Room, but mostly that first year I wandered the streets of London, looking at blue plaques on buildings, checking out bookstores, contemplating pictures in the National Gallery, absorbing quiet in ancient buildings, exploring the stacks at the University of London Library, Senate House. Just off Leicester Square, in Soho, I came across a small Catholic Church that contains a mural dedicated to the Virgin by the French artist and writer, Jean Cocteau. Space here was private and otherworldly. Other places where I spent quiet time were the Courtauld Institute and, of course, the Tate Gallery and the National Gallery. I had taken a one-hour-a-week option in art history when I was an undergraduate, but I had never seen the grand masters outside of bookplates. Here in London, I could see Italian masters, Dutch masters, French masters, English masters, and masters I had never heard of before. I began to know the Romantic and Victorian painters and artists who complemented the work of the writer I was studying: William Blake, John Linnell, John Martin, Richard Dadd, John Constable, J. M. W. Turner, Noel Paton, and of course the Pre-Raphaelites and their circle. The artist closest to the subject of my research was Arthur Hughes; Hughes had illustrated several of MacDonald's books. Just as I had in Toronto, in London I entered a world that thrilled with colour and shape and surprise and ideas and, for me, newness. The old was new to me.

Back in Reading, I discovered not far from where I lived an Oxfam shop that had a book section unlike any book section I had seen in similar shops. Among the books, I found antiquarian books, copies of books from the nineteenth century that tied in with my research in a tangential way. Here I found copies of fiction by Marie Corelli, Mary Molesworth, Charlotte Yonge, Hall Caine, Frederic W. Farrar, G. A. Henty, and others. One day, while I was kneeling by a bookshelf checking for books I could use, an elderly man stood above me and asked what I was looking for. I mentioned George MacDonald, among other Victorian writers. I also mentioned illustrated books. He suggested that I follow him into the back room. I did. There I found stacks and stacks of books. The man told me he kept the really interesting books in here. This was my introduction to Patrick Withers. Over the next nearly three years I got to know Patrick. That first day, he sold me the collected works of George Meredith for two pounds sterling, about five or six dollars back then. That was fourteen volumes for less than ten dollars. And he kept on the lookout for books I would find useful or interesting. It turned out that Patrick was a retired schoolmaster and also a former bookseller. He was now retired from his book business, and volunteering at Oxfam. He was much more than a retired schoolmaster and bookseller. He was a collector and an eccentric. He came by his eccentricity early.

One evening, as Patrick sat with Suzanne and me at our kitchen table after dinner, he told us of his childhood and upbringing. His mother, apparently, had been a strong-willed woman who desperately wanted to have a daughter. I dare say, she was a virago. She and her husband had some difficulty conceiving a child, but when they did the child was Patrick. Patrick's mother had had a boy, not a girl. Undaunted, this woman proceeded to raise her young child as if he was a female. She dressed the infant in dresses and frills, curled his long locks, and when it came time for the child to attend school, she enrolled Pat in a public school for girls. Patrick went to a girls' school until he was an age when it was no longer possible for him to be among girls without scandal. He was in his puberty years when he was removed from the girls' school and placed in a boys' school. Most likely it goes without saying that Patrick had a difficult time adjusting. More surprising was his eventual recruitment in the army. He said that he had no idea how to perform as a male. All he had known was female behaviour until he was about twelve.

Patrick grew to adulthood confused about his sexuality. He never did marry and, as far as I know, he never had a sexual relationship with either sex. He became something of a recluse with an interest in collecting. I have put this mildly. The first time Patrick invited me to his home, I arrived to find a small house surrounded by a high hedge. It looked like a fairy-tale house, and indeed it was. As I approached the front door, I saw that the windows were dark, blocked by heavy curtains. I entered and smelled the musty smell of museums, old newspapers, and books. The place was crowded with things, furniture and piles of books and papers, and knick-knacks, and drawings and paintings on the walls. Patrick ushered me into his sitting room. I sat on a plush chair between a piano piled with papers and a side table covered with books. I never did know why he had a piano, but he could not have played it because it was piled high with stuff. He explained his fascination with Napoleon. Every May 5, he would dress in a black suit, travel over the Channel to Paris, and visit Les Invalides where he mourned at the tomb of Napoleon. His interest in Napoleon had prompted him to collect memorabilia related to Napoleon. He owned several of Napoleon's letters, and one of his most prized possessions was a tooth he said was once Napoleon's, that is, once lodged in the great man's mouth. Patrick had also written not one, but two books on Napoleon. He explained that he was having a difficult time finding a publisher for these books. When he showed one of them to me, I understood why. The manuscript was in long hand, and in a script that was indecipherable. At least I could not penetrate the handwriting. It was neat enough, tiny in the extreme and so streamlined that the letters all ran into each other making it impossible to sort out letters, words, and sentences. The manuscript was also very fat. I felt badly.

Patrick was anxious that I not talk about his place to people I knew, and at first I thought he was just being eccentric. But soon I realized he had a genuine reason for not wanting his place advertised. It was a museum. On the walls were painting by the likes of Dante Gabriel Rossetti, Arthur Hughes, and Edward Burne Jones. He ate from eighteenth-century china that rested on an oak table made during the Restoration. He had many first-edition books. Before I left England, he entertained me in his garden for the first time. The garden contained nineteenth-century roses (I had not known there were such things), and Patrick offered me wine from Victorian crystal glasses. Also on my last visit, he took me to the sitting room where I had first experienced his hospitality. He sat me down and asked me to wait while he went to fetch something. He returned holding two books, one of which he put aside and the other he held out to me. It was a first edition of Christina Rossetti's *Speaking Likenesses* and it was in mint condition. Patrick knew I would be interested in this book because its illustrator is Arthur Hughes, the same person who illustrated many of George MacDonald's books, and it was a book by Rossetti that connected to work by MacDonald and his friend Lewis Carroll. Of course, I admired the book. I coveted it. Patrick asked if I had a copy of the book, and I said no. Back then most of the books I was working with were not in print, and *Speaking Likenesses* was one of these. I handed the book back to Patrick. He took it, put it down, reached over and picked up the other book he had brought and said, "This is for you." I looked down and saw a second copy of the first edition of *Speaking Likenesses*, this one battered with a torn spine. Patrick simply said, "It has a bit of foxing." I said I could not take this gift, but he insisted. As I took hold of the book, I swear I could feel a tug from Patrick as if he was reluctant to let go of this precious possession. But let go he did, and this book graces my bookshelf to this day.

When I left England in 1973, Patrick wrote to me two or three times. I could not read his letters, although I did write back letting him know about my new surroundings and my new job teaching at the university in Calgary. Then the letters stopped arriving. Six years later, in the fall of 1979, I returned to England to spend the year. I was on my first sabbatical, and I lived on the south coast in Bournemouth. But I did make a visit to Reading. The Oxfam shop was no longer where it had been, but I found its new location not far from the train station. It was a much fancier shop than the one I remembered, although it contained very few and very uninteresting books. I asked the person behind the desk if Patrick Withers was still working at the store. Patrick who? This person, and the other two she consulted, had never heard of Patrick Withers. I let quite a few more years elapse before I sought Patrick again. This time I consulted the internet. In fact, I have consulted the internet several times, most recently in 2015. I checked obituaries for Reading, and for Berkshire, and for England, but to no avail. I found no trace of Patrick Withers. This absence strikes me as strange. What happened to his many pieces of history, his art and literature and furniture and glassware and china and manuscripts and that tooth? Some questions will, perforce, remain unanswered.

So far, my education in England consisted of conversations with Patrick, wanderings about London, and desultory reading in the British Museum. I am glad I spent many hours in the British Museum, partly because this is an experience few, if any, of today's students will have. The British Library has long since replaced the old Reading Room. I also cherish my trips on the Northern Line to Colindale to consult the newspaper archive; this venue closed in 2014. As much as I found working in libraries tedious, I am grateful to have had the opportunity to study in a few of the world's great libraries, the British Museum, the Bodleian in Oxford, and the Beineke in New Haven. One evening, as I was returning books to the central hub in the British Museum Reading Room, I overheard a woman at the next window asking the person to whom she was returning her books where Marx sat. I loved this. The library person waved his hand and answered, "Out there in the round." In other words, Karl Marx, like the rest of us, entered the Reading Room and chose a seat, most likely a different seat one day to the next. But this moment was a reminder of all the great voices who had studied in this grand place. Experiences like mine were rare, and are even rarer now. I also recall having to read out loud a card that said I would not smoke or eat or shout or use profanities while working in the Bodleian Library. In the manuscript room of the British Museum, I transcribed the entirety of the first manuscript of George MacDonald's *Lilith*.

My mention of the Bodleian Library conjures memories of Oxford. Oxford was a mere thirty-minute train ride in the other direction from London. As time went on, I would go more often to Oxford because I could use the stacks as well as consult rare books in the Bodleian. And I liked Oxford. I liked the feel of the place, its intensity of buildings with names such as Ashmolean, Magdalen, Christ Church, Queen's, Sheldonian, Balliol, Oriel, and even New College (founded in 1379!). I have a brief story about the Shelley Memorial at University College. I often visited this memorial because I loved Shelley and thought the sculpture of his drowned body sensuous and moving. In my student days, people could simply walk past the porter's gate, turn right, and proceed to the small hall that was home to the Memorial. A lot of years later, I was visiting Oxford with Frances and I wanted to show her the Shelley Memorial. We headed over to University College only to discover that the porter now stopped people from entering unless they could show evidence of belonging to the college. I guess this was to keep the quadrangle quiet and free of pesky tourists. I think the same policy reigned at the other colleges. Undaunted by the halting of the porter, I told him of my student days and my many visits to the memorial and that I was hoping to show the sculpture to Frances. The porter said he would allow us to pass if I could tell him where the memorial was located. I did this, and he was as good as his word. We proceeded to the hall and Frances was, I am happy to report, suitably impressed by the beauty and intensity of the memorial.

I loved wandering the streets and lanes and quads of Oxford. I found the experience of the university buildings more stirring than the experience of the university buildings in Cambridge. I think the reason for this is simply the compactness of the Oxford colleges. They sit cheek by jowl, whereas the colleges in Cambridge seem more spread out. I know, the Backs at Cambridge are famous for their beauty, but Oxford has the Thames and the River Cherwell and enchanting walks behind Christ Church. Perhaps my championing of Oxford over Cambridge has as much to do with familiarity as it has to do with anything else. I remember the stained glass in Magdalen College Chapel, its steely look so different from most stained glass I had seen. Walking the byways of Oxford seemed an education by virtue of sight, sound, and intake of breath. The very air is charged with times gone by.

In my second year in Reading, I sometimes met Muriel Hutton in the British Museum, and we would have tea after the library closed and before I caught the train back home. Muriel was an independent scholar who lived in Redcar, in the northeast of England. She was captivated by MacDonald and devoted her life to studying his work and life. She located the curtains that the

MacDonald family used in their drama production of *The Pilgrim's Progress*. Her interest rose from her piety; she was a devout Christian and found, as many do, spiritual support in MacDonald's writing. Sadly, I lost contact with Muriel after I published an article in the *Scottish Literary Journal* on MacDonald's *Lilith* in which I noted that through the successive rewritings of that book in manuscript, MacDonald excised the word God until it appeared only a few times in the published version. My argument was not that MacDonald removed God, but that his excising of the word served to make his book more accessible to non-Christians, and less overtly homiletic. Muriel wrote a riposte to this article, and the journal asked me to write a reply to Muriel's piece. I did. And sadly that was the last I heard from Muriel. I say "sadly," because not only did I genuinely like her, but also Suzanne and I had visited her in Redcar and benefited from her hospitality. By the way, she treated us to the best fish and chips I ever had in England.

One time, when Muriel and I met after a day at the British Museum, I had an encounter I am compelled to report here. The two of us were seated in a café having tea. In another booth, behind and across from Muriel, a young man caught my eye, not because he hailed me, but because he appeared to be in distress. When we left, this young man was still visibly upset. On the street, I was saying my goodbyes to Muriel when I thought I should return to the café and check on this person I had watched for over an hour. Muriel suggested this was not a good idea, but I went back anyway. I asked the young man if he was all right. He said, no, he was not all right. I sat down and he proceeded to pour out his woes to me. Much of what he said had to do with his girlfriend. The two of them were Americans who had been traveling together when she suddenly dumped him, left and did not return. Anyway, time was passing and I was expected home. Rashly, I asked if this person would like to accompany me home and stay the night. He had indicated that he did not have a place to stay. He demurred, saying he could not make up his mind what to do. So I made his mind up for him, and dragged him from the café. I should mention that he was from Phoenix, and was now on his first trip away from home. His girlfriend, also from Phoenix and also away from home for the first time, had left him in France, and he had made his way to London where he fell apart. He said he had no idea what to do. He was incapable of making decisions. He was quite simply paralyzed. So we went to Paddington and caught the mail train to Reading, arriving quite late.

All the way on the train, Chris kept talking. He obsessed about his girlfriend, telling me that the two of them were God-fearing Catholics who had vowed to remain celibate until after marriage. However, their passion was intense and so they pleasured each other orally. He was telling me, in unnecessary detail, about cunnilingus in the desert, and I was watching faces of the other passengers appear above their papers or up from their books, sporting quizzical or disapproving looks. I felt acutely uncomfortable, but tried my best to provide solace to this tortured soul. He told me that he was paralyzed; he did not know where to turn or what to do next. Had I not approached him, he would be sitting in that café still and would have sat there until they removed him forcibly. When we finally got back to the flat, Chris was still obsessing. Suzanne was not pleased to have an unannounced houseguest so late in the night, and she was less pleased when he just kept talking, ignoring the food she kindly prepared. Chris talked into the night. Suzanne went to bed. In the wee hours, I was fed up and suddenly blurted out that I had had enough, I was going to bed, and in the morning I was taking Chris to the bus station, putting him on a bus and sending him home to America. He was insufferably self-absorbed. He stopped talking. In the morning, I did just that: took him to the bus station, put him on a bus to London with instructions to get a plane back to Phoenix. That was that. Much time elapsed when I received a brief note in the mail from Chris. In the note, he simply said he was home in the U.S. and thanked me for welcoming him into my home. I have never heard from him again.

Since I am reflecting on people I knew in Reading, I must remember Taysir Kamleh, a Palestinian Muslim I met and became friends with for a while. This story recounts the ending of this friendship. Taysir came as a student to Reading University, and I met him through Ian Fletcher. It was not easy to meet people because I did not have an office on campus, and I did not attend classes. The few people I met, I met by luck. Anyway, Taysir became a friend. He had come to Reading from Syria. I no longer remember what he was studying. He had red hair, something I found curious until he explained that not every person in the Middle East had black hair. He also carried papers that listed him as a "stateless person." He was Palestinian, and he told me of his parents taking him to look at a house in what is now Israel, pointing to it, and saying that was once their house, but that it was taken from them when Israel became a state in 1948. He also took me to a meeting on campus of the Palestinian Students' Society. I cannot recall in detail the arguments that took place on the floor of the meeting, but I do remember that there was a Jewish man among those attending and that he dominated the discussion. I also recall Taysir's anger. He insisted that if I were his true friend, then I would support his cause of restoring a Palestinian state, even if this meant taking up arms. We argued and argued—endlessly and without compromise or conclusion. Taysir was, I believe, connected to Fatah.

I suppose the friendship had to end, although I regret that it did. It happened this way. One day, Suzanne and I were out riding our bicycles, and we stopped by Taysir's place. He was living with his wife and two children. They welcomed us warmly. We spent so much time there that the day was waning. We excused ourselves, and prepared to leave. Taysir said that we could not leave because he was inviting us to stay and eat the evening meal with them. I thanked him, but explained that we did not have lights on our bikes and therefore should leave before it became dark outside and dangerous for us to ride home. Taysir explained that I could not refuse an invitation because this would be an insult. I explained that we meant no insult, but that we had to get home by dark for reasons of safety. He said I was not respecting his culture. I said that we were both on neutral ground since England was neither his nor my country. And so it went, back and forth. Taysir went so far as to go outside and remove the hand pumps from our bikes. In the end, I wrested the pumps from him, and we left. But I had done something irrevocable, and the friendship had come to an end. As I say, I regret this. I learned much from Taysir, not least that the situation in the Middle East is not as simple as I had been led to believe by the press in my country. This is something that became even clearer years later when Frances and I visited Israel and Palestine and saw the devastation the conflict brought to the Palestinian people.

Another friend I had in England was the husband of my wife's colleague; this was Dennis Grimshaw, someone else I have lost as a friend over the years. Dennis was a friend when I had no other in England. We used to play tennis and go boating together. He was fun to hang out with, although he would not enter a pub with me if I was wearing shorts. In the pub, he insisted that I drink only bitter, and not Shandys or lager and lime or any other girls' drinks. Definitely not Pims! I also had to have a pint, not a half pint; half pints were for sissies. Dennis was a hydraulic engineer. He was also a musician who later played with a group that called themselves, Vince Green Vipers. Remember that in England what North Americans refer to as a car's windshield is called a "windscreen," and then say Vince Green Vipers very quickly. I enjoyed Dennis's sense of humour.

Finally, there was Michael Sharp. I met Michael in my last year at Reading. He was a Ph.D. student whose work focused on twentieth-century war poets, especially Keith Douglas. His supervisor was Ian Fletcher, and we had this in common. We became mates and Michael encouraged me to write poetry, something I did—very badly. He also inveigled me to co-edit a literary journal. We named this *ZEMZEM*, in homage to Keith Douglas's war memoir, *From Alamein to Zem Zem*, published posthumously in 1946. *ZEMZEM* was short-lived—one issue. We worked hard and managed to bring out just one number, cheaply typed, run off on a Gestetner, and stapled. We had no financial support. But we did receive contributions from bona fide writers: Michael was a published poet, Peter Porter was well known in literary circles, and Ian Fletcher offered us some prose under the name Ian Selwyn. We headed the issue with a quotation from P. B. Shelley, a poet both Michael and I admired intensely. This small journal contains the only poetry of mine ever to dare stand in public; like the Emperor, it wore new clothes. Here is one example:

Three Sisters
(for Michael)

One wears red, one wears blue,
But I go naked in sun and snow
Except for this brooch hanging

Gold and green, like a leaf.
They hate me, those other two;
My limbs are white, my loves true.

Like snakes they insinuate
Round my body, blue and red
Between my thighs in secret.

Our father used daguerreotype
Long ago to record our eyes
Smiling red and blue and green

Like gems sparkling in the sun.
Browned like burlap by the film
That still covered my exposure.

Hiding their moving hands
Like insects they scurry
And enter my helpless body

While I watch horrified
As red and blue contend
For possession; wasps busy

Buzzing about my navel
Stinging beneath my brooch
Until my body hides itself

Giving up greenness and
Shrouding its whiteness
In colour of blue and red.

Three of us now dressed
Make a pretty picture;
In colour we smile in pain.

And our mother is so happy
She combs her hair just right
Then, still looking in the mirror

She watches our frantic dance,
A battleground of red and blue
Instead of tears she laughs anew.

And so, you can see why I never became a poet. Sylvia Plath would not find much to admire in this exercise in revisionary gothic. But the experience of putting together this one number of *ZEMZEM* was useful, and I valued this friendship with Michael.

Years later, I visited Michael in Puerto Rico. He had arranged with his department at the University of Puerto Rico to have me as a visiting speaker. I went for a week, and they put me up in a small bed and breakfast on the beach. They also instructed me not to walk across the city to campus, but to take a taxi. I guess the needle and syringe I saw by my naked foot as I sat on the beach the first morning should have been enough warning. But heedless of this, I walked across San Juan to campus, and on the way I passed an alley. As I peered into the alley, I could hear police sirens and police vehicles pulling up nearby. Down the alley I saw a man who had been stabbed and he was bleeding profusely. I kept going. I thought of Puerto Rico as somehow a premonition of all our futures. People lived behind gates and barred fences and doors with multiple locks, or else they lived across the island in gated communities. I saw similar conditions later in South Africa. 'Tis a pity because Puerto Rico is beautiful. 'Tis a pity that for some reason Michael Sharp stopped communicating with me after I left the island. This was just before the time I was diagnosed with hemochromatosis.

In the spring of our second year in Reading, Suzanne and I traveled to Scotland to visit Huntly, where George MacDonald spent his childhood. In Huntly, we stayed with a Mrs. Robertson. She kept the windows in her house open, although this was only early April and the weather was still damp and cold. When we remarked on the cold, she brought us a "pig" to heat the bed. The pig was a round stoneware hot water container; apparently the word "pig" is a Scottish word for a round pot. Mrs. Robertson was a delight, and I wrote to the local paper to thank her and the other people we met in Huntly for their hospitality. We visited the local library with its useful MacDonald collection. We visited the Farm, the childhood home of MacDonald with its wondrous skylight windows. We visited the ruins of the nearby castle with its broken but fabulous spiral staircase. I had never before connected a writer so nicely with his or her place of birth and childhood haunts. We also saw the dentist's office that once was a home of the MacDonald family. On the same trip, we visited Aberdeen and its university where MacDonald studied as a young man. Scotland impressed me, and I have no doubt informed my work in mysterious ways.

Thus began my meetings with various people connected to George MacDonald and the study of his works. In 1980 when I was in England on sabbatical, I met David Robb. I was in Scotland giving presentations in both Aberdeen and Dundee. David was a young MacDonald scholar working at the University of Dundee. He welcomed me to his home, and while showing me his collection of MacDonald books one evening, he passed me a first edition of *Lilith*. I expressed envy that he owned a copy of this masterpiece. He simply said in reply, "You can have it." I knew how precious this book was and is, and so I said I could not take it. But David insisted. This kindness is typical of MacDonald himself, and I encountered it in many of the people I met in the MacDonald community. That same year, I met William Raeper in Oxford. He was a young independent scholar writing a biography of MacDonald. He had little money, and yet he hosted me in Oxford and took me to lunch and dinner. Some years later, Bill died in a plane crash in Africa while on a goodwill mission. His death was far too soon, and his loss to the MacDonald community was immense.

During the three years in Reading, I somehow managed to get through my thesis. The first year I spent largely acting the flaneur, and feeding the swans down by the Thames. The second year I got down to reading in an organized fashion. My father-in-law made a small cabinet for me designed to take the two sizes of file cards I used for notes. This handcrafted cabinet was about two and a half or maybe three feel high. I filled it with file cards that were replete with notes. Then during the third year, I wrote the thesis. I had, by this time, made one friend in the English Department, Michael Sharp, and I had also worked as a tutorial instructor in my second year. The tutorial consisted of two students, both female. I no longer remember their names. The subject was James Joyce. We met once a week and discussed *Dubliners*, *The Portrait of an Artist as a Young Man*, and *Ulysses*. The experience has largely disappeared from memory, although my reading of *Ulysses* was formative. I did not lead a tutorial in my third year because I received a Canada Council grant that allowed Suzanne to go back to school. We lived sparingly, but well enough to take journeys throughout England and Scotland, and abroad to France and Italy, and to Greece. In England, we visited as many ecclesiastical buildings as we could, seeing the following notable cathedrals: Gloucester, St. David's, Ely, Bath, Salisbury, Worcester, Canterbury, Chichester, Christ Church, Hereford, Durham, Leicester, Lichfield, St. Paul's, Wells, Winchester, York, Ripon, Southwark, and of course Westminster. Another church I admired was Beverley Minster in Yorkshire. This was the first of such buildings I saw and its stone carvings, soaring arches, intricately carved choir stalls, and splendid glass captured my imagination. Beverley was the beginning of a quest to see as many Romanesque and Gothic buildings as I could. Memorable on the trip to Greece was a visit to Cape Sounion and the Temple of Poseidon. Standing on the promontory, gazing at the sun lowering on the Aegean Sea, I turned to one of the beautiful marble columns and there scratched in the stone was the name "Byron." I have no idea whether the graffiti was authentic, but I like to think it is. I was stirred.

Place me on Sunium's marbled steep,
Where nothing, save the waves and I,
May hear our mutual murmurs sweep.
(*Don Juan*, Canto 3)

During these years, we had visitors from home, my mother and an uncle (Uncle Chuck, my mother's brother-in-law), my sister and her husband, and a friend from McMaster, Winston Lindsey and his wife. Winston taught me something about travel. I was taking him on a tour of London, showing him the Houses of Parliament, Big Ben, and Westminster Abbey when I noticed that he was not looking at these historical sites. I remarked on this, asking him why he walked head down while he gabbed away with me. He replied that he could see these sites anytime in a book or on TV, but that he had only a short time to visit with me. I was eager to show the sights; he was eager to see a friend. Those were different days in England. I received catcalls when I wore shorts on the streets of Reading. And I remember the men on campus sunbathing in long sleeve shirts and wearing ties. Food was atrocious.

Egg and peas on a menu meant just that: a plate upon which sat a runny soft-boiled egg garnished with a pile of mushy peas. That was it. No toast or bread unless you asked for it as an extra, and then you received a thin slice of white bread resembling a slab of plastic. Butter was extra, and heaven forbid you should ask for marmalade or jam.

I did not have a strong relationship with either D. J. Gordon or Ian Fletcher. I recall one day when I answered the door of our flat to find Fletcher standing outside. He doffed his hat before he entered. What he wanted, I no longer recall. This was the only time he was in our flat. I was in his house two or maybe three times in three years. In fact, I seldom saw him until my final few months in Reading when he started reading my draft thesis. He was ruthless in his comments on my writing; he made me a writer or at least started the process that resulted in my managing to write with some degree of clarity and perhaps even grace. Fletcher was something of an eccentric; he was Dickensian, a relic, wise but uneasy socially. He had contacted malaria in the war and periodically suffered from relapses. He was also a prodigious writer, who published relatively little. My friend Michael Sharp and I created that short-lived journal, *ZEMZEM*, and Fletcher readily agreed to contribute to the project. His contribution was a section of an unpublished novel he had written. I also remember browsing the stacks in the university library and coming across two books by Harold Bloom that contained inscriptions from Bloom himself to Fletcher. Bloom had inscribed these books to his friend Fletcher and Fletcher had passed the books along to the library. No sentimentality here.

Fletcher's main scholarly interest was in the *fin de siècle*. In fact, this interest explained his willingness to take me on as a student. When he saw the name George MacDonald among the many other names in my Ph.D. proposal, his interest was piqued. He had for some time been curious about a passage in W. B. Yeats's *Letters to the New Island* (1934), in which Yeats mentions seeing in Bedford Square a production of the MacDonald family's play, *The*

Pilgrim's Progress. Yeats's comment is intriguing in that it indicates his interest in drama that is spare and unadorned by elaborate stage sets. Fletcher was a scholar and he wanted to know when and where Yeats saw this production. His idea was that I might just find this information. Alas, he was to be disappointed. I was not a particularly clever scholar. I did, however, meet MacDonald's godson who generously gave me copies of photographs of the MacDonald family production of *The Pilgrim's Progress*. My interests were less in such archeological uncovering than they were in interpretation. From early on I was taken with the creative possibilities of reading, not the minutiae of historical research. In other words, I thought what readers of literature did was to fashion a structure of words influenced by and dependent on what we read. The critical essay was a creative exercise. I will not say that my Ph.D. thesis is successfully creative, but it moves in that direction more than it serves up data that we did not have collected before.

Oh, I did spend hours doing the kind of research Fletcher encouraged. I scanned the pages of nineteenth-century magazines and newspapers looking for references to MacDonald, his writing, and his activities as a lecturer, sermonizer, and actor. I also spent many hours in the manuscript room of the British Museum transcribing the hand-written first version of MacDonald's great work, *Lilith*. This document, annotated, formed the Appendix to my thesis. Suzanne and I also made a trip to MacDonald's birthplace in Huntly, Scotland, where we stayed with Mrs. Robertson. But mostly, I read MacDonald's work, the criticism of MacDonald's work, related historical material (e.g., the writings of the British and German Romanticists), and the theory of the day ranging from Warren and Wellek to Wimsatt and Brooks to the Chicago Aristotelians, to, of course, Frye. Most likely because of my interest in Frye, Fletcher and Gordon dubbed me a "neo-Jungian." I did read some Jung, but the truth is I never really found Jung either convincing or particularly useful. Freud is a more creative thinker, to my mind. But I did not delve as far into Freud then, as I did later, once I had finished my thesis and began to think of moving through and beyond MacDonald. I struggled mostly alone in this work. What I wrote was a rag-and-bone shop of a thesis, a collection of old and dusty ideas and facts that offers an assortment of material, from a review of MacDonald's life, to readings of two of his major works, to the inclusion of the *Lilith* manuscript. The thesis remains unpublished, and I later published just one segment of a chapter from it, a review of the nineteenth-century love affair with the character Lilith, her origins and iterations.

My three years in England were satisfying, despite relative isolation. Seeing much of the country, exploring ancient buildings, learning about Norman (Romanesque) and Gothic architecture, seeing plays in the West End, traveling to the Continent, hosting family and friends, and meeting a few people were invaluable. I might note in passing that I saw many theatre productions in the West End with some of the best-known actors of the day, including Laurence Olivier in *Long Day's Journey into Night*, Paul Scofield in *The Rules of the Game*, Diana Rigg in *Jumpers*, Alan Bates in *Butley*. Many of the performances I saw in my early years have passed from memory, but I might also mention seeing Richard Burton as Hamlet, and attending concerts at Massey Hall with the likes of Joan Sutherland and Gordon Lightfoot while I was a student in Toronto. I had my days as theatre goer and opera aficionado, but I confess to nodding off during many of these performances. Live performance held my attention less than did celluloid performance. I liked the movies. Still and all, this time in England proved formative.

My acquaintance with George MacDonald also proved formative. MacDonald, at the time, was a mostly forgotten nineteenth-century writer of overly didactic novels, turgid poetry, sermons, some worthy children's books, and a couple of well received adult fantasies. His reputation largely depended on comments made by C. S. Lewis who wrote, in *Surprised by Joy*, about MacDonald baptizing his imagination; Lewis also edited a book of MacDonald writings, nuggets Lewis mined from MacDonald's works. For Lewis, MacDonald was an inferior prose writer whose spiritual vision was worth passing on. Lewis called MacDonald a "mythopoeic" writer, a writer worth reading for the spiritual wisdom he offered, not for any literary reason. At that time, history seemed to accept this assessment and MacDonald was mostly remembered by a coterie of Christian readers, those who valued the tradition of the group of writers known as the Oxford Christians or the Inklings: prominent members included J. R. R. Tolkien, C. S. Lewis, Owen Barfield, Charles Williams, and Neville Coghill.

Although I could sympathize with much of MacDonald's Christianity, his belief that everyone and animals would go to heaven (this means everyone, including the Devil), his emphasis on good works, his insistence on a benevolent (non-violent?) God, and the sense he gave of a "feminine" God, I did not have an interest in such an approach to literature. For me, literature was, if related to scripture, then a secular scripture. In fact, for me all scripture is secular in the sense that it tells a human, not a divine, story. Literature has more to do with reminding us of this world and the various possibilities for humanity in this world, than it does with some fabulous place beyond or with plans for human behaviour, designs for living. Even work that dealt with overtly transcendent themes, a work such as Dante's *Divina Commedia* for example, tells us about the human condition in the here and now. How could this be otherwise when we really know nothing of a hereafter? How could we? I had read enough to know that all the literature over all history had not and would not end the nightmare of human weakness and stupidity. Literature was important for what it could remind us of human foibles or of political possibilities or of creative possibility, but it was not going to raise humanity to some transcendent otherworldly place of satisfaction and peace and comfort. What interested me about MacDonald was his sense of literature's availability to everyone; his was a democratic vision. Like the writers who had formed him, MacDonald proffered a vision of hope knowing full well that this hope is always just beyond desire's reach. In other words, MacDonald was a Romantic in heart and mind. The Romantic vision of equality, tolerance, tranquility, good will, and human connectedness to nature spoke to me then, as it does now. The humanist's dream is to wake and find that dream true. We are caught in a series of dreams, and are unable to wake. Should we ever wake, game over. Should our dreams ever be realized, game over. We must, however, continue to dream. Without dreams, we are lost. Our enterprise involves an understanding that literature contributes to the building of a city of words, words that testify to the possibility of the world we want, but words that are never ending. The world we want is always an hour beyond our reach. The only construction worth pursuing endlessly is the construction of the city of words.

Towards the end of my three years in England, I saw a notice in the *Times Educational Supplement*. A visiting scholar from the University of Western Ontario was making himself available to Canadian students in England who might like to discuss job prospects with him. He was staying in London House, Bloomsbury, and I wrote to arrange a day and time to meet with him. I no longer remember his name, but he was helpful. He told me that jobs were few and far between in the profession and that I should not think twice about taking any job I could get. His example was Saskatchewan; he said if I was offered a job at the university in Saskatoon or in Regina, I should take it. Once I was employed in a university, I could begin to write myself out of one institution and into another, more pleasing place. Publication was, he said, the name of the game. Not long after I met with this person, I began writing letters of application to various universities; I wrote many letters, upwards of fifty, and I received only two positive responses, one from a university in Baghdad and one from the University of Calgary. I thought about this for a while and concluded that if I went to Baghdad (I was very interested in the experience such a position offered) I would most likely be stuck there forever. I had a wife to consider as well. I thought that it was very unlikely I would ever write anything of note, and so I would not be able to write myself back to Canada. The only sensible choice was Calgary.

I should interject here a brief account of hiring practices as they exist today. The young scholar seeking gainful employment in the university today faces a daunting task. First, he or she must look far and wide for any opening that might, even in a tangential way, fit his or her research interests. Also, the young scholar must leave graduate school with publications and conference presentations, the more the better. A book would be nice, and some do publish books before they graduate. Should the young person be fortunate (is that the word I want?) enough to land an interview, she or he is in for a grueling time. The interviews now typically take at least one whole day. The prospective professor must submit to a humiliating series of interviews, with the department, with the department's appointments committee, and with the dean. Then she has to deliver herself of a paper to an audience of students and professors. Sometimes the young person also must instruct a class. Even the between times, lunch and dinner, are rife with the tension of the interview. In short, the demands on a young person trying to find a position in the university are arduous in the extreme. And of course, the young person may have to run the interview gauntlet more than once before, if she is lucky, landing a job. Once in the job, the ordeal has just begun. Next comes tenure review, and review for promotion. All this so that the university can claim it has "excellence," a buzzword of the early 2000s. Not only do scholars in my discipline study the best that has been thought and said in the language, but they themselves are also, as Miss Jean Brodie has it, the *crème de la crème*. Or so the story goes. Now what about my interview back in 1973?

We did not have a phone in England and so I had to make arrangements to be on campus at a specific time to receive a call from Calgary. When the call came, I spoke with Anthony Petti, head of the English department. He said they were interested in my application, if I was willing and able to teach children's literature. I said I was. After all, George MacDonald had written well-known children's books and he was a friend of Lewis Carroll's. Dr. Petti said I should meet with Dr. Roger Peattie, who was on study leave in London. Dr. Peattie would interview me for the

University of Calgary position. Arrangements were made and I met Roger Peattie at Paddington train station for lunch. It turned out that Peattie was a Victorian scholar specializing in the letters of William Michael Rossetti. For much of the time we spent together, Peattie told me of his research, and we chatted about the Pre-Raphaelite painters and poets. Mostly, I listened. When we parted, Peattie told me I would hear from the university in due course. Well, I did hear in due course. They offered me an initial contract as assistant professor, starting at $14,000 a year, beginning in September 1973. I was on cloud nine. I had a job, and the salary seemed beyond possibility.

First, however, I had to complete the thesis and sit the viva. The viva was as quirky as everything else in my passage from callow small-town youth to university instructor. Fletcher invited a young scholar from Edinburgh to be my examiner; this was Colin Manlove, who was just at the beginning of what would be a very productive career publishing many books on British fantasy literature. The oral examination was set for a weekday morning, probably Friday, but I am not certain. The three of us met in Fletcher's office and sat in plush chairs drinking tea. The affair lasted an hour or two and the only memorable thing I recall was the moment near the end when Professor Manlove pointed out that I had misquoted him in the thesis. I was nonplussed. From this distance, I do not know how I talked myself out of this one; perhaps I didn't; perhaps Colin Manlove was simply generous. But this moment passed and soon Fletcher was breaking out the sherry. I was through. I did not see Professor Manlove again until 2005 when we were both speakers at a conference on George MacDonald at Baylor University in Waco, Texas. But two years after my Ph.D. examination, Manlove published the first of his many books. This was *Modern Fantasy*, and it is noteworthy here because in the notes on the chapter on MacDonald, Manlove cites me as an authority on German Romantic literature. Two things I will note: this was the first time my name had appeared in a published book or essay, and I am not an authority on German Romantic literature. Yes, my thesis is sprinkled with references to the likes of E. T. A. Hoffmann, Ludwig Tieck, Adelbert von Chamisso, de la Motte Fouqué, Jean Paul, Novalis, Goethe, and other German writers of Kunstmärchen. But I had read all this material in translation. I could not read German. Academia is a strange land, a land not meant for the innocent.

In any case, I now had more letters behind my name, should I want to use them. I did not attend convocation at Reading, nor did I pay the five pounds to have my name on the rolls. The parchment came in the mail some months later and it disappeared in a drawer somewhere until it turned up folded some thirty years later when I moved from one house to another in Calgary. Years later, as I write this, I have no idea where that document might be. I suspect it will turn up again if I move again or after I am no longer here to see it. As for my first two degrees, they are long gone, as far as I know. My B.A. just might hang on a wall in my sister's house. I ought to ask.

CHAPTER TEN

Return to Canada and Calgary

Late in August of 1973, we returned to Canada. We flew to Ottawa where my sister had arranged a party to introduce her newly minted doctor brother. I have always felt uncomfortable with this honorific. I am, of course, proud to have achieved the education I have, but I have also felt that titles promote self-importance. More often than I would like, I see in the academic profession a sense of entitlement, as if "Doctor" or "Professor" somehow means that the person using such titles is important, different from and even better than those without such titles. Honorifics smack of hierarchies. And academia is a hierarchical profession (perhaps all professions are, I don't know). Once on the ladder as assistant professor, the desire is to move up to associate professor and finally to full professor. The term "full" says it all. Each rank carries with it a sense of importance, and all ranks enjoy knowing they are above another rank. Assistant professors have sessional and other adjunct instructors "below" them. I am not sure that this is the time to launch a diatribe against the treatment of sessionals in departments of English (and by extension, in universities generally). But let me briefly rant. I can do so by recounting a story. Some years after I had taken up a teaching position at the University of Calgary and had advanced into the second rank—associate professor—I received a letter from a colleague in the state university system in California. The person writing to me was Mitzi Myers. Now Mitzi Myers was already a force in late eighteenth- and early nineteenth-century women's writing. Her work on such writers as Maria Edgeworth, Dorothy Kilner, and Mary Wollstonecraft was groundbreaking. Naomi Wood referred to her as "unquestionably *the* founding mother of eighteenth-century children's literature criticism." Quite simply, Mitzi Myers was at the forefront of the feminist recovery of late eighteenth century women writers.

The letter I received from Mitzi Myers deeply saddened me.

She wrote to me as Professor McGillis, and she beseeched me to help her retain her job at the University of California. She said she was on a contract that was due to expire and she feared she would be let go. Her duties mostly had her teaching composition to undergraduates, and her research work was not valued. She hoped that I could see my way clear to write a letter of support for her. Her livelihood was at stake, not to mention the continuation of her work in eighteenth-century women's writing. To this day, I cannot fathom how a scholar of this prominence and importance could have been in such a vulnerable position. I wrote a letter. When next my path crossed Mitzi Myers's path at a conference, she expressed her heartfelt gratitude for my letter. I felt both honoured and embarrassed. She was thanking me, when in truth it was the likes of me who ought to have been thanking her for her groundbreaking work. Too many fine scholars find themselves on the adjunct treadmill.

This story should remind us of the countless hard-working and gifted persons universities rely on to do the bulk of undergraduate teaching, who are overworked, underpaid, and underappreciated. In my department, at one time, sessional instructors did not have a vote in department meetings. They serve eight-month contracts for a minimal wage and no job security. Often, they are not contracted to teach until just before a term begins. The majority of sessionals are women, some single mothers trying to eke out a living in the profession they love. Both men and women sessionals cling to the hope that one day they will get full-time employment in the professorial ranks. Some wait years for this opportunity; some spend their careers hoping for that faculty position that never comes. And universities are content to keep these adjunct workers in their place. They provide cheap labour. At one time in my department, we had twenty-eight sessionals out of a faculty of eighty or so. These workers who taught the majority of undergraduates in English had little or no say in curriculum matters. They were distinctly second-class citizens in the department. In the years when first-year composition classes were taught, sessionals taught the majority of the sections of this subject, a subject that full time faculty members thought beneath them.

As I write this, I see a news item posted online by the CBC concerning the plight of sessionals in our universities. Here is one short paragraph: "A full course load for professors teaching at most Canadian universities is four courses a year. Depending on the faculty, their salary will range between $80,000 and $150,000 a year. A contract faculty person teaching those same four courses will earn about $28,000" (Ira Basen, "Most university undergrads now taught by poorly paid part-timers," CBC News, September 7, 2014). Zane Schwarz, in the *Globe and Mail*, March 4, 2015, notes that, "Underpaid part-time staff teach a majority of undergraduates in Canada. For example, at U of T contract faculty and teaching assistants do 60 per cent of the teaching but make up 3.5 per cent of the budget. This is not an isolated problem. According to one study, the number of contract faculty in Ontario increased 87 per cent in between 2000 and 2014." The situation has not improved during the more than forty years I have been associated with the university system. Nor will it improve as long as we continue to value a system that is hierarchical, underfunded, and blind to economic realities. As long as universities can convince people who love their subjects that a real job just might be waiting after long years of apprenticeship, universities will find a full pool of willing participants in a system that thrives on exploitation.

I might note in passing that the faculty at my university does not have a union. The situation is different in other provinces, but in Alberta government workers are barred from forming unions. What faculty have in this province are associations, a word that simply means that, by the generosity of the government, faculty may have meetings and an administrative body that looks out for grievances and negotiates contracts with the board of governors. The government, represented by the board of governors, may, and often does, reject the association's requests. In fact, way back in the early 1990s the Alberta government, led by Premier Ralph Klein, under pressure from impending deficits, imposed a 5 percent cut to all university faculty salaries. The associations at the various universities and colleges had no recourse. I recall sitting in a meeting of the association in which members complained about wages and working conditions. The complaints were long and loud. But when someone suggested that our only recourse was to go on strike the tone of the meeting changed. Now we heard woeful fears of job loss from the untenured and fear of losing money from those tenured. In short, solidarity was impossible. Job insecurity prevailed. Members of the association caved to government abuse.

Just this morning, I read a news item in the *Ottawa Citizen* that underlines the weakness of university faculties and shows how governments and administrations disrespect them. Here is the first paragraph of that item: "The association representing Canada's university professors condemned Carleton University's board of governors Saturday for a new policy that will ban board members from speaking publicly about the meetings they attend" (November 28, 2015). The article goes on to note that this ban is for life. In effect, this is a permanent gag order. It puts a stay to free speech and frees the board of governors from accountability. Universities like Carleton or the University of Calgary are, or at least used to be, public institutions, and their workings both financially and in policy were open and above board. This appears no longer to be the case. More and more universities function the way private corporations function; more and more, the most important factor in the life of a university is not knowledge, but rather money. And money dictates the knowledge that universities will pursue and disseminate. Perhaps the best-known example of the influence of big corporations on university research is the case of the University of Toronto's Nancy Fern Olivieri and her dispute with the pharmaceutical company Apotex beginning in 1996. More recently, a controversy surfaced at the University of Calgary involving the president of the university, Dr. Elizabeth Cannon, and the Enbridge Corporation. Enbridge funded a research centre on campus and Dr. Cannon sat on the board of Enbridge. The controversy had to do with an alleged conflict of interest as well as the influence of Enbridge on the research being carried out in the centre it funded.

The influence of money on research and dissemination has increased over the years, alarmingly to my mind, raising concerns that academic freedom too often can be compromised. When I began teaching at the university, the most important feature of one's curriculum vitae was one's publication record. This is no longer the case. What comes first now in these documents is a listing of grant moneys. All research now, it seems, has to be funded. Why, I am not sure. Money keeps the institution going, I guess. The more money, the more prestige; the more money, the more successful the institution is at attracting the best researchers and students. The more money, the more one can identify as someone at the top of the heap. The more money, the more important we are. It was back in the mid- to late 1990s that the shift from research for the sake of research to research for the sake of money took hold. I recall sitting in a department meeting and hearing the head urge each of us to cultivate our "wealthy friends," and seek to have these wealthy friends fund the department in various ways: for research projects, for scholarships, for technological support, and so on. Once again, my innocence went missing. I had always thought that what we did when we researched and wrote and developed ideas was simply to fulfill what we had been contracted to do on the understanding that this was part of our job and that our job was in a publicly funded institution. The kind of research we did, as humanists, involved reading books and other relevant documents, perhaps traveling to a research library to consult an archive, and then organizing the material we gathered into a meaningful structure of words. To undertake such research did and does not take a lot of monetary support.

And yet, we were encouraged, if not forced, to seek out funding for our research and writing. Here is another story. Sometime in the middle of the first decade of this century, the associate dean of my faculty invited me to lunch. How nice. I went, curious to know why I had received this invitation. It turned out that the dean wanted to convince me to apply for a SSHRC (Social Sciences and Humanities Research Council) grant. I asked why I would do this. The dean's initial response was: because I would be successful in my application. I said that may or may not be so, but why do I need the money? The dean knew I was engaged in a research project that involved movies, and she said that I could hire a student to watch films for me and take notes. I countered that I could watch the films for myself, that I enjoyed watching the films. I thought that we ought to enjoy the research that we undertook. She said this was closed-minded; I should understand that research-intensive work demanded assistance and that my hiring a student would help that student pursue his or her education. Now the student the dean was suggesting was a Ph.D. student, not an undergraduate or an M.A. student. I told her that I would prefer that the Ph.D. student receive a grant to pursue her or his own research. I further noted that we were prolonging the time it took for candidates to complete post-graduate work needlessly, or only to keep these people in the system as long as possible to get the most money from them that we could. In short, I did not like the way things worked. I was told I simply did not understand. I had become a dinosaur in the profession.

I return to the dean's remark that my application would be successful. She went so far as to say that someone else would fill out the application and I would merely have to sign it. Success has its privileges.

Indeed, the work environment fosters privilege. The privileged are, from the top down, academic administrators of various stripes, full professors, associate professors, assistant professors, lecturers, sessionals, graduate teaching assistants, graduate students, undergraduates, and staff. All groups have their pecking order. Among the professoriate, those who brought in the most money were the most privileged. I found this distasteful. And I always thought that such divisions were antithetical to what we represented: educated people who had learned that to be human was to be part of a community of equals. What made us equal, or ought to have made us equal, was a sense of fairness, an understanding of desires, needs, and differences, a sharing of time and space, and a giving of whatever was needful for others. Of course, I was an innocent. Human beings seem incapable of sharing time and space on an equal footing with others. I sometimes recall my late adolescence when I railed against humanity for its laziness, its narcissism, its selfishness, its myopia, its insensitivity, and its slovenliness. And I regularly remind myself that I was not far wrong in my assessment. Power and greed and corruptible seed seem to be all there is, the man sings.

I cannot forbear shifting from faculty to staff. In 2005, the university where I worked, in its wisdom, and in its rush to embrace the private sector, decided to privatize Food Services. Privatization was a great fad, and the university embraced the fad. Up until then all the food outlets on campus were run by the central university administration. Those who worked for Food Services had full-time jobs with benefits; they were union workers. Outsourcing was supposed to save the university money, and also to reduce costs for those purchasing food by bringing in competition—the usual capitalist argument. Against vigorous protest, privatization went ahead. Everyone who had worked for Food Services found themselves without a job. The new private firms offered jobs to many former employees; however, the new jobs were part-time and without benefits. I knew a woman who worked in the coffee kiosk closest to my office. She depended on her job for the support of her family. Her husband was unable to work because of a disability. She was the sole wage earner. Suddenly she found herself without a job and with the offer of a new part-time position at greatly reduced salary and no benefits. Her story was just one among many such stories. Of course, the institution did not care. Its only concern was for the "bottom line." As always, the cash nexus won the day.

Anyhow, I return to 1973. We were back in Canada. Once again, as she had all my life, my mother helped me. She lent me

$2,000 and I bought a brand-new red VW Beetle. I do not recall what happened to my old green Beetle. This new one, however, would take us across Canada to our new life in Calgary. We packed it and set off for the west. When we arrived, we found a place to live in the basement of a house in Parkdale. We lived in this place that first academic year, and then we moved into a rented house in Sunnyside. We stayed in Sunnyside from 1974 to 1976, when we bought a house in Brentwood, not far from the university. I am not certain how long we stayed in this place, but probably until about 1980 when we returned from a year in Bournemouth, England. We had by then moved to Mount Pleasant with our young daughter, Kyla Anne. We were in Mount Pleasant until 1983 when things got rough for a while, with marriage breakup and moving.

Let's review those first ten years in Calgary. My first conference paper came in the summer of 1975, at the Mythopoeic Society Conference in Los Angeles. Suzanne and I drove down to Los Angeles. I really knew nothing about the society or the conference, but when we arrived, I discovered that this was as much a fan conference as it was an academic conference. Arriving at the Claremont College campus for the conference, we saw characters out of Tolkien and other fantasy works wandering about. I have few memories of the occasion except for a breakfast I shared with Walter Hooper, the erstwhile (or so he claimed) secretary of C. S. Lewis in his last months of life. When I arrived at the breakfast table in the dorm, Hooper was holding forth to a group of young acolytes. I sat and listened as he told a story of Lewis's distaste for the manner in which Homer presents Helen of Troy in *The Odyssey*. What he was describing did not match my sense of the redoubtable Helen as she descends the stairs to confront Telemachus and his comrades, and then drugs their drinks. She is a mature woman, completely in charge of the occasion. I got the sense from Hooper that Helen was a middle-aged woman of little interest. I made the mistake of saying I disagreed. The table went silent. I had gainsaid the great man, I guess. What I was encountering was the celebrity system at work in academia, something I would encounter again over the years. I did not, and do not, like it. And a coda begs for a hearing at this point: some years later Walter Hooper became embroiled in a plagiarism controversy set out in Kathryn Lindskoog's *The C.S. Lewis Hoax* (Multnomah, 1988). Apparently, Lindskoog was in error in her charges against Hooper, and I really have no information one way or the other. However, I confess to harbouring an affection for Lindskoog's work, even though I have not read it! How's that for impartiality. Actually, this incident just goes to show how petty and uncharitable academics are. Mea culpa.

The next year, 1976, I attended my second conference, this time with a paper on Lewis Carroll. The conference was the annual meeting of the Popular Culture Association, and it took place in Chicago. This conference was more fully academic than the one the year before; however, it had vestiges of popularity. In the evenings, we could attend the screening of films, and the array of papers struck me as odd for academia. For example, I noticed a late afternoon session on pornography and this piqued my interest. I went to find a room filled to standing with eager people. I can recall clearly two of the three papers. One was a presentation by a middle-aged, pot-bellied male professor from Buffalo; he described the course he taught in pornography. This course, apparently, was not a study of pornographic materials, say a study of work from de Sade to Bataille, but rather a "hands-on" course. Students had to do a project of some kind. One assignment had two members of the class demonstrate sado-masochism, and as they were performing, a student from the audience jumped up and hurled the words, "Knock her down, slap her tits." This seemed to amuse the speaker and his audience. In the question period, someone asked the speaker how he evaluated such projects. He replied by saying that he gave an A to two students who had made a film of each other performing fellatio on one another. He gave an A, he said, because they managed to hold the camera steady during the performance. I am not making this up. The second paper I remember from this session was on bondage magazines. The speaker passed out several magazines for the audience to peruse; they contained pictures of women tied up in various ways, wearing leather contraptions including masks, hanging from ceilings, folded in tires, bound in ropes. At the end of the session, two men were at the exit to make sure no one absconded with a magazine.

I recount this memory not to make fun of academics—after all, I am an academic—but to indicate the vagaries of the profession. Some of the things we do and study strike me as less than intellectually rigorous. This is not to say that the study of pornography cannot be intellectually rigorous, as the work of Morse Peckham, among others, indicates. And some pornography is well worthy of study—I mentioned de Sade and Bataille, but I might also mention the sixteenth-century writer Pietro Aretino or our contemporaries Alan Moore and Melinda Gebbie whose *Lost Girls* is a masterpiece of erotica. But if I reflect on the movement of the profession from my time as an undergraduate in the 1960s to where we are today, I can note several things.

1. The Popular Culture Association was a healthy sign of the profession embracing both high and low culture, rather than just the great books of the past. The humanities embraced a democratizing tendency.
2. The rise of theory from 1966 onwards was an uneasy sign that the profession felt it needed to do something to be taken seriously in a world that privileged science over the arts. In other words, the democratizing tendency found opposition in the elitist tendency of theory.
3. The expansion, partly fostered by theory, of subject areas from the tradition of great books to women's writing, to children's literature, to queer writing, to world literature was a healthy sign of the humanities grasping its political importance and its political imperative.
4. The movement from the democratic embrace of the Popular Culture Society to the rarefied air of the high-theory period

was a sign of the profession circling the wagons, fearing the loss of importance and attempting through the obfuscations of theoretical language and the outreach of the study of popular culture to prove its importance. These shifts from canonical literature reflected the desire to maintain prominence in a world that no longer took the humanities seriously.

5. The passage from theory to a post-theory return to close reading and new historical exploration is a sign of acceptance of diminishment. Departments of English are following in the steps of departments of philosophy and classics, growing smaller, specialized, and on the periphery of university life.

But the changes sketched above were just underway in 1976 when I attended the Popular Culture Association Conference in Chicago.

This same conference also began my taking advantage of travel opportunities provided by the conference circuit. I spent much of my time wandering the streets of Chicago, visiting the Chicago Art Institute, exploring bookstores, gazing at the Sears Tower, and generally enjoying a place I had never seen before. In these first years of my working life, I took advantage of travel opportunities to explore such cities as New York, Charleston, Seattle, Philadelphia, Las Vegas, Berkeley, Waco, Boca Raton, Charlotte, Frankfurt am Main, Paris, Salamanca. By the mid 1980s, however, I was becoming involved in two of the associations whose conferences I attended, and it was becoming more difficult to slip away. A colleague from the United States, Anne McLeod, once referred to me as "elusive." Well, I became less elusive as time went on. But those early wanderings, like my wanderings in Toronto as an undergraduate and then in London as a graduate, were an important part of my education. I had a peripatetic education, the education of a flaneur.

That same year, I attended my first Modern Language Association (MLA) conference. It was held in New York, between Christmas and New Year 1976. This was also my first trip to New York, and as usual back then, I spent as much time wandering the streets of the city as I did attending sessions at the conference. I did, however, give a paper. The paper was on George MacDonald, and the experience ought to have sunk my innocence yet again. The session was the last session of the evening; it was to end around ten. My session, for some reason, had five papers instead of the usual four, and mine was to be the last. By the time the four previous speakers had finished, it was late and people were anxious to get to the bars. You should know that academics generally do not think about others when they present papers, and they regularly take more time than they are allotted. Had people stayed to time, I would not have felt so pressured. But I could sense everyone's weariness with the proceedings. I tried to speak briskly, but I had managed to read perhaps half my paper when the moderator interrupted me to say, "That's all, folks, let's go have a drink." Before I could collect my paper and my thoughts, the room was empty. Such was my first experience as a speaker at the vaunted MLA conference, the premier conference in my profession. I would be remiss not to say that I had much better luck with the MLA conference in future years.

That first MLA in New York also allowed me to visit the Museum of Modern Art, the New York Public Library, the Frick Collection, Lincoln Center (I saw a production of Humperdinck's *Hansel and Gretel*), and wander the streets of Greenwich Village, and even hear some Blues. Speaking of Greenwich, I must recount my experience having dinner there. I had met a fellow named Eric at the conference, and he invited me to have dinner with him and a few others in Greenwich Village. We did. The dinner is memorable only for Eric sending the wine back because it was "corked." Anyway, Eric told me his life story. He was from a wealthy New England family, and he claimed that his parents were friends with the screen actor, Misha Auer, known for films such as Frank Capra's *You Can't Take it With You* (1938) and Gregory La Cava's *My Man Godfrey* (1936), among many other films. Eric was trying to find permanent work as an academic, but failing. He was a charmer, at least on first meeting him. I thanked him for the dinner and said if he was ever in Calgary to look me up. I didn't think much more about him.

That is, until I received his phone call a year or two later. He called to say he was planning to come to Calgary and he was going to stay with us. In other words, he invited himself to stay as our houseguest. Suzanne was uneasy. As for me, I dutifully went out to the airport to meet him when he arrived. What I saw coming through the doors from International Arrivals was a person carrying a fishing rod and fishing basket and wearing a plaid shirt. All that was missing was the fishing net. I asked if he was going fishing and he replied that I was a Canadian and therefore would know where the good fishing was. We were, apparently, both going fishing. Perhaps I should interject here to say, I do not fish. Things had not begun well. Back at the house, Suzanne met Eric. He gabbed away, and said I was taking him fishing the next day. I had no idea where to go fishing, but I had seen people fishing at Smith Lake, a small lake not far off the road near Castle Junction. It was an easy hike into the lake south of the highway, although it did involve a bit of elevation. I told Eric about this place, and he seemed content. The next morning, when he saw me getting my hiking boots on, he began mithering about what to wear on his feet. I indicated that his brogues would serve, but he wanted to know if Suzanne's boots would fit him. They did. He wore them without asking. I think both Suzanne and myself were too shocked to say anything. Off we went, but all the way to Banff, Eric kept saying we should stop at the Banff Ranger offices and ask about places to fish. He was irritating me, and so I stopped at park headquarters in Banff. Inside, Eric asked the person at the information station to tell us a good place to fish. The answer came back that Smith Lake was a popular spot. Vindicated, I smiled inwardly as we got back in the car.

We drove to the trailhead and began the trek into the lake. Eric fussed about the possibility of encountering a bear. I tried to calm his anxiety, secretly hoping a black bear would suddenly appear about four feet from Eric. We got to the lake, Eric prepared his gear, I slouched by a tree with a book. Sometime later, I heard a call from Eric, and when I looked toward the shore, I saw him holding out his fishing rod. Dangling from the end of his line was a mid-sized trout. I waved and smiled, offering encouragement and congratulations. Later that day, Eric had some three or four fish struggling on a line in the water. It was time to go home. As I got up to leave, Eric hauled his fish onto dry land and said to me firmly: "I don't like to clean them." Frankly, I was fed up. I replied: "You caught them, you clean them." The next bit is the point of this story. Eric proceeded to sit down, take off Suzanne's boots, take off his socks, pull the socks over his hands, and then using his socks as surgical gloves, he cleaned the fish. Once the fish were cleaned, Eric took the socks off his hands, put them back on his feet, and put the boots back on. We hiked out and drove home. I debated all the way whether to mention the socks and fish cleaning to Suzanne.

Back home, Eric insisted that Suzanne fry the fish for dinner, and he demonstrated how to fork and eat the cheeks from the fish heads. It was a pleasant starry August evening, and we sat outside after dinner. The sun went down and darkness enfolded us. Out of the dark, I said I had to be honest, and I told Eric I did not enjoy his visit. He said nothing for a while, and then resumed his usual patter about himself and his wonderful family. Next day, he flew out of our lives. I have not heard from Eric Hatch since that time, although some weeks after his visit Suzanne received a short note in the mail. It was from Eric, and it simply said, "Thanks for your hospitality." All this from a chance meeting at the MLA.

In fact, I enjoyed MLA conferences. Many of my colleagues complained that these gatherings were too large (some 10,000 registrants), that too many papers were dull, and that the whole affair was just a large "meat market." The meat market charge had to do with the job interviews that took place at this conference. I never had the occasion to be part of the job interviewing process at the MLA, and so I really do not have an opinion on the matter. What did interest me was the variety of papers and the opportunity to see and hear people whose work I had read and admired. In my years attending this conference, I heard such luminaries as Paul de Man (before his star had fallen), J. Hillis Miller, David

Malouf, Geoffrey Hartman, and the redoubtable Stanley Fish. I also enjoyed touring the huge book display. Of course, the *raison d'être* for many was the opportunity to network, and I confess that networking did help me to make contacts and participate in projects I would not have participated in had I not met and talked with colleagues at conferences. The MLA also provided the critic and novelist David Lodge with grist for his satirical mill in the novel *Small World* (1984).

One last note regarding conferences. In 1983 I arranged to meet the writer Alan Garner at the ChLA conference in Edmonton. I had been asked to interview Garner for the journal, *Children's Literature in Education*. Anyway, by the time of the conference I was experiencing personal problems, and I was not in the frame of mind to conduct an interview. I did meet Alan Garner, and I explained that I could not go on with the interview we had planned. He said that was okay. We could have lunch, I could ask questions that came to mind, then I could write up the conversation and he would review it. I tried to reiterate my difficulty, but he insisted we have lunch. We did. It was a pleasant lunch and we got on well. I did not write up the conversation. That was that. Then in 1996, I crossed paths with Alan Garner once again. This was in Charlotte, North Carolina. I was attending another ChLA conference and one day I passed by the tables where authors were signing their books. Alan Garner had a new book, *Strandloper*, and he was signing copies. A long line was at his table. I bought the book because I admired his writing, but I never did stand in line to have an author sign a book I had purchased. I was on my way out of the room when I heard someone call my name. It was Alan Garner. He called me over, saw that I had his book in my hand, asked to see it, and proceeded to inscribe it. The inscription reads: "For Rod the son of the Slave from Alan." Then below he signed his full name, and below that where the Harvill Press's signature Lion Rampant was, he made fart marks coming from the lion's rear and placed the word "Rubbish" next to these marks. I cherish this book.

CHAPTER ELEVEN
Mexico, Mother, and More

Over the Christmas holidays in 1978, Suzanne and I took my mother and my Aunt Ann to Mexico. We went first to Mexico City and then on to Merida in the Yucatan Peninsula. In the city we were confronted with lines of beggars, something none of us had experienced before. Every street corner had a mournful-looking woman with several children, all of them holding out their hands for coins. We also saw men who carried cans of petrol or kerosene; they would take a swig from the can, light fire to what was in their mouths, and walk backwards so the flame went outward and did not burn them. Perspiration gleamed on their red faces and bodies. We found these sights disturbing. Mexico City felt huge and it bustled with colourful people and buildings. Murals by Diego Rivera in the Palacio Nacional de Mexico were deeply impressive, stunning in their size, shapes, and colours. Especially impressive were the ones devoted to class struggle; in one, I am sure I saw the image of Frida Kahlo. And speaking of Frida Kahlo, I first saw her work at this time. We toured the Blue House (Frida Kahlo Museum) swathed in colour from works by Kahlo, Rivera, and others.

In the Yucatan, we visited Uxmal and Chichen Itza, two important Mayan sites. These ancient cities are fascinating. I can recall scampering up one of the pyramids and admiring sculpture on the buildings, but much of the experience has now left me. I do recall not taking to the guide we had and Suzanne and I leaving the group to wander about on our own. On the bus ride back to Merida, my mother asked whether she should tip the guide when we got off the bus. I said that people would most likely give him something, and that he would be waiting at the exit to receive whatever people gave him. I also said that I was not going to tip him because I had not taken advantage of what he had to say at the sites we visited. My mother held up a peso and asked if this would be enough. I said no. He would expect more than that. My mother was stubborn and when she got off the bus, she gave the guide a peso. He looked at the coin in his hand, turned and without a word placed his free hand on my mother's shoulder, and when she turned to face him he pressed the peso back in her hand. She was mortified. This incident made me remember a story my mother had told me about a trip she and Aunt Ann took to New York. They ate in a restaurant and did not enjoy the experience; they both decided not to leave a tip, but when they were leaving and just about at the door, the waiter came over, stood in front of the door, and asked: "What's wrong, ladies? Did you not enjoy your meal?"

I cannot leave Mexico without mentioning that nine months after we returned from that trip, on September 15, 1978, Kyla Anne, our first daughter, was born. I remember Kyla's arrival vividly. Dr. Gregory was the doctor's name, and he, a nurse, and myself were dressed in hospital gowns, surgical masks, and booties. Kyla arrived red and wrinkled, with a bruise on her eye and her head slightly askew because of the clamps that drew her into the air. I will not describe the scene in vivid detail, but I remember it well. And I remember mother and daughter meeting for the first time. After a time, I went home and did something I had never done before and have not done since: poured myself a stiff glass of scotch. I wish I could report that I had a repeat of this experience two and a half years later when Kate Ferguson made her arrival, but the truth is that I was on a trip when she made her entrance on March 18, 1981. I regret that I missed this auspicious event. But by the end of March 1981, I had two daughters, two precious daughters who have over the years continued to surprise me, make me proud, and demonstrate the beauty of humanity. I cannot imagine being without them.

I say I cannot imagine being without them because prior to their arrival in my life I was adamant that I did not want children. I thought back then, as I think now, that we can place the cause of much of the world's woes on overpopulation. Too many people on a finite globe make for food shortages, water shortages, pollution of both food and water resources, loss of arable land, depletion of finite natural resources such as fossil fuels, encroachment on nature, extinction of animal species, crowded spaces where the push for more space inevitably occurs resulting in violence of one kind and another, most ferociously in open war. Jonathan Franzen's novel, *Freedom* (2010), contains a discussion of the problems related to overpopulation. As the novel's title suggests, our freedom is precarious in a world in which too many people occupy too little space. The problem has prompted a leading scientist, Steven Hawking, to prophesy that humanity will have to vacate the planet sometime in the future in order to survive.

Just as I do not think children are a necessity in order for men or women to feel fully realized, I do not think marriage is a necessary institution. Marriage, with its attendant economic activities such as the purchasing of expensive clothes meant to be worn once or perhaps twice, the fees for licenses and for those to perform the ceremony, the doling out of money for food and drink and for places in which to hold receptions, the providing of entertainment (in some cases), and the after travel called a honeymoon, all this is capitalism at its fullest and most counterhuman. The vows spoken are, as often as not, broken. As an institution, marriage is as corrupt as any institution. And while I am on this harangue, I might notice just how nonsensical, if not downright obscene, capitalism itself is. Capitalism depends on production and consumption, and on the constant increase in production and consumption. More production means more consumption means more profit for those who supervise the production of that which is consumed. The profit makers want to maximize profits and therefore will attempt (successfully most of the time) to pay the lowest wages possible, just enough so that those who produce the consumable goods can afford to buy some of these goods. More production means more consumption and more consumption means more material waste. Anything consumed eventually turns into waste. More waste takes up more space. We live in a finite space that simply cannot withstand more and more production, more and more waste, and more and more division of that which labour supplies.

Capitalism pretends to give us a natural way of organizing our needs. We need food, clothing, transportation, and shelter from the storm. And so, we produce food through agriculture and the food industry that follows from farm produce. And so, we produce clothing in factories and make this available in stores. So, we make cars, ships, trains, and planes to move people and goods about. We produce more and more until we have an island of garbage the size of Texas floating in the Pacific Ocean. Capitalism depends on such buzzwords as production, consumption, value, competition, worker, manager, labour, and so on. The value we place on both labour and that which labour produces is artificial. We pay workers as little as we can pay without causing revolt; we charge as much as possible for the goods produced without causing a refusal or inability to pay. We say that competition keeps the order of things manageable; competition keeps prices fair and in line with what people can pay. But in this stage of late capitalism, competition is a mirage. We have no genuine competition in a world where most of the consumer goods have been consolidated under a few giant corporations. What competition is there when Best Buy and Future Shop are owned by the same corporation (since I wrote this Future Shop has closed)? The same can be asked of the huge grocery store chains. Capitalism is all smoke and mirrors. Union support of workers is in ruins. Pension schemes are fast becoming a thing of the past. Part-time labour is the preferred form of labour because employers do not have to pay benefits or provide job security. This is one reason for the plethora of part-time people working in universities. Universities are complicit in the exploitations inherent in an economic system that thrives on making the most from giving out the least.

From children to capitalism, I have made a great shift. Or have I? Children too become annexed to the capitalist grind. Children mean money for the capitalist marketplace. Just about everything produced has its form of appeal to the young, from a dazzling array of toys to electronic gadgets to clothing to fast foods and candy to films and music. Even guns have their place in items marketed to the young. The market knows no limits, and its ethics are dubious at best.

The end of the 1970s was a time in my life of children and economic security. I received tenure around 1978, and we purchased a house in Brentwood, not far from the university. Then in the fall of 1979, I received my first sabbatical and we moved to England for a year. Before we left Canada, we spent some time in Peterborough with my mother and I cherish this time. She had an opportunity to spoil her granddaughter, Kyla. This was great. I only wish she had had the time to enjoy Kate as well, and that both Kyla and Kate had memories of their paternal grandmother. She was a special person, and I have no doubt that she has passed along something of her fierce spirit, generosity, and subtle sense of humour to her grandchildren.

After that short time in Peterborough, we flew to England and took up residence in Bournemouth on the south coast. This sabbatical year truly was a rest. I had great plans to transform my Ph.D. thesis into a book, but truth to tell I spent much of my time with my one-year-old daughter. The flat where we stayed (owned by a colleague of mine, Bill Magee), had, in one of its closets, an alphabet of plastic letters, and we used these letters when we read picture books with Kyla. During that year, she learned the alphabet. We also took Kyla to Europe visiting France and her northern neighbours, Luxembourg, Belgium, and the Netherlands. I cherish this year as a time with family. I do not remember enough about my work that year to know what I accomplished. I did take a two-week trip to Texas and Florida for conferences. And I spent a couple of days with a colleague from the University of Alberta who was on sabbatical in Tampa, Florida. This friend was Jon Stott; he set me in a floating chair in his swimming pool and made sure I had a beer in my hand. Jon was one of the creators of the Children's Literature Association, a group that became crucial to my career in the next several years. He was gregarious and kind. Back in England, we traveled about, saw ecclesiastical buildings, castles, fortified houses, and other historical monuments. As the year wound down, we decided not to fly back to Canada, but rather to take a boat. This way we would take a trunk with our belongings and have an experience.

The boat that took us to Montreal was the *Stefan Batory*, a Polish ship that had served in the war, had been refurbished, and now took passengers across the North Atlantic from the Tilbury Docks in London to Montreal. The journey took nine days. At least this information about the boat is what we were led to believe when we took the trip. Checking the history of the ship, I now find that the original *Stefan Batory* was scrapped in 1971, and that she was replaced by a larger ship that was built in 1952. The ship we sailed on was not luxurious in the manner of the various incarnations of the *Queen Mary*. It was a rather modest affair, but it did have exquisite food. I never missed a meal, despite the rolling waters of the brisk North Atlantic. I mention food, not only because it was good, but also because many passengers did miss meal times. During the first couple of days, as the ship eased down the Thames and out into the Channel, the water was calm. On the third morning, I woke to a strange feeling of rise and fall. As I stepped out of the bunk, the floor came up to meet my feet. It was about 6:00 a.m., and I thought I would go for a morning walk. I dressed and departed the room leaving Suzanne and Kyla sleeping. As I walked down the corridor, I noticed small paper bags lining the handrails both along the corridor and up the stairs. These bags were like the ones you find in seat pockets on airplanes. I did not think much about this until a bit later when I went to breakfast. The dining room was close to empty, although a fellow I befriended on the voyage was there. I do not recall the fellow's name, but he was a First Nations man who wore a large belt buckle with the word "BOSS" emblazoned on it. I called him the Boss. Neither he nor I missed a meal on the voyage. Many others, however, did. By the time breakfast was over, most of those small bags had disappeared and the decks had few people walking about and those that were walking looked green.

The North Atlantic is not a kindly ocean. I can recall waves crashing over the bow of the boat, just like you see in movies. The ship did have a swimming pool, but no one was allowed to swim in it because the boat rolled so much that water would slosh over the sides. Also, the decks were lined with chairs and blankets, but few of these chairs had occupants. The weather was cool and damp. We did see porpoises, and this was a highlight, but mostly the trip dragged on to its ninth day. By the time we docked in Montreal, we were ready to leave the ship. Stepping onto solid ground was an experience; it seemed to move under our feel for a while. Anyhow, my sister and brother-in-law met us and took us to their place in Ottawa. After a few days there, seeing family and arranging for luggage to be sent to Calgary, we headed west. The 1980s had begun.

CHAPTER TWELVE
An Academic Career

a. My Mother

The 1980s were both satisfying and difficult. Kate arrived in 1981, just as the decade got underway and just as my life was about to change. I am not completely clear on the dates here, but around 1982 my mother was scheduled to have her carotid artery cleaned. This involved an operation, and I arranged to travel to Peterborough to stay with her for a few days after the operation. I arrived the day she had the operation, and she was to go home not long after she woke up. At the hospital, I found my mother with a large dressing on her neck. She was somewhat unsteady as I helped her out of the hospital and into her car. On the drive to her place, she was mostly quiet. She seemed a little disoriented. When we got to the Lansdowne Street house, she sat in the great leather chair I remember her father, my grandfather, sitting in smoking his pipe. Mom took out a cigarette and began to light it on the wrong end, the end with the filter. Before long, she said she was tired and would go upstairs for a rest. She rejected my offer to help her up the stairs, but I followed her over to watch her climb up to her room. She got perhaps a quarter of the way up when she collapsed and tumbled down. I caught her and, with difficulty, carried her to the sofa. She seemed lost. I was beside myself, but I had the wherewithal to phone 911. I asked for an ambulance, telling the person on the other end that my mother had fallen and was unconscious. I don't remember the specifics of the conversation, but I do know that I was confounded by what I was hearing. The upshot was that I carried Mom out to her car and drove her to Emergency. The next twenty-four hours are a blur. My mother ended up on a gurney in a hallway, and she was there all night and all the next day. I was furious, not knowing what was happening, I went to her doctor's office hoping to get an answer as to what had happened and what was going to happen. My consultation with this man was as frustrating as hell. He explained the procedure she had undergone, but he did not tell me why she had collapsed or what was going to happen to her now. About the only thing he had to say was that my mother's condition was genetic and I had better take care of my health. I lost my temper and stormed out. Finally, Mom was placed in the chronic ward.

My cousin Denise drove to Peterborough from London to spend a day or two with me and to see Mom in the hospital. Denise could tell how stressed I was and she responded heroically. She made me laugh. The one story I remember her telling, that got me laughing uproariously, was the tale of her escapade with some friends one night they went bar hopping. Now, Denise was a large person, and consequently her story was even funnier to me than it might have been. She said that she got very inebriated that night. As the evening wore on, she became woozier and woozier until, when they were driving home, she knew she was going to be sick, but she did not want her friends to know. In order not to allow her friends to know what was happening, she caught her vomit in her hands as it spewed forth, and then she swallowed it again. By this time, I was rollicking. But then she said, "I even licked my hands." Denise was a born storyteller and a kind person. By the time she left, I had calmed down somewhat, but I still did not know what was going to happen to Mom. As far as I could tell, the chronic ward was where they shelved people they did not think they could cure. Mom was simply going to be looked after until she passed. She was just in her very early sixties.

During these days, I visited with Mom for hours. She did not say much, and once as I was looking at her distorted face, I noticed that she was looking intently in front of her. I turned to see what she might be looking at and saw her face staring at me from the mirror on the bed tray. She had opened this and was examining my reaction to her condition. I winked. I do not know whether a flicker of a smile crossed her face or not, but she closed the lid of the tray and kept staring ahead. From this time forward, I did not see the mother I had known; she had changed and begun her descent.

Well, what I say above is not exactly true. I did see, for a brief moment, the mother I had known. The hospital arranged for an Anglican minister to visit with Mom. He came when I was sitting with her. He asked me if he could have some time alone with Mom. I left, but I did not go so far that I could not hear what transpired. The minister spoke to Mom about what you might expect, God and the hereafter, and forgiveness, and so on. He then asked if she might like to take communion. He did not say the last rites, but I knew what he meant. My mother had not talked up to this point, but when he offered to administer the Eucharist, she spoke firmly: "Not just now, thank you." When I heard this, I knew that was Mom, strong-willed as always. And I knew she was not ready to go gently into the good night. I felt suddenly strong.

What happened next prolonged my mother's life for another six or seven years, although she was never again the bright and quick person she had been. My sister got to work in Ottawa. Since my mother had been the director of the Bronson Home, a residence for elderly Anglican women, she had had contact with several influential people in Ottawa, people who had sat on the board of directors of the Bronson Home. My sister contacted one of the women my mother had known and informed her of my mother's condition. Before you could shake a leg, a helicopter was landing at the Peterborough Hospital to fetch my mother and take her to a rehabilitation center in Ottawa. I have forgotten the name of this place, but my mother was a patient here for a few months. After these months, however, she was moved into the Glebe Centre in Ottawa, a high-rise apartment building especially for seniors. Mom was not happy. She had grown dependent on the rehabilitation routine, and this new place where she was much on her own made her anxious. She expressed a wish to move in with my sister, but my sister—rightly, I think—refused to take her in full time. Before long, my mother was deteriorating again. By the mid-1980s she found herself in what we used to call an old folks' home, in Embrun, some 20 or so miles from Ottawa. Here she remained until the end on April 1, 1989.

During these dark years for my mom, I traveled to Ottawa every few months to see her. When I arrived at the home in Embrun, I would see her across the room sitting in a chair. As I approached her, she always greeted me in the same way: "Have you got a cigarette?" I would answer no and then she would sit in silence, a vacant look in her eyes, or perhaps a haunted look. I have no idea where she was in her mind. She had had a difficult life, and now she had this: a chair in an old folks' lounge surrounded by other elderly people in various stages of decline. She deserved better. Once I took her for a drive in my sister's car. As we drove along the country road, I remarked that I did not know how she and my father met. Her reply was a curt "No, you don't." That was it. Now I will never know how my mother and father met. I only know that they had troubled times, like so many people, and that my sister was born, as they used to say, out of wedlock. For the remaining years of her life, my mother was silent and what I would call sullen. I never again had a conversation with her.

On April Fool's Day of 1989, I received a call from my sister informing me that mother had died. This news came, as such news always does, as a shock. My mother had been the most important person in my life, never wavering in her affection even as I continued to do things she would have preferred I not do. She taught me many things, including the act I am now performing—typing. She had an old portable typewriter and in the summer near the end of my high school years, she placed a table in our backyard, placed the typewriter on it and me in front of it, and proceeded to instruct me on the proper way to type. When I went to university, she gave me that small plastic typewriter; it served me right through to my years in England when I was writing my Ph.D. thesis. My mother also gave me a sense of the importance of ministering. She was unflagging in her ministry to others, helping the elderly and the infirm whenever and wherever she could. She had a difficult life, but she also had an indomitable sense of humour. I wish now that I had seen more of her over the years. That last morning does, however, have a story.

As I understand it, my mother was sitting in the front hallway of the Embrun home on the morning of April 1, 1989. An attendant came to see how she was, and my mother said she had soiled herself. Since the attendant was familiar with such soiling, she went off in a huff to get something to help her clean my mother. When she returned ready to help my mother recover her dignity, my mother just looked and said, "April fool." I like this story because it does reflect my mother's sense of humour and willingness to self-deprecate. She was, without doubt, a person of rare gifts of tolerance and generosity and sensitivity. She was also stubborn and principled. I recall when she bought her first car in the late 1950s. She bought a car in order not to be dependent on my father. That first car was a 1956 Pontiac, and when the used car dealer came to the house to complete the deal, my mother hauled out a wad of bills and paid cash for the car. She hated debt. She was grateful for the small things life can offer and she made sure her children grew up with a similar sense of gratitude.

I suppose I should mention my mother's funeral. When she died in 1989, I flew to Ottawa to help my sister arrange for my mother's funeral. Much of this time is a blur, but I remember sitting in my sister's kitchen when she asked me to phone our father to give him the news. My mother and father had been separated for twenty-five years, but they never did divorce. I dialed the number my sister gave me and waited. Then I heard my father's voice. The conversation went like this:

"Hello."

"This is Rod."

"Who?"

"Your son, Rod."

"Oh, how are you?"

"Not too good. Mom died."

"Who?"

"My mother. Your wife. Betty. She died."

"Oh, that's too bad. I'm not feeling very well myself lately."

I handed the phone to my brother-in-law. To be fair, I had not talked with my father for quite a few years, and I had not seen him since 1969. Anyhow, the funeral was disappointing, to say the least. Not many people came to celebrate what had been a life of giving to others. The service was in Ottawa, but after the service my mother was conveyed to Peterborough where she had grown up, and was buried in the Little Lake Cemetery. I miss her every day.

b. University Life

I became an academic because I thought life in the university was a kind of pastoral, a life devoted to nurture, a life removed from the hustle and flow we associated at the time with rats in a maze. The academic did not have to negotiate a maze; he or she did not have a minotaur lurking to gobble her up. The life of the mind was the good life. At least this is what I thought. And I was not completely wrong. For the fortunate, the groves of academe served as a retreat, a sort of monastic stay against confusion, a refuge from the cold world. I entered the profession at a juncture. This comfortable life, some called it a sinecure, was still possible, but the comfort was on the wane. Things were changing, and to my mind not for the better. When I arrived at the university, quite a few of my senior colleagues had not published a lot (a few had published nothing) during their years of teaching. For example, a previous head of my department was not far from retirement, and over his lengthy career he had published one article, a good article, one that had proven influential. But that was it. Of course, he had served the university as department head for several years. People respected him, or at least the "old guard" respected him. Another senior colleague published an article now and then, but he concentrated on a research project, collecting and collating the letters of a famous literary figure, that took years to complete. Projects of this magnitude are becoming rare precisely because administrations do not want to wait to see the results of scholarly research. What they want is first money in the form of research grants, and second publication fast and furious, the more the merrier, the more it looks as if university professors earn their living. Teaching, despite the lip service given to its importance, is simply not visible enough to trump publication. What catches the eye is the professor's name in print, and especially on the cover of books.

Over the years, the importance of teaching became more prominent in the university, or at least we became more aware of the need for positive peer evaluations and student evaluations. The annual report form included a section where we were to explain our teaching philosophy and describe our innovations in our teaching methods the previous year. One year, I tried everything from group work, to straight lecturing, to handing teaching duties over to the students themselves. I also took the Gregorc Style Delineator. This is a test designed to show you how you best learn, what style of learning an individual has. According to the delineator, an individual will exhibit one of four learning styles: abstract sequential, concrete sequential, abstract random, and concrete random. I fell into the last category, concrete random. This means that I like to begin with specifics, with a concrete idea or image or word or whatever, but that I then wander all over the place when discussing this concrete thing. This makes perfect sense when I think of my classroom performance. However, the idea is that instructors learn about the various learning styles in order to best meet students' needs. Knowing about learning styles will allow us to teach to all the students in an effective manner. No student left behind! Well, it don't work out that way, as the Duke says in the film *El Dorado*. Teaching is an imperfect craft. The message we received from the administration was that whenever things go awry in the classroom, the fault will be the instructor's. Little or no emphasis falls on the students despite the fact that the students we are dealing with are adults, or supposed to be adults. It seems to me a simple fact that we cannot reach all of the students all of the time.

But my point is that the growing emphasis on good teaching in the university is a public relations trick. Smoke and mirrors. I saw firsthand that teaching only mattered when it came to annual assessments or promotion when administrators, for one reason or another, did not want someone to get ahead. In other words, teaching evaluations only figured in negative assessments of work performance. Whether someone was well published or not, teaching made its impact on assessment only when the person being assessed was disliked. I saw this when I served as faculty advisor for colleagues who were appealing denial of promotion or tenure decisions. In two cases, I saw reports from the heads of department that flaunted the evidence of student teaching evaluations and argued that the appellants were poor teachers. In assessing their colleagues, heads of departments can cherry pick the student comments that serve their purposes best. The normal way of proceeding in evaluations of faculty members is to look for publications.

Even here, we have institutional quirks. The annual assessment form I was familiar with asked faculty to list the number of articles, reviews, papers, or books published in a given year. Faculty members were advised to hand in with their reports copies of their publications so that the head and then the faculty promotions committees could check the quality of the work. No one, however, is silly enough to think that the head of a department can read all this material in the time she or he has to get the work done. What happens is a quick totting of numbers and an assessment based on these numbers. Oh, the head and the committees will check to see what journals articles appear in and what presses publish books; some journals and some presses are more prestigious than others. The manner of proceeding leads to squabbles over whether one book is better than another because the one book has a prestigious imprint while another does not. Squabbles even occurred regarding whether a press such as the Edwin Mellen Press was a vanity press or not. Heads and committee members spent more time raising spurious objections to publication records than encouraging collegial interchange. The assessment process is and was guaranteed to lower morale and raise anxiety needlessly. I remember a colleague who had not published much of anything, but who did serve the university on many and important committees, including the budget committee. She had also won teaching excellence awards. I valued her as a colleague. She confided in me that she often was sick to her stomach when she left her house for work in the morning. She fretted and fretted over receiving low increments in annual assessments; she was convinced the university did not value her work. She felt like a second-class member of faculty. She finally took early retirement, and the university—so concerned over "retainment"—lost a valuable member who could have given the university another ten years. Instead, the university lost a gifted teacher and gained a bench with her name on it.

When I began my work at the University of Calgary, we taught nine hours a week, we did not have a dress code, we did not have to be in our offices nine to five, and we did not have to work forty-eight or fifty weeks a year. Spending days reading, writing, and professing was satisfying. Of course, there were expectations and these expectations could, and often did, create anxiety. We were expected to generate positive student evaluations and we were expected to serve on committees both within the department, and also within the faculty. Serving on committees happened either by a professor being voted onto a committee by his or her peers or by being appointed by the head of department or the dean. Like everything else in the university, committees took hierarchical form, some deemed more important than others. Diminishment came to those who did not manage to find themselves on the important committees. Indeed, the diminishment of the small and meek was a regular activity in these groves, and nothing served diminishment more than the pressure to publish. The most intense of expectations was the infamous publish-or-perish imperative. When I arrived in the university as a young professor, my older colleagues were not particularly productive, and many thought of the professoriate as a sinecure. Things were changing, and the so-called old guard found themselves referred to as "turkeys." The pressure to publish was growing more intense than it had been, and tenure was coming under scrutiny. To the uninitiated tenure equaled sinecure. Once tenured, a professor could rest on his or her laurels and do little for the rest of his or her career. I recall a student once mentioning the old yellowed lecture notes of an older professor. I suspect some professors did coast, rest on their laurels, use the same lecture notes year after year, and generally enjoy the good life without much in the way of stress.

But, as I say, the salad days were ending. Now young people coming into the profession felt the need to publish and publish often. Here is how things worked at my university. Every year, around the beginning of December, each member of the teaching faculty had to submit an annual report. The report form contained three sections, one for each of the areas of work we had to fulfill: teaching, service, and publication. The form asked for numbers: (1) how many classes, how many students in each class, how many students filled out evaluations forms, how many graduate supervisions, and so on, (2) how many committees, how much time allotted to each committee, and (3) how many books, articles, reviews, conference papers, presentations, invitations to speak. We filled in boxes with numbers. The form allowed for titles of publications, and we were instructed to turn in with our form copies of publications and copies of student evaluations, plus any other relevant documents (course syllabi, examination papers, notes from students telling us how wonderful we were, etc.). The head of department gathered all this material from some forty department members. He or she then read through all the documents (!) in order to evaluate each individual. Evaluation came in the form of an increment allotment. One increment was worth a dollar figure differing for each rank, assistant, associate, and full professor. The dollar figure amounted to pocket money. Increments came in stages: 0, 0.4, 0.6, 0.8, 1.0, 1.2, 1.4 and so on. Significant numbers were 0.4, 1.0 and anything above 1.2. Why? Well, 0.4 was "satisfactory career progress," but anything below 0.4 was considered unsatisfactory and if an individual received an unsatisfactory increment two years running, the dean of his or her faculty had to initiate dismissal proceedings. So much for tenure ensuring employment security. And anything over 1.2 was exceptional.

In mid-career, I sat on the General Promotions Committee

(GPC). Someone told me that this was an honour because the GPC was the highest committee on campus, responsible for vetting faculty promotions committees' decisions regarding annual increments, tenure decisions, and promotions to the various ranks. The committee not only oversaw these affairs, but it also heard appeals. Regarding the annual report and the two-year rule of below 0.4, I witnessed just how devastating and unjust this system could be. One person from my faculty had received zero increments two years running, and as a consequence he was brought before the GPC to explain why he thought he should not be dismissed. When he arrived in the room, he was a wreck, nervous and shaking. He had no defence to offer other than that he was a good teacher and he was working on various research projects. I had, of course, read his file. His file contained the past two years' annual report forms. I looked closely at these forms and concluded that this person had no idea how to fill out the forms in a manner that would best serve his interests. These forms call for, after all, self-promotion, and self-promotion depends upon one's sense of confidence as well as one's cunning. Buried in what this person had provided on the form were indications not only that he was active in researching in his area of expertise, but also that he had published entries in a French dictionary. He just did not know how to showcase what he had accomplished. True, what he accomplished was not a lot, but it was, to my mind, worth more than zero. Anyone could see this. However, the head of this person's department and also the FPC that vetted his annual report had not, for whatever reasons, seen fit to credit what was under a bushel. GPC heard both the person who had hidden his light and also his head of department. It was clear to me that the head of department simply did not like this person. We debated, and finally decided that this person had received unfair treatment. I was pleased at the outcome, but displeased that we had to deal with this case in the first place. The emotional damage was uncalled for, unjust, and downright unfair.

While I am speaking of GPC, I might as well recount another

case that highlights just how fraught the system of evaluation is despite the claim of objectivity. As I indicated, GPC considered appeals for denial of promotion. One case that came before us was that of a man from one of the science disciplines who had been denied promotion to full professor. I spent much time reading the file, and I was puzzled. The man's curriculum vita was fulsome. He had many publications, and a comparison with others in his discipline at the same point in their careers showed he was not only well published, but that he was above average in the number of his publications. His letters of reference from established scholars were uniformly positive, and even glowing. His teaching appeared to be satisfactory and he served his department on the requisite number of committees. I could not understand the head of department's negative assessment. When we convened to deal with this case, I had no idea what to expect. First, we heard from the head of the appellant's department; he set out his reasons for denying promotion "at this time." He seemed measured and thoughtful. Yet I remained puzzled. Then the appellant entered the room to put his case before the committee. I turned to see him enter, and in a flash I knew why he had been refused promotion. He wore a turban. I guess his name ought to have been an indication, but I had not twigged, not until I actually saw the person. I had seen this sort of discrimination at work in my own department, but I had not thought of it here until the moment the man walked in the room. Without labouring the point, I note simply that this person won his appeal and was promoted to full professor. Once again, I was pleased at the outcome, but displeased that we had to waste time on what was a clear case of prejudice.

What I chronicle here does not indicate the changes in the university. Some things do not change and the claim of objectivity is one of these things. Let me give another example since I am on a roll. This is a different example in that it deals with the examining of Ph.D. candidates. I am going to narrate my first experience as an external examiner of a Ph.D. candidate. I had been working at my university for about ten years, and was just beginning to show signs of publishing, when I received an invitation from a university in Ontario to examine someone's Ph.D. thesis on the poet Ted Hughes. The letter of invitation included a sample piece of writing from the candidate along with a request that I read this sample and let the supervisor know whether I thought the candidate would pass or not. This struck me as odd, but what did I know back then? I also noticed that the candidate was someone I had met at a conference. I wrote back saying I would not comment on the student's chances of passing, but I would accept the task of evaluating the full thesis and then examining the candidate. They accepted and I got myself ready for this new experience in academic life. The thesis arrived in the mail. I read it and wrote a lengthy report. In fact, I wrote two lengthy reports, one for the student and one for the supervisor and members of the examining committee. This was a dumb thing to do. But I had, I think, good intentions. The thesis was poorly written and loosely argued, and I wanted to be as blunt as possible without hurting the student. My aim was simple: to seek a stay of execution, as it were, and to suggest the student do major revisions and resubmit. Therefore, I wrote a harsh report for the committee and a more measured report for the student; in this second report I set out a list of revisions the candidate might undertake.

The time came and I flew down to Ontario. No one was at the airport to meet me and so I made my way to the hotel where they had booked a room for me. I found no note. The only information I had was the time and place of the oral examination to take place early the next morning, a long way from the hotel. Came the morning and I made my way via public transport to the campus and, after some meandering, found the venue for the examination. When I arrived at the room, I found some dozen people sitting around a long table. This struck me as odd since any oral examinations or vivas that I had experienced had a maximum of five people. As soon as I entered the room, a person approached me and asked if I was the external examiner, and if so did I have a report. I said yes, and this person asked to see my report. I hauled it from my briefcase, she took it, and then she left the room with it, returning some minutes later with copies for everyone around the table. I had had no opportunity to explain about the two reports. People began to pore over what I had written in the harsh version of my report. After a few minutes during which I sat nonplussed, someone asked me to explain something I had written. I answered and then came more questions until I stopped and asked who was being examined here. Thus began an awkward couple of hours. The student came in, and as convention dictates, I, as external examiner, asked the first question. I tried to begin on a light note to put the student at ease, but this did not work. We plodded on until things came to a natural end and hour and a half later. The student withdrew and as soon as the door was closed, the Supervisor (a well-known Canadian writer and academic, by the way) looked me in the eye and said: "All of us think the candidate has passed. What do you think, Dr. McGillis?" I must say here that this is not a fiction because what followed is the stuff of fiction. We debated back and forth for quite some time. I heard comments such as, "She is a good-looking young woman," "She won't be teaching in the profession; she has a job with CBC," and "Sometimes we have to give a student the benefit of the doubt." Finally, much to my chagrin, I gave up and followed the pack. I was not a happy camper. But the proceedings were not over.

I hesitate to continue. The student was ushered back into the room, and immediately her supervisor handed her a copy of the harsh report. She sat, began to read, and burst into tears. Then she got up and hastily exited the room. Everyone sat still. The person who had first greeted me said she would go after the student and bring her back for a celebratory drink. Off she went. The rest of us shuffled to the outer room where I stood by myself across the room from ten others. Before long, the person who had gone after the student returned alone. The student refused to come back. The awkwardness continued until someone from the group across the room approached me, and in lowered voice asked me if I would like to go for lunch. Gratefully, I said yes. The two of us made our way out of the room, out of the building, and eventually to a small restaurant where my rescuer told me the back-story to the day's events. In a nutshell, the department wanted the student to pass and go away. This explained why they had asked me to read a sample of her writing and say whether I thought she would pass or not. They had wanted assurance that she would pass and they would be rid of her successfully. This was my initiation into the wonderland of Ph.D. orals. The person who took me to lunch, by the way, was Barry Olshen. I am grateful to him. I have never seen him or corresponded with him since.

The story, however, is still not quite over. The candidate that day passed and went on to have a successful, almost distinguished, career in academia. We have crossed paths many times over the intervening years, and she has never forgiven me, once even accusing me in public of plagiarism. I wish I could say that was the last time I was the bad guy, but, well, then I would have no more stories.

But I do have more stories. At the risk of flogging the proverbial dead horse, I shall quickly recount a few. First is the Ph.D. thesis I examined for a colleague and friend of mine from Australia. His student was one of the best, he assured me. The thesis arrived. I read it. And yes, the writer was strong intellectually; I could see this. However, the thesis was poorly written, replete with grammar errors and lumpen prose. The thesis had to do with subjectivity and identity in young adult fiction, but the verb form of choice was the passive one, effectively taking the writer and her subjectivity out of the language. Anyway, I wrote a lengthy, very lengthy, report, including a page-by-page scrutiny of grammar problems. The student passed and went on to have a relatively strong career. A couple of years after I had examined her thesis, I met the person in England. When we were introduced, she remarked: "Oh, you are the pedantic one." After a pause, she added: "And I still don't know what a dangling modifier is." She seemed proud to announce this lack of knowledge. The story is noteworthy because it is a small indication of what I take as a huge problem in the profession. English professors, or at least too many of them, do not know how to write, do not understand how language and grammar work, do not love language, and do not care that they lack knowledge or the ability to write in public with grace. Over the years, I have seen the standard in writing deteriorate lamentably.

I have other less than happy stories concerning Ph.D. theses and examinations. I shall save the worst for last and offer a moment of sweetness and light. In the mid 1990s, I received an email asking me if I would examine a Ph.D. thesis by a student from the University of Umea in northern Sweden. I said yes, and the follow-up email gave details of travel; they wanted me to stay a week to save on flight costs. They also noted that my job was to be "opponent" in a sort of public debate. Accordingly, they said, would I please wear a suit for the occasion. Not only would a panel of judges be in attendance, but also the candidate's family and any other interested parties. In short, the occasion was open to the public. I wrote back saying, "Suit?" Quickly I received another message asking me to take their request for proper attire seriously since this was an important event in the student's and the university's life. When the thesis arrived, it did so in the form of a published book. I scoured my closets and found an old three-piece suit I had acquired way back in the early 1970s. It fit! And so I wore this suit on that auspicious day. The day, by the way, was in mid-November, and the place was just a few hundred kilometres from the Arctic Circle. When I arrived, daylight lasted just a few hours. But the weather was not cold and I saw no snow. People were friendly and the student was nervous. On the day of the examination, I found myself in a theatre on a stage equipped with two lecterns, one for me and one for the student. The seats below held some thirty or forty people. My task was to deliver myself of a talk based on my reading of the thesis, and then to begin questioning the student. As I had way back when I first began serving as external examiner for Ph.D. theses, I began on a light note, making a joke. The student did not get the joke, and we had a rough few minutes at the outset of the debate. But we got on more smoothly as we went on.

After we ended the discussion, the panel of judges repaired to a room to adjudicate what had transpired. Apparently the "opponent" did not take part in the deliberations, although he or she could attend the meeting. I was surprised to learn that these rather ambitious affairs had become over the years pro forma, but that in this case the judges were perplexed. They did not know whether the candidate had acquitted himself successfully or not. Consequently, they broke convention and asked me to give an opinion as to whether the student should pass or not. As far as I was concerned, the student had done all that was asked of him, and he had shown sufficient familiarity and dexterity with his subject that he should pass. So, he did. Later that evening, I was a guest at a large party that took place at a drinking establishment across from the hotel where I was staying. The place was rocking. At one point, a man approached me, introduced himself as the candidate's uncle, and complimented me on my performance earlier in the day. I thanked him. And then he said: "But Clarence [the student] won." What could I say but "Yes, he did."

Over the years, I examined Ph.D. theses from eight countries, and I supervised six Ph.D. students to completion. I mention this because my final supervision was the most contentious. You would think that I had learned by then, but I was always a slow learner. I had agreed to serve on the examining committee for a Ph.D. candidate in our department. This candidate had written his candidacy examinations, and I was one of four who read these examinations and then participated in the oral exam that followed. I hesitate, but I think I have to divulge that this student was from the Middle East, a foreign national. The oral did not go well, and the student was told he had failed. Protocol dictates that students have a second chance to write these exams and make oral defence. But the supervisor in this case was adamant that she did not want anything more to do with the student. He was, she argued, unteachable, not smart enough, and also sexist. The department was prepared simply to tell the student to go away. He had cost us nothing since he had the wherewithal to pay for his own education, supported by the government of his country on the understanding that he would return to teach there once he successfully completed his degree. I felt that the department had not treated the student fairly, that they were just going to dump him. Accordingly, I offered to take the student on as his supervisor and prepare him for re-sitting the candidacy exams.

As we began to meet and discuss the exams, I saw that the student was certainly smart enough to undertake advanced study; however, he did not understand just what advanced study means in our discipline. He was prepared to work hard, to take direction, and to memorize all the data necessary. Herein lay the problem. In this student's world, the teacher told the student what to think and what to say and the student did what he was told. Independent or creative thought was beyond his comprehension. In this sense, the former supervisor was correct; the student had a mental block that, in the end, proved impossible to dislodge. To compound the difficulties, the student told me that he had to pass because, if he did not, he would have to repay his government all the money they had invested in his education, some $200,000. He told me about this financial situation while showering me and my family with gifts, a partial list of which includes clothing, two silk carpets, a model boat, a battery-run power drill, a gas-powered lawnmower, and various accessories for my daughters and my wife. I endeavoured to explain that such gifts were not appropriate, that I did not want them, and that he must not do this. The gifts kept coming. As time went by, the student became more anxious to finish; his government, he told me, was pressuring him to complete his studies and return home. He had a draft of his thesis, but I did not think this was an acceptable draft. Students can, however, insist on submitting their work for examination, and this student insisted. I was not pleased. But I arranged for examiners and set a date for the oral, making certain that the student knew I thought his work was not ready for submission.

Before the oral examination, I thought long and hard about this student and his arrival at this stage. He had completed his M.A. at a university in Michigan, and I discovered that his supervisor there was a former student in my department; I had taught her when she was an undergraduate. I had also written a reference letter for her application to graduate school, and I had made it clear to her that my letter would be "tepid." His move from Michigan to Calgary struck me as problematic in that he came as the student of a former graduate of our school. Such things ought not to matter, but as my narrative demonstrates, they more often than not do matter. In any case, he came to Calgary where he passed his three courses without problem, as far as I know. Then he faced his first stumbling block when he failed his candidacy examination. This was when I entered the picture and all I knew was that he was a student the department was looking to unload. What struck me as unfair was that up to now the student had an unbroken progression toward the degree he sought. The university had been willing to take his money (he was a rare student in that he was not receiving grant money from the institution), but up to now it had been unwilling to give him an honest assessment of his abilities and achievements. To my mind, he had been treated differently from other students, and unfairly dismissed when he was just about at the end of the line. He never should have received the M. A. degree; he never should have been accepted into the Ph.D. program; he never should have passed all three of his courses. And yet he moved through the system without impediment until the final reckoning.

So, we convened for the oral examination. It went along as one might expect; the student acquitted himself with assurance, if not with the alertness one might have hoped for. Then came the committee's discussion. The local examiners felt the student should fail the examination and be instructed to leave the program. I argued that the student had been passed along a line by people who had refused to evaluate him honestly and openly, and who had given him the impression that his work was acceptable.

In other words, the institution had served the student badly, while accepting his money. I also knew that he would not be teaching outside his government-approved job in his home country. I made it clear to the committee, and later to the student, that I could not write him a positive reference, should he seek a position other than the one waiting for him back home. The debate went on, and to my surprise the external examiner agreed with me. Together we convinced the others to pass this student. I am not proud of passing this student, but I am pleased that what I saw as an injustice was righted in some way. Coda: the student never did request a reference from me, but he did leave one more present: a kayak and paddle.

One final story because it demonstrates how egregious the institution can be. First, I note that the university in which I worked made it clear in its calendar that plagiarism was a serious offence: "In cases in which the dean and/or faculty is satisfied that a student is guilty of plagiarism, cheating or other academic misconduct in circumstances which suggest a clear intention to deceive or otherwise commit an academic offence, the normal penalty will be either suspension or expulsion from the faculty." A second sentence states: "In cases in which the dean and/or faculty is satisfied that an offence has been committed, but doubt is left as to the existence of a clear intention to deceive or otherwise commit an academic offence, the normal penalty will be probation." These penalties seem clear to me. Okay, let me recount one time I received an invitation to examine a Masters thesis in the Faculty of Education at my university. The thesis came, and it was hefty. I began reading, but before I got very far into it, I began to sense voices that I knew from my own reading. I pulled Michel Foucault, Wolfgang Iser, and Louise Rosenblatt off my shelves and compared passages in their books with passages in the thesis. Bingo! I discovered complete paragraphs lifted from these writers throughout the student's work. The case was clear: this student had plagiarized and plagiarized a lot.

What was I to do? I could turn up at the oral and simply say that I found plagiarism and the student must fail. But this seemed harsh to me. Over the years, I saw that many students had no clue what plagiarism was. I was willing to give this student the benefit of the doubt. Accordingly, I phoned the student's supervisor and informed him about my finding. His response caught me off guard. He denied my "allegations." Taken aback, I said okay, but I was clear about what I had to do. He grumbled, and I suggested he come to my office to see what I had found. He came. I showed him my evidence and he blanched. He said he did not know what to do, and I suggested that he postpone the oral examination, have the student correct her work and resubmit. This way no one would be the wiser, she would learn a lesson, and everything would go according to Hoyle. Away he went. Later that evening, at home, I received a phone call from the associate dean of the Faculty of Education. She said that she heard about my accusation of plagiarism and she wondered if we could go ahead with the oral and simply have the student make corrections after the fact, as it were. The assumption was that the student would pass the oral. This was stunning. First, the dean's comments implied that the student's work was worthy of passing, and second, her remarks made light of what the university calendar termed "serious" misconduct. Once again, my innocence went the way of all flesh. I was flabbergasted. I know, I ought not to have been flabbergasted, but I was. In effect, this dean was telling me they were going ahead with the oral as scheduled and she was expecting me to fall in line. You see that initial experience examining a graduate thesis at a university in Ontario was not an aberration.

Fast forward to the oral examination. Things went along until the examiners' deliberations. I stated my case, but the others demurred. Of course, the evidence was clear. What was less clear was the degree of seriousness the others felt regarding this evidence. The others suggested the student could pass with what amounted to minor revisions. I thought this was completely unacceptable both because it made light of plagiarism and second because it would give the wrong message to the student. They were prepared to wait me out. I lost this one, just as I had lost the one in Ontario. When the student returned to the room, I made an attempt to let her know how serious her borrowings were. She smiled. Sometime later I received a copy of the student's thesis with a brief note thanking me for my advice on her work.

Over the years, I experienced many other instances of the institution's failure to act honourably, justly, or fairly. A couple of times I served as faculty advisor for colleagues who appealed a denial of promotion or tenure, and both times I saw just how personalities got in the way of fair treatment. Both times the faculty member I advised was female, one a female of colour. The profession likes to present an image of intellectual honesty and objectivity, fairness and equality, but this image is a veneer, a covering for inflated egos and personal vendettas. I hesitate to use the words "sexism" and "racism," but you will grasp my sense of things. Often what passes for thorough vetting turns out to be thorough dislike. And such subjective decision-making can even take place when, as far as I know, personal dislike is not an issue; rather what is at issue is the sense of intellectual superiority, a sort of academic snobbishness. How else to interpret a faculty promotions committee failing to award merit for books published by presses the committee deems "vanity" presses? This happens with regularity. Or take the following anecdote: I am walking through an airport with a colleague who teaches in a university across the world from where I teach. We are chatting about our professional work, as people do, and as we speak, we become aware that we had both served as an external assessor for the same person at a university in a country neither of us comes from. We assessed this person for promotion and tenure. We found ourselves comparing notes, as it were. My colleague had not recommended the person be awarded promotion and tenure, arguing that the person had not shown sufficient intellectual rigour in his or her publications. The case for negative recommendation rested on a book the person had published with Routledge, one of the most active publishers of academic books in our area. In fact, both of us had published books with Routledge. My colleague noted that Routledge was very uneven as a publisher, turning out some very good books and also turning out duds. This particular book was a dud, he opined. I had taken a very different position, and had recommended the person be awarded promotion and tenure. My reasons were simple: the candidate for promotion and tenure was still a relatively junior member of the profession; he or she had amassed a suitable number of publications; everything else in the file was positive—teaching and service records; and the book, whatever we might think of it, was with a reputable press and did indicate the person's ability to bring a book-length project to completion. The book was researched adequately; it dealt with an important and timely subject. It was not my place to say whether the book was not good enough. Please do not get me wrong. I do not argue that shoddy research and poor writing should be acceptable in the profession, but this book was neither poorly written nor shoddily researched. The argument was tepid and I might find things to disagree with, as my colleague certainly did, but for me this was no reason to deny this person movement through the ranks or some modicum of job security. As for the book, reviews would do the job of pointing out its weaknesses.

And while I mention job security, I might as well say a word or two about tenure. I know that some, both inside and outside the profession, think of tenure as a sinecure. Once tenured, never insecure. Well, my earlier story about two consecutive years of zero increments ought to have indicated just how precarious security actually is. Tenure does not guarantee a job for life. People lose jobs for one reason or another, incompetence or inappropriate behaviour or simply the chopping of positions as a result of budget cuts or shortfalls. Then why is tenure important? The answer is clear and crucial. Tenure protects, or should protect, academic freedom. It is a sort of first amendment right for academics. It means that we cannot be punished (fired) for holding and professing views inimical to prevailing orthodoxies. In other words, tenure assures employment without recrimination. Tenure is a way of saying, okay, you (the faculty member) have demonstrated competence in the three areas of responsibility in your job, teaching, service, and research, and consequently we place faith in you that you will continue to perform competently, grow in your profession, and do what a professor does: profess. To profess means to affirm, to declare allegiance to something, to vow, and a professor's job is to be affirmative, to declare his or her sense of things as related to his or her discipline. This is why we can think of university teaching as a calling. The professor has the burden of passing on knowledge, and often knowledge comes with the faith that knowledge supports the human enterprise in all its promise of betterment and cohesion and community and rightness. The pursuit of knowledge has something to do with the pursuit of the world we want.

Sometimes this means the university must tolerate divisive and downright repulsive ideas. Here is an example. Some years back a controversy arose when an academic named John Philippe Rushton published a plethora of articles and books on genetic similarity theory. In short, Rushton argued that various races could be categorized according to their brain sizes and genital sizes. Since "genital" here refers to the penis, we already have a sexist problem. Anyway, those with the largest brains and smallest genitalia (supposedly Asians) were more intelligent than those with the largest genitalia and smallest brains (supposedly Africans). My aim here is not to explore or debate this silly and, more importantly, insidious theory, but to point out that some called for Rushton's removal from his academic position. He was a tenured full professor at a prestigious university in Ontario. Arguments for Rushton's removal cited his poor research methods, but ultimately the calls for his dismissal rested on his alleged racism. I say "alleged," but really, as far as I am concerned, he was the ugliest of ugly racists, hiding his hatred of others under the guise of research and scholarship. However, according to the dictates of tenure, he had a right to say and do what he was doing. He could say what he wanted short of openly inciting hatred of others. The university had no real grounds on which to terminate his contract. The same cannot be said for the profession at large. Rushton's work, like all academic work, was subject to scrutiny by his peers. It is up to others in the profession to evaluate the importance of work. Had Rushton's work received the attention it deserved, then he would have found himself isolated to such an extent that he would have found it well-nigh impossible to function in the profession. He certainly had a right to espouse the views he did, but these views were rightly scorned by many. As for the validity of his research, this was criticized by many of his peers. I cannot comment with authority on this aspect of the Rushton case; I can only point out that even had Rushton's work been researched fairly and thoroughly, his conclusions were hateful and unnecessary in the light of human and humane progress. Had the profession done its work, ideas such as Rushton's would have received nothing but ridicule, and ridicule should have sufficed to silence the pseudoscience. Had Rushton been working in a system such as the one I knew firsthand, then he well might have received zero increments and suffered the scrutiny that zero increments in two successive years brought. Why zero increments when he did publish? The answer is simple: if his work was decried by his peers in the profession, then his university could fairly judge this work as inadequate. Also, peer-reviewed journals would likely have rejected his submissions leaving him with little or nothing to report each year. A zero increment or two might then have prompted this researcher to alter his focus, sharpen his conclusions. Or he might have found himself without a job, having lost this because of a failure to produce acceptable research.

I am trying to argue for a range of ideas in university teaching. I am not trying to argue for the acceptance of hate speech. Rushton's conclusions may have been hateful, but they did not constitute out and out hate speech. Therefore, these despicable conclusions needed to be called out for the untenable foundation upon which they were constructed. And they were. People also noted the sources of Rushton's research funding, and this information should have and did undermine his research project. We might worry that work such as Rushton's could increase racial division, and in this sense, it was work that promoted hate, if it did not overtly speak hate. The reply to this argument must be that in an environment where all opinions are available, free speech will inevitably allow for the truth or untruth of scientific research to be demonstrated. We might argue further that even if Rushton's research were accurate (which it apparently is not), we ought to discount it for reasons of human community. But this argument is fraught with difficulty. Why censor accurate findings? What is more important is dealing with such uncomfortable findings in ways that promote justice and equality, not division and disparity. The point is that once all voices are heard, we can hear the ones that are humanly acceptable and the ones that are not. Let the Rushtons of this world voice their terrible slander, and let them find their voices quieted by stronger sensible and sensitive voices.

(As recently as June 2020, the psychology department at the university where Rushton worked issued a statement on his work. You can read it here: https://psychology.uwo.ca/people/faculty/remembrance/rushton.html.)

The point here is important for pedagogic reasons. Often students in the humanities fear that their views will cause them to receive lower grades than they should if these views go counter to the views of their instructors. And who knows, perhaps this fear is well founded in a few cases. For the most part, however, what we look for in our students is not particular points of view, but rather well-argued and well-researched, well-considered, and well-written essays (i.e. attempts to convince). One can value an attempt to convince without being convinced.

And so university life was, for a while, a good life. The university allowed for open debate, examination of ideas, and time for thoughtful consideration of the human condition. Time and space suited the life of the mind. What Newman called the idea of a university was conducive to the well-examined life. What went on in the university did not, however, stay within the university. The life lived here produced ideas that tempered life beyond the campus. The university was the omphalos, the anchor, the source. What the university student, and especially the university student in the humanities, gained was perspective, an understanding of the complexities of human existence, and along with this perspective came the possibility for urbanity, tolerance, sensitivity, and vision. By vision, I mean, the hope and struggle to better the world in which we live. What the humanities offer is a blueprint for Golgonooza. At least this is the way it once was.

c. Networking

Recently I read an essay in the *New York Times* that argued the era of the academic conference was over. I doubt this, but I can understand the concerns regarding conferences. Papers are often stultifying, delivered in monotone, head lowered to peer at paper. For me, however, the academic conference was a boon; conference life offered an education precious in its expanse. I met many good friends at conferences, and made many productive connections. Sometimes just being at a particular place was somehow educative; I think of Princeton, Cambridge, the Sorbonne, and the Goethe Institute. But perhaps the most lasting education came from travel itself. Over the years, I visited many countries and I think I am the better for having done so. I shall, in the next section, review some of the travels I undertook because of conferences.

But before the next section, I want to describe my experience organizing a conference. Because conferences had been so helpful to my career, leading to lasting friendships and positions on boards, and opportunities to publish, I wanted to somehow return the favour. The two organizations that had helped me the most were the Children's Literature Association (ChLA) and the International Research Society for Children's Literature (IRSCL), and what better way to show my appreciation than holding a conference that brought these two organizations together. Accordingly, in 1999 I organized a conference on the theme "Children's Literature and the *Fin de siècle*." We brought to the university campus some three hundred delegates from twenty-four countries. The conference lasted a week, and it was the most exhausting week of my life. Okay, preparations for the conference were not that taxing. I worked with my colleague from the French department, Claude Romney, and with the conference center on campus. We arranged for an opening night at the Nickle Art Gallery with guest speaker Tololwa Mollel. Other guest speakers included Sheila Egoff, E. L. Konigsberg, Laurent Chabin, and Jack Zipes. The week was split by a mid-week day off when excursions to Banff and in the evening to Boundary Ranch took place. One of my colleagues from the French department, Glen Campbell, agreed to give lessons in line dancing during our evening at Boundary Ranch. All in all, it was a memorable conference.

And for me, the memories are not all of the positive variety. The trial began that first Sunday evening when I was just about ten minutes away from introducing Tololwa Mollel as our opening speaker. Suddenly, a frantic woman approached me saying that she feared being murdered in her dorm room. This was a delegate from France, and she insisted that she had been robbed; she said a skirt and a pair of shoes had been stolen from her dorm room, and she feared the perpetrator would return in the night to do worse. She wanted to call the police. I had to find someone to introduce Tololwa before I headed off with this woman to check her story. On the way to her room, we picked up campus security, and when we got to her room, there on her bed were her purse and an expensive camera. My first question was: why would a thief steal a pair of shoes and a skirt when a purse and camera were easily available? Of course, the answer is: he or she would not do this. Sometime later, both skirt and shoes turned up on the stairs into the dorm. As for the intruder this beset-upon woman feared she had seen, this turned out to be the person who was sharing the room with her. Anyway, by the time all got sorted out, I had missed the opening talk and following reception.

The rest of the week offered a series of crises. I won't detail everything that happened, but I must mention the arrival of E. L. Konigsberg, famous award-winning writer. I had not long arrived at the reception desk on the second morning of the conference when a phone call came for me. On the other end I heard a troubled voice; this was the voice of Ms Konigsberg, and she was not happy. She was at the airport and her luggage had not arrived with her. More egregiously, she had received treatment she did not take kindly to. This was Stampede Week in Calgary, and as part of the festivities, people arriving at the airport might find themselves lassoed in a friendly gesture of welcome. As fate would have it, Ms Konigsberg found herself lassoed. She did not find this gesture of welcome friendly. And for some reason I no longer remember, no one from the conference was there to meet her. Oh, we had sent a person, but this person had been stalled in traffic and was late. I got busy and sent a fellow named John Snow out to the airport. John was a gracious host and he found the celebrity and calmed her down. For the rest of her time at the conference, Ms Konigsberg would only deal with John. She did not speak to me.

To make matters worse, Air Canada threatened to go on strike that week (and I believe they did), making life difficult for everyone. We had guests staying in our house who wanted to return to France in time for their granddaughter's birthday party, but their return was put in jeopardy by the impending strike. I found myself called upon to be travel agent as well as conference convener. We nearly lost dear friends because of this problem with the airlines.

Every day something happened. There was the woman who tumbled on some stairs and had to go to hospital, the demands for xeroxing or technical support that we had not been forewarned about, the complaints about rooms or food or whatever. But I ought not dwell on the stresses involved in organizing what was a terrific conference. Jack Zipes was a wonderful guest speaker. I met and became close friends with Laurent Chabin. And Sheila Egoff was a charmer. Professor Egoff arrived and I met her at the airport. She entered hauling behind her an oxygen tank and accompanied by a young assistant. I immediately had visions of another conference person ending up in hospital. But Professor Egoff was a brick. She soldiered on. She gave her talk reading from huge Bristol boards, each with just a few words in a huge font so she could read what she had written. Her assistant held these for her. She reminded me of Bob Dylan with his cue cards for "Subterranean Homesick Blues."

According to my c.v., I gave presentations at seventy conferences over the years, and public lectures forty more times. Many of these have become a blur, but I know the conference circuit served me well. Despite the failure of many, if not most, papers to stick in memory, I can say that the meeting of minds offered by such get-togethers does provide the opportunity for productive collaboration. The people I have collaborated with over the years—Kerry Mallan, John Pennington, Karen Coats, Anna Jackson—I met at conferences. And many of my publications came about because of my attendance at conferences where someone suggested I contribute to this or that project. I know that funding for travel is less these days than when I was in mid-career, but I would argue that any funding available for conference travel is funding well placed. The travel itself enhances our ability to be effective instructors. I have no doubt we bring our travels into the classroom with us.

Conferences not only provide the opportunity to disseminate ideas, but they also usefully remind each of us that the work we do is communal. It is both bracing and humbling to hear our colleagues grappling with ideas. Conferences are carnivalesque in that they are an outlet for enthusiasts. These meetings are a time out from the routine of term and teaching, a time out that celebrates our activities as researchers and writers. The meetings combine the social with the academic. They remind us, had we forgotten, that what we do is fun or ought to be fun. Like anything else, conferences can become stale, they can suffer from an overflow of inflated egos, and they can weary with repetition. But they can also be stimulating, informative, and playful. Finally, they give people a chance to see and experience another place.

CHAPTER THIRTEEN
Travel in No Particular Order

Here is a series of adventures of an innocent abroad. The academic is privileged to have opportunities such as the ones I recount below.

a. South Africa

I travelled to South Africa twice, the first time in April 1995, just one year after the ANC came to power and Nelson Mandela became president. I was attending a conference in Pretoria, and I stayed with a family during the days of the conference. This was a well-to-do family of three. The father was a lawyer and the mother was a teacher. They welcomed me into their spacious home, but told me that while I was staying, the security system would be compromised. Normally, all three slept in a central room that was locked, guns nearby. The house was locked and so was the gate in the surrounding wall. Outside the wall and down the street was a vehicle with two armed guards. They assured me if any trouble occurred, the armed guards would be there within ten minutes. I thought back to Puerto Rico and the walls and gates I saw there. Anyway, this couple was very kind, arranging for me to play squash with a friend of theirs, followed by a dinner party. The fellow I played squash with was a blustering sort, who railed against the "New South Africa," assuring me that "you can take the Kaffa out of the bush, but you can't take the bush out of the Kaffa." I did not like this person. I liked him even less at the dinner party.

I can't remember how many people were at this dinner, but it was a good-sized group. Waiting on us was a young Black woman named Biddy. I learned that Biddy had grown up on the same ranch as my hostess. Near the end of the meal, my squash "friend" suddenly blurted out: "There is visible proof of the inferiority of the Black person." He was looking directly at me when he said this. I had no idea how to respond, first because I had no idea what he was talking about and second because I was a guest in this house. He went on. He said that these two women—gesturing to my hostess and Biddy—grew up in the same place and one had made something of herself and the other was, and I quote, "nothing." I had only encountered such overt race hatred and bigotry once before in Mississippi.

At the conference, the majority of delegates were white; the people who served coffee and cleaned up the rooms were black. Each morning, I went to the same place to get a coffee, and I had friendly conversation with the same fellow each day. He remarked one morning that he admired my tie. I was wearing a tie my grandmother had given me; it was Ferguson tartan (my mother's maiden name was Ferguson). I thought of it as my lucky tie. I asked him if he really liked it or if he was simply saying this to be pleasant. He assured me he coveted the tie. I told him that I would not give it away because it was a gift from my grandmother, but if he gave me his address, I would send him one from Canada (I now see how this was a mistake; I should have just given him the tie). He took a scrap of paper and scribbled his name on it. I said I would need an address, and he took the paper back and scribbled some more. I took this paper back home, went shopping and found a Ferguson tartan tie, placed it in an envelope and sent it. I have never heard back.

This first trip to South Africa was a series of emotional encounters. Where to begin? While at the conference, I gave a talk to open an art exhibition. The artists were from South Africa and Namibia. After my talk, I was going through the gallery and a young woman from Namibia came up to me. She told me of the travails encountered by Black artists and writers in South Africa. Despite the majority of people being Black in this country and despite the momentous change in government that had taken place, the arts were still largely controlled by white people, and these white people continued to privilege white artists and writers. I was disappointed to hear this, but not surprised. After all, I was attending a conference where the vast majority of registrants were white. And I come from a country where First Nations voices have found difficulty being heard.

Also at this conference, I attended a panel discussion on race in the profession. Up to then, I was of the opinion that jobs should go to the best-qualified person—period. At this panel, I heard explanations of affirmative action that made sense. We all know that the profession was (and is) male dominated, and white male dominated at that. White privilege is something I had to get clear in my mind, and I think I did. People on this panel, including Rhonda Bunbury, a friend and colleague from Australia, argued that until such time that gender and colour were not an issue, it was incumbent on employers to seek out qualified women and minority people for jobs. If we expect to achieve the world we want, a world of equal opportunity, then we have to build this world and we can start building by making room for the disenfranchised and discriminated against. Leaving that panel discussion, I changed my opinion. Affirmative action does not mean hiring incompetence; it means choosing to hire those from groups historically neglected and even overlooked whenever opportunity arrives. The idea is to build a workforce that is truly representative of the people who make up our populace. Diversity is the goal here, as it ought to be everywhere.

A group of some six people at this conference were board members of the IRSCL (International Research Society for Children's Literature), and they planned on going to Kruger Park for a few nights and then going on to Cape Town. They planned to have their board meeting in Kruger Park. I had been a member of this board only a couple of years back, and so they asked me to come along as mascot. I did. We drove from Pretoria to Kruger, and stopped in a small town. Here we accessed an ATM. I marveled at this: here we were in rural South Africa, in a small town colourful and strange to my eyes, and through the pressing of a few buttons I could access my bank account. The countryside was fabulous even when what we were seeing on distant hills were what our host called "homelands." These were areas set aside for

Black people under apartheid, and the houses were rudimentary at best. Similar places in urban areas were referred to as townships. More about the townships later.

Our small band arrived at Kruger Park, where we stayed in cabins and met around an outside fire in the evenings. During the day, we went on safari. Safari constituted a day's ride in a small bus-like vehicle on the many roads throughout the park on a quest to see animals, especially the big five: lion, elephant, Cape buffalo, leopard, and rhinoceros. On our daily journeys we saw only two of these, elephant and buffalo. We did see clear evidence of the rhinoceros, but we saw neither hide nor hair of the two cats. In the evenings, however, we did hear the lions growling not far from our gated camping area, and this was very reminiscent of Rider Haggard. Other animals we saw included giraffe, hyena, crocodile, hippopotamus, kudu, sable, impala, and springbok. Most amazing was the dung beetle. The only time we were allowed out of the vehicle was when we came upon hippopotamus near a river; we were instructed to stay well away from them. The experience of seeing these animals in the wild was powerful. They looked healthy and huge and high-stepping. They looked as if they did not have a care in the world. I guess they looked free. I know the illusion that lurks here; nevertheless these animals put on a show of the way things should be.

I mentioned the sound of lions in the evening and Rider Haggard. Well, one evening Rhonda Bunbury and I went for a walk in the gathering dark. It was the crepuscular time. As we wandered, we noticed ahead a couple of large white open-sided tents and a young man setting long tables nearly covered in white tablecloths. As we approached, the young man nodded to us and asked me if we were looking for something. He referred to me as "Boss." We began chatting, and it became clear that he was setting the table for a party of people, white people, and that he thought we were members of this party arrived early. We assured him that we were not. And so we talked for a while. He told us he came from a nearby homeland, that he was working for a white master, and that his brother had been shot by the authorities. Hearing all this was unsettling. Whether what we heard was true or whether what we heard was what the young man thought we wanted to hear does not matter. We were experiencing years of aparteid injustice manifested in the age-old Hegelian way. We were masters and he was servant. I felt very uncomfortable.

The trip to Kruger was good; the group was close and the time together relaxed. I decided to extend my trip and travel to Cape Town where I would meet three of the group for a few more days in this beautiful yet disturbing country. We drove back to Pretoria and I caught a plane for Cape Town. As the plane descended toward the Cape Town Airport, I gazed out the window at a large area adjacent to the airport of what we would think of as slums in North America, only these places were worse than anything I had seen before. As I looked out the window, I felt a tap on my shoulder. The man next to me was clearly a businessman, well-dressed and supremely white. He had not spoken during the flight from Johannesburg. Now he spoke to tell me that what I was looking at was a place where country people stayed. They came, he said, from the country looking for work. They had no money and so they gravitated to this place where they could find a place to stay for little or nothing. I nodded, but did not speak in reply. We landed and as I entered the main entranceway, I saw a man holding a sign with my name on it. During this visit to South Africa, I was rarely on my own. Anyway, I indicated that I was the person he was looking for and he turned and walked toward the exit. I followed. Outside, he went to a van and opened the rear door for my luggage and leaving this open, he went and got in the driver's seat. I put my two pieces of luggage into the van, shut the door, and then got in the side door to sit down because someone else was in the front passenger seat. Off we went.

We drove by the place I had seen from the air. This was a township, and I was to learn more about it before long. We stopped at a hotel and the passenger in the front seat got out. So too did the driver. I sat for a moment, and then got out and moved to the front passenger seat. The driver returned, got in, took a glance at me, and drove off. He had not spoken all the time I had been with him. As we drove along, I looked out the window at what in the U.S. south would be antebellum homes, beautiful places with pillars and two or three floors and handsome lawns and gardens. I asked the driver about the place we had passed on the way from the airport. He asked me if I really wanted to know, and I said I would not have asked had I not wanted to know. Then he asked why I wanted to know. I told him about the man on the airplane and what he had said. I also told him I thought the man on the plan was not telling the truth, or certainly not telling me the whole story. He surprised me by pulling the van over to the curb and stopping. He turned the van off, and sat with his back on the door. Then he began to tell me about this place, a township where under apartheid Black people like himself had to live. They had to have papers to leave the township for jobs in the city. It was as if they were prisoners there, he said. He then told me that he lived there in a zinc-lined shack with fourteen other people. Conditions, he said, had not altered greatly for those who lived there despite the change in government. I guess my eyes became moist because he abruptly stopped talking and started the van and drove off. We came to the hotel and we both exited the van. At the back, the driver opened the doors and I reached in to get my luggage. I was startled by the driver's hand and arm coming down over mine. I looked at him and withdrew my arms. He reached in to get the luggage, and I did the same as he had done. He looked at me, and I said, "You take one, and I'll take one." He grinned as we each took a piece of luggage. Inside at the check-in, I said thanks and he embraced me quickly and left.

Cape Town is beautiful, but the way a city such as Charleston is beautiful. This is a terrible beauty. This is a beauty that exists because of suffering and brutality and injustice and the unkindness of human beings. Everywhere are reminders of history's nightmare. I spent a few days here with John, Maria, and Sandra. One day we rented a car to drive along the coast, right to the Cape of

Good Hope, the southern tip of Africa. Before we got clear of the city, we got lost and found ourselves in an eerie place reminiscent of the place I had seen near the airport. As we drove down a dirt street, no one was in sight. The area looked deserted. But before we came to a place to turn round, people slowly began to appear from behind shacks and from side roads. Soon there were many people just standing in a large crowd watching us as we stopped and turned around and drove back from where we had come. This was a strange experience. It was silent and eerie, the crowd of people just staring as we retreated.

Soon we were on the highway and drove along the coast, rugged and beautiful. We came to the Cape and took pictures. I can't recall much more of that trip, except the return journey to Cape Town. By the time we were on the way back, darkness had fallen and with it came a dense fog. Driving was difficult and slow. We did not arrive back in the city until nearly eleven. When we drove to the place where Sandra was staying, we saw someone seated on the porch holding a rifle across his lap. This was the landlord. He was on the porch waiting for Sandra, worried that something dire had happened. He said that he was on the verge of calling the police. Such is South Africa. Such beauty. Such danger.

My second trip to South Africa occurred six years later in 2001. After my first trip, I told myself I would not go back to South Africa because it was too emotional. My friend from Pretoria, Thomas Van Der Walt, wrote and asked me to give a talk at the conference he was organizing, and at the end of his letter he said, "Don't say no." He knew my feelings after the first trip. Anyway, I agreed to go. When I arrived, Thomas met me and he asked if I would mind waiting with a woman from Zimbabwe while he went to look for someone else who was arriving. The person from Zimbabwe was Miriam, and when Thomas introduced us, she asked me what I thought of South Africa. I said that when I first came to this country back in 1995, I expected to enter the airport and feel a bit self-conscious because everyone would look different from me. However, that was not the case. Now that it was six years later, I said that I departed the plane expecting to enter the airport and feel self-conscious because I would look different from everyone else. Lo and behold, that was not the case. I said she was the one who looked different. Her reply was: "Some things take a long time to change."

This time the conference was to take place at a country resort, a place called Klein Kariba, some sixty-five or seventy kilometres north of Johannesburg. Here we stayed in brick units, and closed our windows to keep out the baboons that moved about freely among the dorms. As had been the case in 1995, registrants at the conference were largely white and the service people were black. Some things change slowly, as Miriam had said. Evidence of this occurred on the day of the excursion to visit the San people, also known as the Bushmen. I did not wish to go on this excursion because I suspected I would find the whole set-up objectionable. But a friend convinced me to go along. We got to a ranch where we were given a brochure telling us of "the happy little people," the Bushmen. A guide then told us how these small people were reduced in number and they had been given sanctuary on this ranch. "Sanctuary"? Here they lived in their traditional way, fashioning items to sell to eager tourists such as ourselves. I doubted that traditionally these people fashioned baskets and other things for tourists. I was already on edge. Then we arrived at a clearing where there were three or four grass huts, in front of which were smiling people with their wares to sell. Some things take time to change. Here was evidence that exploitation was alive and well in South Africa. Exploitation is not the preserve of South Africa; it is ubiquitous.

On this same trip, I met Elana Bregin. Elana is a South African writer, and I found her story compelling. She told me that her work had been, prior to 1994, focused on and directly engaged with the political and racial problems in her country, but after the end of aparteid she found herself without a voice. She has, since then, returned to writing, but when I met her, she was still working through what it meant for her as a white South African to be a writer. She understood the importance of standing down so that other voices might be heard. She also told me of her experience as a student hearing Juluka for the first time. Juluka was a South African band formed by Johnny Clegg and Sipho Mchunu, and in their early days together they had difficulty because it was against the law for a white person to perform with a black person. Elana told me that once when she was in university, she went to a concert not knowing who was playing. When the curtain pulled back, a black person walked on stage from one side and a white person walked on from the other side. They came together and began to play. She said the experience was electric. I got shivers just thinking about this event.

Also on this same trip, I had occasion to talk with my friend Thomas and hear of his fears and worries, and his hope that his daughter would relocate outside South Africa. As for himself, he told me of his deep connection to this country. He said that as a white person, he was encouraged to leave, to go back to where he came from. The problem, he noted, was that he came from South Africa. This was his home. He could understand the anger of the Black population, but he also wanted people to acknowledge that he only knew this place as his home. This is where he had been born and brought up. Race matters are, I guess, complicated, but we might remove the complication by accepting difference, celebrating difference, and acknowledging that difference is the future.

I left South Africa, but I carry it with me even now.

b. Russia

In the spring of 1991 (March) I traveled to Russia to attend a board meeting of the IRSCL. Later that same year, on August 19, Boris Yeltsin famously addressed a crowd from atop a tank outside the parliament building. This was the time of perestroika ("restructuring") and glasnost ("openness"). Russia was in turmoil. Those were interesting times. I flew from Canada to Geneva where I changed planes for Moscow. When I went aboard the plane for Moscow, I was confronted with a nearly empty double row of seats. This was a Boeing 747 and I saw only half a dozen people seated here and there. I took my seat thinking I was in the Twilight Zone. The plane left with just a few passengers, no more than six or eight, in this huge tube. When we landed in Moscow, I saw two or three planes on the sides of the runway, appearing as if they had slipped there and were abandoned. This was my introduction to Russia. I got through customs and made my way to the hotel, the Peking Hotel. As I entered the lobby, a woman approached and greeted me. She said I should check in, go to my room, and stay there until someone called me. I asked how long this would be and she said she did not know; she was waiting for the others to arrive. I checked in and went to my room, a closet of a room with a strange elevated toilet. The single bed was hard, and the room was dark. It was about three-thirty in the afternoon, and I was excited. Here I was in Moscow—sitting in a hotel room. I decided to go for a walk.

I left the hotel and began to walk up a wide avenue. I was wearing a long black coat, blue jeans, and hiking boots. As I walked, I noticed people going by carrying huge rings with rolls of toilet paper on the rings. I also noticed people carrying five and six ice cream cones. These were strange sights to me. I thought I would follow the trail of ice cream carrying people back to the source, and eventually I came across a small kiosk with a long line of people waiting for ice cream cones. The small kiosk was adorned with a cartoon penguin. Having found this place, I thought I would check out the subway because I had heard that the subway stations were worth seeing. I went down some stairs and entered a station. It was huge. An army could have marched in there. The walls were decorated with beautiful tiles that carried pictures of heroic looking workers, farm workers, industrial workers, just the kind of thing one might expect as stereotypical of Russia. Amazing really. Clean and bright.

By this time, it was growing dark outside. It was March and the days closed early. I thought best to return to the hotel. When I got back, the woman who had first greeted me was waiting, and she was furious. I had not followed her instructions. She gave me a lecture about following orders, but what she was really expressing was anxiety that I might have been whisked away by someone because I was visibly a foreigner and a foreigner means hard currency. At the time, the ruble was pretty much worthless and people were looking for American dollars or German marks. This woman feared I had been taken out to the woods by a taxi driver or someone else looking to score some hard currency, and left there a cold carcass. These were the days when Russian stores were empty. I entered one store and saw the empty shelves and the short line-up of customers proceeding to a glass-protected counter to purchase whatever few items were available. As I had wandered the streets, I had noticed that some stores had nothing in them but empty shelves, whereas others had everything one could wish for. These latter stores also had signs in the windows that read, "Hard Currency Only." I found this fascinating. This was a country with two economies, one official and the other the black market. The black market, however, seemed acceptable as it functioned so openly.

Once back in the hotel, I met the other six board members, and also our interpreters. The interpreter assigned to me was a tall student named Oleg. I was to spend quite a bit of time with Oleg over the next week, and I gave him various gifts—blue jeans, cigarettes, and chocolate. The next day we traveled to a writer's retreat some ninety miles outside of Moscow. This retreat was a handsome, if somewhat worn, eighteenth-century mansion. Here we had our meetings, until mid-week when we decided we should take a break and do some sightseeing. Accordingly, we asked to go back to Moscow on the Thursday. We were informed that we could not go on Thursday because gasoline had not been rationed for the van that day. In short, we got the runaround. We were stubborn, and on Thursday we simply took ourselves out to a main road and waited for a bus. We climbed aboard the first bus that came along and traveled to a nearby small town where we found a huge supermarket. This was a large concrete two-story building with little in the way of decoration or signage. We went inside, and what we saw was dramatic. Imagine a Walmart store with nothing in it but the employees and empty shelves. This huge space contained nothing but empty shelves. Well almost nothing; where televisions might have been we saw a few scattered LPs, including ones by Lionel Ritchie, David Bowie, and the Rolling Stones, all rather old and with the lettering on the sleeves in Cyrillic script. At the far end of the ground floor was a glass cabinet, the kind you see in butcher shops. A man was standing by this cabinet haggling with a couple of women who stood behind the cabinet. One of our group, Tony from England, said he was going to go and see what was happening. I went with him, and as we approached, we could see that the man was haggling over the price of a small fish, the only item on display. Tony said he was going to get a picture, but I felt uneasy and began to walk away. Behind me I could hear yelling from one of the ladies. Then Irina, our host and one of the board members, came forward talking loudly. When I got back to the rest of the group, my friend Jean Perrot, who could speak Russian, asked if I knew what was being said. Of course, I did not. Jean translated: the Russian woman behind the cabinet yelled at Tony that he was a spy and he could not take pictures; Irina replied that Russia was a free country and he could take pictures wherever he wanted to take pictures. As I said to Jean, the real point was that Tony was embarrassing the people in the store. He should not have tried to take photographs here.

Russia was fascinating. We met people, such as Oleg, who were excited by the changing times. They saw the new openness as beneficial and genuinely hopeful. On the other hand, someone such as our host Irina complained of this new Russia. She looked back to the days of Stalin as the salad days. Why? Well, she had been a member of the privileged class, having a car and driver and a place outside the city. She feared losing these luxuries. The new Russia brought openness, but it also had its corruption. One story I heard at the time was that shortages of meat were artificially created. Trucks carrying meat were purloined by criminals and the meat tossed in the woods to rot, just to keep availability scarce and prices at a premium. We saw evidence of unrest on the streets; rallies with people carrying placards and hollering.

When the time came to return to Moscow for a final dinner before departure, we had a small adventure. The van we were taking back to the city broke down on the highway. A replacement might take some time to arrive, the person in charge said. We decided to hitchhike back to the city. The person in charge, and Irina, were shocked. They advised us strongly not to do this, but we ignored their advice. Well, they might have relaxed because we had no luck whatsoever in finding a ride. Our thumbs simply elicited perplexed looks from drivers who passed by and a few honks. Our effort was in vain. However, I do have a couple of pictures of our intrepid group on the highway, thumbs extended.

The night of my departure came. I was to leave for the airport around four in the morning and Oleg was to come to the hotel to take me. The time came, Oleg arrived, and the two of us got into a taxi. It was raining as we drove through the quiet early morning streets of Moscow. Then Oleg turned to me and in the dark he extended his hand, telling me he had a gift for me. I took what he offered; it was a candy in a paper wrapper. I knew that after a week of conversing with me and receiving things from me, Oleg wanted to give something back. I thanked him and said I had something for him in return. I reached in my pocket and found a couple of twenty-dollar bills in U.S. currency. These I handed over to Oleg. He took them, and I could see tears in his eyes. We did not speak. Arriving at the airport, I saw a huge crowd of people inside. The crowd was so large that I told Oleg I could not go through all those people. He said they were Armenians trying to get out of the country, and he grabbed my hand and pulled me through the teeming throng, pushing people aside as he went. We got to a security point and he pushed me through. Once on the other side of the barrier, all was quiet. I looked back to see Oleg (he was very tall) disappearing back through the frantic crowd. I have never heard from him since.

I check my journal from that time, and I see my notes from this trip are mostly about food. Here is a summary of what we ate:

potatoes, watery soup, pancakes and sour cream, boiled fish, something that looked like perogies but was supposed to be potato and was sickly sweet, coffee made from wheat, junket-like pudding, stew, fish bun (bun with boiled fish and egg inside), mashed zucchini, and cabbage cabbage cabbage. We had cabbage at breakfast, lunch, and dinner. Near the end of the trip, we were treated to lunch at the Writer's Union in Moscow. The place resembled the coffee shop at the British Museum, except that it had works of art displayed on the yellow walls. The outer foyer also had an art exhibition, Spanish work that was garish and slightly grotesque. My memory of this work has faded. The food, however, remains in my memory probably because it was almost edible: salty raw fish again, good fresh salad, lots of roast potatoes and vegetables, breaded chicken. For dessert we had ice cream, and chocolate cake. To drink, we had what may have been real coffee, Pepsi, and wine. No vodka! And all week, no milk.

After that lunch, my journal reminds me that we went to see Tolstoy's statue, and then we walked to the Kremlin. At the Tomb of the Unknown Soldier, we witnessed a bride and groom place flowers on the monument. Apparently, this is a tradition to honour those who kept fascist rule out of Russia. Then we went into Red Square with its display of onion domes, Lenin's Tomb, and St. Basil's Cathedral (a museum now). Seeing St. Basil's is one of the great experiences of my life. The colours are stunning, absolutely breathtaking. Sadly, the building was closed when we were there, but an elderly Russian man accosted me and asked to exchange coins. This is why travel matters.

I end this rumination on Russia with a few quotations from the journal I kept at that time. "Americanism creeps into (inexorably) Russian life. Signs, music, products, people. A strange world teetering on the edge of something horrendous—either collapse and civil war or Bush's new world order" (that would be the first President Bush). "At times Moscow seemed so familiar and then the realization that it is profoundly different from what we know." "Huge buildings empty. Line-ups are a way of life." "Dirt everywhere. Things falling apart; obviously the centre has not held." My last note has proven to be wrong, of course. "Few vegetables. Little meat. Some neon." "Dreary, dark, low, spiritless airport." "Green, pinkish beige, blue (sky) are prevailing colours. People dour, square, full of phlegm—but there is great warmth. Humiliated by the apparent chaos." In short, I enjoyed this experience and have often thought I would like to return, especially to visit St. Petersburg.

c. Spain

I have meandered through two countries and noted that in both South Africa and Russia I was participating in IRSCL activities. I should tell you how I came to be a member of this organization. In 1989, Frances and I traveled to Salamanca, Spain, to attend my first IRSCL conference. Of course, we took the opportunity to travel some in Spain, visiting such places as Córdoba, Toledo, and Malaga. We rented a car, and in Toledo I had an emasculating moment when I turned up a very narrow street, a narrow street that grew narrower the farther we drove, until we came to a 'T' intersection. The walls were so close to the car that turning was impossible. My only recourse was to back up and return to the square from whence we had driven. I did this—gingerly. People began to appear peering at us from windows. The car scraped the walls making a noise that caused goosebumps to rise on the skin. Then came a terrible scrunching noise as the left side mirror cracked and broke free; it dangled sickeningly as the car finally left the narrow alley and came to rest in the square. I got out to check the damage, remarking rather loudly that my manhood had been compromised. Then I noticed all the people staring at the car, staring at me, looking blankly, but behind that blankness I knew they were laughing, enjoying the plight of this innocent from abroad who could not navigate their ancient streets.

For the rest of the trip, I worried about that broken mirror and remarked on all the cars with perfectly fine mirrors. When we finally returned the car to the airport, I was sure the rental people would make me pay for the damage. Arriving at the airport, I found the requisite parking spot and then found that this was a long way from the rental desk. By the time we got to the desk, our time to get to the plane was running out. I mentioned this. The person at the desk asked if we had filled the gas tank. I said yes. Anything else, she asked. I am not sure now what I said, but I think I prevaricated. Then I heard the magic words, "Okay, thank you, sir, for your business. I hope you choose our company the next time you rent a car." Off we went.

Having had such an unsettling experience, I needed something to offset the diminishment of my confidence. This came at the IRSCL conference. Here's what happened. I had never been to one of these conferences before, and I was not a member of the society. But I found the people genial, and got along well. Before the general meeting on the penultimate morning of the conference, someone approached me to ask if I would like to stand for the board. If I agreed, then I would say something about myself at the general meeting and wait for the results of the vote. I was flattered, and agreed to stand for office. The general meeting came, I spoke, members voted, and lo and behold I found myself a newly elected member of the board. This is when things began to get interesting. On the final morning of the conference, the new board met, along with outgoing members. As I sat at this my first meeting as a member of the board of IRSCL, I discovered that the society accepted members only after a vetting process. Prospective members had to apply for membership. This meant sending in a letter accompanied by a c.v. and perhaps a letter of support. I realized with a jolt that not only was I not a paid member of the society, but I certainly had never been vetted in the usual manner. Never had I applied for membership. I sheepishly raised my hand, and then pointed out that I was not a member. The others in the room went silent. They looked at each other. I said I could understand that a mistake had taken place, and I would quietly depart. Before I could get up from my chair, the president assured me that they would like me to stay, and that had I applied in the usual manner I would most definitely have been accepted into the society. As long as I paid my dues, all would be well and we could simply proceed.

Well and good, but then the rest of the meeting went ahead and we began the process of vetting applicants. I found this process pretentious and elitist. I recall one applicant who had written a well-known textbook on children's literature. The board rejected her application because they did not respect her scholarship. I was aghast. And I said so. What ensued was a heated discussion not only of this application, but of the entire process of vetting people for membership. I could not, and still cannot, grasp the sense in this way of conducting business. I thought we should embrace any and all who wanted to become part of this community of researchers. As far as I could see, ours was not the task to judge the scholarship of others, but rather to encourage it. If we had any mandate, then this should be to bring people together to share research and perhaps to strengthen research. The society was truly international, and as such, we understood that research in various parts of the world was at a different stage than it was in other parts of the world. Because of this, I saw a strange situation in which a researcher such as the lady who published the textbook found herself rejected, whereas someone else from a country the board wished to encourage was accepted when this person clearly did not have the academic credentials of the person we had rejected. I found this bizarre. I also noted over the years I was associated with the society a growing influence of English-speaking countries to the detriment of membership from non-English-speaking countries.

What I am setting out here is the presumptive character of academics. Not all academics, of course, but enough to make the atmosphere on campuses charged with a sense of privilege. When I began teaching, everyone taught at least one first-year undergraduate course. By the time I retired thirty-eight years later, some full professors did not teach any undergraduate courses. Or let me recount two stories of academic celebrity. The first is rather fluffy, but I will tell it anyway. In the mid-1990s I was in Sweden for a conference, and one day I found myself taking a walk with a junior colleague (see, there I go with terms that smack of hierarchy) from Australia. As we strolled along, she remarked how lovely it was to be among famous people. The remark stopped me for a moment. Then I asked what she meant and to whom she was referring. She said she was talking about the stars of the profession, and she mentioned two or three people, ending with me. Oh, I said, let's go across the street to that small shop and when we enter let's see which one of us the shopkeeper or any shoppers there recognize. She laughed and said they would be unlikely to recognize either of us, and that I was simply being modest. So, I said, I wonder if we were at another academic conference, one where a different crowd gathered, would either of us be recognized? And so we bantered. But my real point, understated, was how distasteful such categorizing of people, academics or otherwise, is.

My second story is more pointed. It has to do with two of the most well-known people in my profession: one of these I will call Henry Borstein and the other is Jack Zipes. In 1999, I organized a conference at my university, bringing together for the first and so far only time both the IRSCL and another group I have yet to discuss, the Children's Literature Association (ChLA). I wanted our plenary speakers to be people whose work I admired and I had recently been reading the work of Borstein. He is an academic whose work crosses disciplines, touching on literature, education, the media, and politics. His voice was a voice for the dispossessed, and I admired what I read. It seemed a good choice to ask him if he would give a plenary talk at our conference. I emailed him, asking him if he would speak and offering $1000, plus travel and accommodation in a hotel close to campus. He wrote back and said he was interested, but he wanted more information about the conference. So, I wrote again telling him about the two organizations, other possible speakers, and anything else I could think of. He wrote back a curt note declining my invitation. His note was so cool after his genial first message that I felt compelled to write back and ask: "Was it something I said?" I hoped that I had not offended him. He replied to say that no, I had not offended him, but that the fee I had mentioned was "far below my usual fee." "Far below"? I checked out the amounts some of the more prominent names in the profession received for talks, and I saw that some would receive $10,000 (and even more). Not only was I shocked, but I was also outraged. These people had day jobs, and as far as I knew one aspect of their day job was to give talks. Heck, I would go places for nothing more than airfare and accommodation, and I did. Anything above that I might receive was a gift, not a salary. We call this an "honorarium," a payment made in lieu of a legal or required fee. An honorarium is a show of gratitude, not a requirement. I decided that I did not want this fellow as a speaker.

Anyway, I said this story was about two academics. Jack Zipes is even better known than Henry Borstein. He is the author of thirty books or more; he is also someone who works with children in schools and elsewhere. He lives a life to match the values he expresses in his writing. I had met him some fifteen years before our conference, and as fate would have it, I saw him at a party the year before the conference I was planning and just after I had communicated unsuccessfully with Professor Borstein. We were both attending the annual MLA conference in Toronto. We had an informal chat and I mentioned my recent dealings with Professor Burstein. Jack simply said: "You tell Henry Borstein to go fuck himself. And you can quote me." Hearing this, I smiled and asked if his remark meant that he would be a plenary speaker at our conference. He countered by asking me to repeat the conditions. I said we had $1000 Canadian (minus GST) as an honorarium and that we would put him up in the dorms. He gave me the evil eye and said he would be in Rome at the time of the conference (at that time Zipes spent six months a year in Rome), but that he would fly back to Minneapolis (he worked at the University of Minnesota at the time), change his shirt, and fly on to Calgary. We could pay for his flight from Minneapolis to Calgary. He also stipulated that he wanted a kettle in his room to make tea, and that he would stay for the seven days of the conference (an unusually long conference) if we left him undisturbed when he wanted to work. The deal was sealed with a handshake.

Jack Zipes is as good a model as we have for the academic: a prolific scholar, dedicated teacher, and active participant in the lives of young people both of university age and younger. I witnessed a workshop he gave on storytelling, and I was agog with pleasure. We need many more of Jack Zipes's ilk, and many fewer who exhibit Henry Borstein's pretence.

And so, I found myself on the board of IRSCL, an opponent to the very manner in which they conducted business, and perhaps even living proof that their system was silly. The system of vetting applicants may have been silly, but it continued for many more years. Despite that, IRSCL is a worthwhile organization. It brings together people from disparate countries, it provides a bit of financial help to young scholars, it encourages international cooperation, and it has a familial feel that I found attractive. As a member of IRSCL, I made several lifelong friendships. Dieter Petzold and his wife Renate have hosted us in their home and visited us in ours. Through Dieter, I also made connections with another group, the German Society named the Inklings, after the Oxford group of the 1920s and '30s. It was at one of the Inklings conferences that I met John Docherty, a MacDonald scholar who also invited us into his home in England. Dieter is from a small town in Germany, Haroldsbach, 35 kilometres north of Nuremberg. In 1998, the Catholic Church officially designated Heroldsbach a holy site. It has a history of holy visions dating back to 1949. Without IRSCL, I would not have had the occasion to visit this strange place, and I would not have met Dieter and Renate.

Another important friend from IRSCL is the French scholar Jean Perrot. He and his wife, Annie, became good friends and we have exchanged visits several times. Jean and Annie live in Eaubonne, just ten minutes from the Gare du Nord in Paris. Back in 1994, Jean created the Charles Perreault Institute for the study of children's literature. He is also the author of numerous books, including books on Henry James, the Baroque, and game theory. He is truly one of the major voices in international children's literature studies. With Jean, I attended a small gathering in the hills outside of Rome, but this is a story for another place in this memoir. Suffice to say that Jean and Annie have been important people in our lives, and we have shared many good times.

Other people I met in IRSCL include Maria Nikolajeva (Sweden and England), Clare Bradford (Australia), Tony Watkins (England), Gunvor Risa (Norway), Marisol Dorao (Spain), Rhonda Bunbury (Australia), and Sandra Beckett (Canada). In fact, members of the board were in my house back around 1990 when the phone rang. It was someone I did not know, Sandra Beckett. She was phoning to enquire about IRSCL, and I had the pleasure of saying she could talk to the president, Rhonda Bunbury, who just happened to be sitting across from me. Yes, the board met in Calgary that year, and I can recall taking them to Banff where the members from Spain and Australia had not experienced snow before. We were a merry group in the Banff Hot Springs, where Marisol did a dance to express her joy. IRSCL is an important organization and I am proud to have been a member, and to have served on their board of directors.

This section began by announcing Spain as the subject, and so I had best return to that country. And I did return. In 2001, I was invited to speak at a conference in Ciudad Real, Spain. My host was the redoubtable Cristina Perez Valverde. She brought me to Cervantes country, and there to tilt at windmills. I remember Cristina and a male friend of hers took me to see some sight (just what I no longer remember), and when we left the tourist place, we wandered several streets looking for the parked car. And when I say several streets, I am not exaggerating. We wandered and we wandered in a manner that seemed aimless to me. I felt as if we were in a film by Luis Bunuel. I was amused. I also remember a feast one evening. The food was plentiful and exotic, including what appeared to me to be a large plate of steaming white shoelaces that was placed before me. Usually prepared to try anything, I passed on this delicacy. A small group of people from this dinner invited me to go to a bar with them afterwards.

Saying "no" was unacceptable, and so I went. The group did not have anyone who spoke English with any degree of clarity, but we were a merry bunch nonetheless. They took me to a crowded bar with music, and they ordered a special drink that sent the man behind the bar out through a side door. When he emerged from this door, he was carrying tumblers filled with some exotic brew. I have no idea what it was, but I drank it. Before long, a tall severe-looking woman stepped up and asked me to dance. Again, I could not say no, and the two of us proceeded to dance—the salsa! Seconds after I had begun to gyrate, this tall dark woman stopped, glared at me, and stomped off, but not before she clearly spoke the words: "Salsa is a dance of passion!" Her tone was defiant. Apparently, I was not passionate enough! This trip was short but intense, and my admiration for Spanish culture is strong. Cristina, by the way, has become a good friend. Since the time I met her in Ciudad Real, she has transformed herself into a novelist. She has also become an acquaintance of my daughter Kate who spent a year in Spain.

This section on Spain has too little to say about Spain. I will close by noting that Frances and I had occasion to see Picasso's magnificent *Guernica* in Madrid, and to visit the Prado Museum. We also saw the El Greco House, the Mosque-Cathedral of Córdoba, the aqueduct in Segovia, and much more. Our experiences in Spain were enjoyable, memorable, and informative.

d. Italy

I mentioned above a trip to Italy arranged by my friend Jean Perrot. This happened in May 1989. We traveled to a small Italian town named Roviano. The conference was on "Aesthetic Education," and took us to three small towns in a region some 60 or 70 kilometers north of Rome. The towns were Roviano, Riofreddo, and Arsoli. We delivered our talks in a castle in the third of these towns. And the castle was still lived in and the owners, a local Prince and his wife, attended each talk. The room for these talks boasted a piano once owned by Franz Liszt. Our host was the flamboyant Giulio Sforza, whom I first met in Eaubonne, at Jean Perrot's house a year or so earlier. I remember hijinks in Jean's garden that involved parodying the holy sacrament. Giulio was a big man, in every sense. He gathered some eight or ten people for the conference on aesthetic education; I was the only North American and the only person who was pathetically unilingual. Well, I could stumble through a conversation in French, but I certainly could not translate my paper into French and deliver it. Giulio told me not to worry. The working languages of the conference were Italian and French. On the day I was to give a talk, Giulio told me that I should speak in English, but pause after a couple of sentences, then Jean would translate these sentences into French, and he (Giulio) would translate from the French into Italian. By the time I gave my talk, I had heard enough Italian that I was beginning to grasp some of what was said. As I listened to my words change into French and then Italian, I could sense the meaning of what I had said in English changing. My guess is that Giulio simply said what he wanted to say regardless of what I may have been arguing. But everyone was kind. I saw smiles all round!

I am tempted to call the experience at this conference *jouissance*. We were assigned cars to transport us from town to town, and the driver of my car was Rita. I have far too little memory of Rita; I know I should remember her more sharply because I know that she was hilarious, telling us of burial places when we passed terraced containers with candles and turning to look at us in the back seat as she drove, keeping up a constant patter. We drove from town to town for events such as a chorale concert or a tour of an ancient mansion. Meals too were taken in the streets of these towns; we walked from square to square having one course—salad, say, or pasta—in one square and another course in another square. But always wine. A young man stayed close to me and kept assuring me that the food was "pas industriel." At least this is what I think he was saying. He also assured me the Mafia had nothing to do with the conference. You can imagine how relieved I was. But I began to suspect that he protested too much.

For some strange reason I no longer remember the other speakers, aside from Jean, Giulio, and Rita, but I have fond memories of the places and the food and the genial company. On the last morning, before we could take our leave, the local women appeared in traditional clothing to give us bread. I took home several loaves, but by the time I made it back to Calgary, these loaves had hardened beyond use. In any case, I recall sitting in the back seat of the car that was taking us to the airport. I looked wistfully out the window at the castle in Arsoli where we had met and given talks. From the front seat I heard my friend Jean remark: "Roderick, it was a dream." And he was right. If only all conferences could be dreams. Our life is no dream, but it should and perhaps will become one; well, for this one time it did become one.

That trip was not my first to Italy. When I was studying for my Ph.D. in England, I decided to travel to Bordighera, on the Italian Riviera, to visit the home of the writer I was working on, George MacDonald. Suzanne and I traveled to the south of France, through Marseilles and Nice, and through Monaco, to Bordighera. When we arrived in Bordighera, we were on a city bus and we happened to strike up a conversation with a woman. We asked for advice regarding places to stay and she suggested we go to such and such an address. We did. When the person who lived there came to greet us, it was the same lady we had met on the bus. This was our introduction to Italy. We spent a couple of days in Bordighera, saw MacDonald's gravesite and his big house, Casa Coraggio, now expanded and recast as an apartment building.

During the rest of our trip, we visited Pisa, Florence, Venice, and Rome. Pisa had that leaning tower; since the tower is an ecclesiastical building, I could not enter it wearing shorts. Florence had the Ponte Vecchio, the great dome, and of course the Uffizi Gallery. The crush of people here irritated me, and I recall trying to see Botticelli's *Birth of Venus* while people jostled about. This was just about the worst gallery experience I ever had, rivaled only by trying to see the *Mona Lisa* in the Louvre. And then there was Venice. Ah, Venice, "La Dominante," "Serenissima," "City of Water," "City of Masks," "City of Bridges," "The Floating City," and "City of Canals," it was all of this and more. I was very taken with Venice. It was so quiet. No cars, and the gondolas do not have motors. Yes, St. Mark's Square was crowded, but the small side streets were not. The city is so beautiful in a melancholy way. Crumbling beauty, beauty tarnished and faded and in disrepair. Time hangs on this city like a shroud, and yet the splendour is a reminder of possible glories, of human capacity for building Golgonooza, great city of science and art, great city of human possibility. Here is a story of Venice that, for me, captures the city's charm.

One evening, we were heading home late but had yet to stop for dinner. We saw a small trattoria on a side street, its humble neon word blinking. In we went to find a spare place empty of customers. The tables were arborite, the walls unadorned, the menu turistico basic and uninspiring. The small elderly man who served us had a tear in the seat of his trousers. We ate quickly and left. What we ate was okay for the money. Anyhow, the next evening we found ourselves in the same area at the same time as the previous evening. We thought, what the heck, we might just as well save money and go to the same place we had frequented the day before. When we entered, the man with the trouser tear recognized us, and before we could take seats, he came over and indicated that we should follow him. He took us to the back of the restaurant and through a beaded curtain into an amazing garden with tables among the flowers and shrubs. The tables were crowded with people, but he took us to a table and introduced us to the local English teacher who in turn introduced us to the local pharmacist. They welcomed us to their table. No menu this night. The food simply arrived, and it was splendid. The servers were the man we first met and his son. We had a splendid meal and a heartwarming human exchange. But the evening had not ended.

When time came to pay, our spondulicks were waved off with a smile and a song. Yes, a song. Father and son began to sing as they ushered us back through the beaded curtain and then out the front door. As we walked alongside the canal in the darkness of the late evening, I looked back to see the two men silhouetted in the light from their doorway, singing some cheerful ditty and waving us on our way. How could I not like Venice? For the next few years, one of my persistent fantasies was of me spending months in this city working and wandering the ancient streets and waterways.

I suppose that before I leave Italy, I ought to say a word about Rome. Ancient footsteps are everywhere. Rome is undoubtedly magnificent. The Colosseum, the Baths of Caracalla, Vatican City, the Spanish Steps, the Capuchin Crypt all made a profound impression on me. The Capuchin Crypt was especially intriguing, chilly, weird, haunting, and funny. Mortality has never looked so pervasive or absurd. And they danced in their bones, in their bare bare bones, to the chitter and the chatter, the click and the clack, they danced in their bare bare bones. I should also mention the Protestant Cemetery where both John Keats and Percy Shelley are buried. Shelley's gravestone marks his ashes, and has the following inscription from Shakespeare's *The Tempest*:

> Nothing of him that doth fade,
> But doth suffer a sea change,
> Into something rich and strange.

I found this moving. Rich and strange, indeed. I admired Shelley for his willingness to give up position and wealth, to give away his shoes to a poor person on the streets of Dublin, to promote the "Necessity of Atheism," to write such intensely political poetry, and to have an inconsumable heart.

But my time in Rome was short. After a cheap meal there, I came down with sickness. I was so sick that we decided to get on a train and return to England.

e. Israel

In 1982, I was excited to have a paper accepted for a conference in Jerusalem, but the war with Lebanon caused the cancellation of the conference. I was deeply disappointed, not least because this would have been my first truly international experience and I would have been on the program with Isaac Asimov. But there you are. Then in 1998 I had a paper accepted for a conference hosted by the International Society for the Study of European Ideas (ISSEI) to take place in Haifa. Frances and I got ready and flew to Tel Aviv, arriving on Tuesday, August 11. We took a bus to Jerusalem where we stayed in the Shalom Hotel, quite a distance from the Old City. We took a shuttle into the Old City, and I shall allow my journal to take over from here.

> Walk through narrow bazaar streets until we come to the "Wall." Make our way up to Temple Mount (Mount Moriah) where we saw the Dome of the Rock. Get rooked by a portly Muslim man who says he is a guide. Oh, and we both have to wear green skirts to cover our sinfully bare legs. The guide tells us forgettable stuff for $20.00. See prayer-square, Mosque, shrine for Rock (Abraham and Isaac and also Muhammad's ascent to heaven). View of Mount of Olives in the distance, Gethsemane, etc. Walk back into city and try vainly to get some money. People very unconcerned and even rude. They take no interest or notice. Walk the Cardo, and into a maze of streets fending off street vendors. Find Dome of the Sepulchre (supposedly site of the crucifixion on Calvary). Fend. Fend. Back to Jaffa Gate. Buy cards. Have beer. Walk to Armenian section, to Dormition Abbey. See camels. Australian busker dressed as Arabian Knight playing harp. Decide to find bank. Outside Jaffa Gate. Get shekels which we'll probably never get rid of. Take 4:30 shuttle back. Evening at hotel. More disco.

I interject here to mention the Western (or Wailing) Wall. We see a bar mitzvah; the men approach the wall, but the women must remain onlookers from the entrance. We also see many people placing slips of paper, prayer papers, into cracks in the wall. Many orthodox men stand about praying. I must confess this all seems strange and unproductive of anything worthwhile. I have much difficulty thinking anything positive about religion, and seeing this spectacle does nothing to alter my frame of mind.

Here is just a bit more from the Journal. "For me, the churches are forgettable, a mixture of architectural styles and sects. Tension everywhere. Money. Crowds. Disarray. And tremendous wealth squandered on censors, mosaics, marble, and useless fakery."

Despite the tone of these journal entries, I found our time in Israel fascinating. We visited such sights as the Israeli-Lebanese border, Masada, the Dead Sea (where we sat on top of the water and burned the souls of our feet on the hot sand), and of course Jerusalem and Bethlehem. As I note in my journal, we visited the Western Wall (also known as the Wailing Wall), the market, and the Dome of the Rock where a man invited us to his home for coffee. We declined. We declined because we were encouraged to be suspicious of people's motives. Under no circumstances, we were instructed at customs, should we accept articles from strangers or take anything we purchased that was wrapped out of our sight. We had ample evidence of trouble during the trip. Once we were denied access to our hotel because of a threat of some kind; we had to wait until the threat was cleared. We regularly saw young men with machine guns getting on public transportation, and when we were at the airport to depart, the building was evacuated because of a bomb threat. The grilling we received at airport security was also worrying. But the most disturbing sight was our passage from Jerusalem across the line into Bethlehem in the Palestinian territory. Once we passed the checkpoint into Bethlehem, the streets were little more than rubble, and the poverty was tangible. We went there to visit the Church of the Nativity, but I had little heart for this tourist sight, especially once I saw the crush of people pushing to enter the small enclave where Christ was supposed to have been born.

We met Steve and Karen DeLue on this trip, and they became friends. The four of us wandered the streets of Haifa together and enjoyed getting to know each other. We later saw Steve and Karen in Norway and also at our home in Calgary. I am not sure if we were with this couple when we had dinner in Bethlehem, but I do remember the hookah passed around the table at that dinner. I reflected on the nonsensical aspect of this world. At the Western Wall we witnessed a bar mitzvah; the men attended the ceremony, while their wives waited outside the entrance. The division of the sexes does nothing to endear this practice to me. And, of course, everywhere we saw the orthodox in their black outfits and ringlets; apparently these people do not work and are supported by the state. On the Sabbath, we were told to use only one elevator in our hotel because only one was programmed so that no one would have to push a button to reach a floor. Apparently pushing a button is considered work, and no work is to take place on the Sabbath. Food must be prepared prior to sundown at the beginning of the Sabbath. All this was intriguing. All over the world, people believe and do crazy things.

f. Scandinavia

Scandinavia had never been an area of the world that interested me. I doubt I would have ever gone had I not attended a conference in Sweden in 1995. The conference was in Stockholm, and during the time there, delegates traveled to Uppsala, birthplace of the great filmmaker, Ingmar Bergman. I was greatly taken with what I saw. My impression was of cities clean and open, and countryside similar to what I experienced growing up in eastern Ontario. The air was soft. The people were unfailingly familiar and warm. Despite the lack of gothic buildings and southern European baroque splendors, the architecture was interesting and somehow noble. One activity at the conference was an evening boat trip through the archipelago, and a short ramble on one of the islands where the farmlands were lush and fresh. I enjoyed Stockholm and recall an impressive reception at the venue for the Nobel Prize ceremonies. In a way, it is a wonder I ever returned to this country because my departure was something of a felony. Another delegate and I were to leave very early in the morning and we asked about paying our accommodation bill the previous day. We were told not to do this because someone would be there on the morning of our departure to take our money. The morning came. No one was about. The place was quiet and closed and still. We looked hither and yon, high and low, inside and out, but to no avail. Finally, we had to get in the taxi and leave in order to catch our flights. All the way home, I felt like a criminal, and I was certain that in due course I would receive a nasty note from someone in authority demanding I pay my bill. The feeling was even more intense than when I returned the damaged car to the airport in Spain. I guess I should have written myself to express my contrition, but I confess I never did. And I never did hear from anyone asking for payment of my bill.

Despite this bump in events, I enjoyed this introduction to Scandinavia, and within a year I was back to serve as the opponent to a Ph.D. student in Umea in the north of Sweden. I wrote of this experience earlier, but I may not have mentioned walking through the town and into the nearby countryside. It was the second week of November and here I was not many kilometres from the Arctic Circle, yet the days were not particularly cold and there was no snow. The sun tried to shine for only about six hours a day, but somehow this did not bother me, or I did not think it bothered me. I did see strange rooms in the campus building, rooms that had one bed with lights above the beds. I learned that these were rooms for simulating sunlight. In the darkness of winter, people could use these rooms to ward off depression. I am not sure if the short days had anything to do with it, but when I returned home, I experienced insomnia for the first time. A week without sleep was debilitating. The good thing is that I now can understand the agonies of those who live with sleep deprivation.

In 2000, I made my first trip to Norway. This was to Bergen for another ISSEI conference. In Bergen it rains. And rains. And rains. Despite the torrential downpour, Bergen was beautiful. And I happened to know someone there too. This was Kristina Fliflet, a former graduate student of mine. We spent some time with Kristina and her family, and on meeting her husband I shook his hand and stared resolutely into his eyes. He laughed and said I must be Norwegian because I greeted him in the Norwegian manner. I confessed that I had been primed to give the firm handshake and unwavering stare. Anyway, dinner with these folks and a trip to their island retreat were highlights of this trip. We also spent some time with Karen and Steve DeLue. Before leaving Norway, we took a cruise on the *Hurtigruten*, sometimes known as the Norwegian Coastal Express, a cruise ship that visits the fjords while traveling north, above the Arctic Circle and close to the Russian border. This trip was a revelation. The isolated villages and towns scattered along the coast were charming, the land pastoral and green. Flowers bloomed and livestock fed in the pastures that came down to the shore. And yet, there are also huge cliffs with waterfalls hundreds of feet high. The pastoral and the sublime come in contact along this amazing coastline. This is a stark and amazingly beautiful country, nothing like I imagine the tundra in northern Canada to look like. Some of the places we saw had only a connection by water with the wide world. On the sea we saw fish farms.

We flew back to Bergen and caught a train to Oslo. This trip too was stunning. The train crossed the country, and this means that it crossed mountains. By the time it arrived in Oslo seven hours after departing Bergen, we had crossed spectacular mountain passes and descended to the coast again. Oslo is a bustling city with large and lovely parks. I remember the park near the university with its sundial, and Frogner Park with its impressive collection of sculptures by Gustav Vigeland. Oslo is a comfortable city, more cosmopolitan than Stockholm. And it did not rain there.

I returned to Norway in 2003 to attend a conference and also to participate in a Nordic children's literature group. The venue was in Kristiansand. I spent the next few years in Nordchilit, a group of scholars and graduate students that met every so often to critique the work of the young scholars. This was a happy group with a noteworthy agenda: to encourage and assist graduate students to achieve at the highest level. The meeting in Kristiansand was in August 2003, but earlier in March the group met in Copenhagen, Denmark. This was my only trip to Denmark. I remember huge wind turbines as we drove in from the airport, wet streets with many bicycles day and night, a huge anti–Iraq War protest in the town center, the canal, the very small Little Mermaid statue, and my reception at the Centre for Børnelitteratur. The director at the time, Nina Christensen, presented me with a book. It was a picture book in Danish about a young boy who refused to take a shit. Pictures showed his stubbornness and also the accumulation of fecal matter—turds with happy faces—in his intestines. The fecal matter grows larger and larger until the final page when the boy lets go and sits on a huge pile of turds. I thanked Nina for this present, but she replied that thanks were not needed because they wanted to get rid of this repulsive book. You should know that at the time I had garnered a small degree of fame by writing on scatological elements in children's literature. Nina indicated that I was a suitable recipient of this book. I am not entirely certain what she meant by this remark.

In any case, I found my time in Scandinavia pleasurable. Perhaps one final story before I leave Scandinavia. Finland is the only Scandinavian country I have not visited. However, I did make contact with colleagues from that country, and one of these, the redoubtable Aino Koskinen, invited herself to Calgary and to my house. She came to give a talk and make connections. I did not know her well at all when she came; shades of Eric the fisherman! Oh, this lets you know something of what is coming. Anyway, I went to the airport to meet her, arriving just when I thought passengers from her plane would be disembarking. The first half hour of parking at the Calgary Airport is free, and I am Scottish enough to want to take advantage of this free time. I watched as the doors opened and passengers came through with their luggage in tow and their smiles ready to greet friends and loved ones. I waited until no more passengers came through the doors. I did not think this odd until some twenty minutes had passed with no one else coming through the doors. I kept waiting, wondering what I ought to do. I waited another forty minutes. Then over the intercom I heard a voice paging Dr. McGillis. I was summoned to Customs where I was allowed entrance through a locked door and found myself in a small cubicle with a chair placed in front of a glass panel. The glass had a hole in it to speak through. I sat in the chair as a man with a clipboard appeared on the other side of the glass and sat opposite me. He looked stern. He asked me if I was Dr. McGilis, and if I knew a person named Professor Aino Koskinen. I said I was the person he was seeking, and I did know Professor Koskinen. He asked me why she was coming to Canada. He did not smile. I explained she was our guest at the university and she would be giving one or more talks over the next week. He shuffled a paper or two on his clipboard. Then he told me to return to from where I had come and wait for this Koskinen woman. I did as he instructed.

Another half-hour elapsed and I was completely befuddled. Finally, after another twenty or so minutes the double doors opened and a woman with flaming red hair came skedaddling towards me. She was visibly distressed. No, furious in a Red Queen sort of way is more accurate. She was in high dudgeon. As soon as she was within earshot, she began to rail against Canada, the customs officer she had dealt with, and the world she found herself in. It took me some time to get a clear story from her. She wanted to get to my place and straight away write a letter to a suitable government official to complain about the treatment she had received upon arriving in Canada. It seems that when she got to Canadian customs, she had broken the line in order to ask for a drink of water because she was parched. The customs officer had informed her that she would find a fountain inside the terminal. She had countered by saying she could not wait until she had negotiated the line and then entered the main terminal. The officer said she had no other recourse. She informed him that she was an important person and deserved better treatment, whereupon he told her to go over to a table and unpack her luggage for inspection. And apparently it got worse from there. And that is all I know about Finland.

Well, not exactly. I know about saunas and snow and even friendly persons. I would be wrong to evaluate Finland on the basis of my experience hosting this one visitor. And really, once she calmed down (this did take some time), her visit went fine. She gave her talk, and she went shopping. Frances took her shopping, and apparently Aino is a whirlwind of a shopper. Frances was most impressed with her ability to move swiftly and successfully through a mall, exiting with bags and bags of stuff.

g. Australia
FIRST TRIP

I have been to Australia three times. The first time was in 1993, and to tell the story of this visit will lead me into matters that have nothing to do with Australia. Here goes. Frances and I went to a conference in Geelong, in the south of Australia not too far from Melbourne. When we arrived, someone approached me and asked if I could assist them. It seemed that a colleague of mine, I will call him Blackie, had arrived early and was causing some consternation with the people setting up the conference. Now I have to tell you about Blackie. He arrived at the University of Calgary one year after I arrived, and so he sought me out as a possible friend because I was new and of his generation. He had impressive credentials, having done his Ph.D. at Yale with J. Hillis Miller. Blackie would often appear in my office and talk in a manner that was cocky and smart. What he said always seemed to be laced with irony. I did not feel all that comfortable with him. He was, I should also say, tall and swarthy. I thought of him as a cross between Lord Byron and Charles Manson. He had these dark piercing eyes that glared right at you, even through you. And he did not reveal much. Well, one day I had occasion to go to his office, and while I was standing by one of his bookshelves, I happened to notice J. Hillis Miller's *Dickens's World*, a book I had thought I had lost. Not really thinking, I took the book from the shelf and opened it. There in front of me was my handwriting, my notes in the margins. I was taken aback and quickly closed the book and put it back on the shelf. All the time Blackie kept his gaze upon me. A few days later, he brought me two ratty paperback books and said they were a gift. Only later did I surmise that this was a trade, my Hillis Miller for his two battered paperbacks.

Anyway, this was my first experience of Blackie's kleptomania. Not long after, he became well known for his purloining of various things from various places. People stopped having him to their homes because he would show up wearing a long deep-pocketed coat and proceed to wander throughout the place lifting this or that like some magpie. He was caught shoplifting on more than one occasion. Kleptomania, however, was only one of Blackie's problems. He had a collection of various types of weaponry—guns, knives, martial arts materials. Did I mention that he taught martial arts at a local studio? Our secretaries in the department marveled at him because he would hop over the waist-high counter that separated the office from the corridor without touching it. Once I saw evidence of his prowess at the airport. It happened like this. I quite often found myself at conferences with Blackie, and one time we traveled to Stanford together. Usually, Blackie would stay close to me until he met a lovely blond woman, and then he was gone. This time, however, I did not wait for a blond woman to appear; I took myself away from him as soon as we landed. At the airport after the conference, Blackie arranged to sit beside me on the plane. Once we were airborne, he asked what had happened to me at the conference, and I sloughed this off with some innocuous remark, a remark that he decided to take as anything but innocuous. He said we were friends and therefore I ought to have stayed with him. I replied that I did not know what he meant by "friends." His response to this was that he only had his close friends to dinner and I had been his dinner guest more than once. To this I noted that he also had had to dinner a colleague of ours whom Blackie had on more than one occasion singled out for his disapproval. His rejoinder was that he did not know whether to kiss me or hit me. I requested that he do neither. The rest of the flight passed in silence, a tense silence. As we taxied on the runway, Blackie asked if I wanted to share a taxi and I said that a colleague was meeting me and I could not very well invite him to catch a ride since it was not my place to do so. At the baggage carousels, Bill began to kick about suitcases gathered in a corner. Not having to wait for luggage, I hotfooted it out and away to find my colleague.

Speaking of dinner at Blackie's, I can describe one evening that fits with the portrait I am sketching here. I went to Blackie's one evening to find his partner at the time, Marie, agitated. Blackie was already in his cups, and when he left the room to look to his cooking, Marie said she was taking her fourteen-year-old daughter and leaving for the night. I followed them to her car and asked where they were going to stay. She indicated that she would go to her office on campus and spend the night there. She said it was not the first time she had done this. Quickly, I handed her the keys to my apartment and told her she could go there and fix a place for herself and her daughter to sleep. I went back inside and endured the evening with Blackie, who was glowering and sullen. He railed against womankind. Before he served dinner, he disappeared. I waited until I heard a great pounding accompanied by hollers. Investigating, I found Blackie in his basement chopping cooked duck with a huge meat cleaver. This was our main dish for dinner.

You will not be surprised, then, to learn that Blackie found himself in remand once in a while. One such occasion happened when I was second-in-command in the department. I decided to take one of his classes myself while he was unavailable; he had been arrested on a weapons charge after police answered a domestic dispute call and found Blackie's arsenal. When I went to the first class, I informed the students that their professor was away for a few days, and this information elicited much laughter. It turned out that most of the students had already learned of Blackie's arrest because it was in the newspaper that morning. The students just thought this was cool. For reasons I could never fathom, students loved him; they enjoyed his sarcasm and insults, and they rewarded him with more than one Teaching Excellence Award.

This despite the fact that he turned up for class too often in his cups. Blackie had a substance abuse problem: alcohol, hashish, pot, and I don't know what all. Once I mentioned the film *Midnight Express* while Blackie and I were going through security at the airport. Once safely on the other side, he glowered at me and told me in no uncertain terms never to do such a thing again. You can guess why.

One final memory of Blackie. He received "voluntary severance" from the university well before the age of retirement. Rumours flew about campus as to the reason for his dismissal, but we really do not know the reason. Universities used to have more tolerance for troubled faculty than they do now, and Blackie had been given a long rope. I guess he had come to the end of his tether. He left the university and took up with a young blond woman and the two of them went to teach in Korea. Not long after they went there, a colleague received a message from Blackie saying the food was great and vodka was five dollars a bottle. Then the young blond woman left and Blackie moved on to China where he died a couple of years later, alone in a small apartment. No one brought his body back to Canada. One of his ex-wives/partners hosted a gathering to remember him. A house full assembled to say farewell to Blackie. When the host invited people to step forward and offer memories of him, no one came forth. It was awkward for a while. I decided to say something, although when I got up to speak, I had no idea what to say. When I stood and began to talk, out came the story of how I discovered that Blackie had purloined one of my books. The silence after I stopped talking lasted only a few seconds. My story seemed to have broken the ice and more people came to say words about Blackie, one fellow even reciting his apocryphal tale of fighting in Vietnam during that infamous war as if it were true.

Anyway, back to Geelong and the conference in Australia. It seemed that Blackie had arrived early at the conference venue and he had been caught stealing one or two things. The conference organizers did not know how to cope with him and they asked if I could "look after" him. In other words, they wanted me to be my brother's keeper even though Blackie was not, and never would be, my brother. I have few memories of that conference, but one memory I do have is of a short bus trip about eight of us took to visit a waterfall. Blackie, myself, Frances, and a woman from England sat in the back seat, and Blackie charmed this woman even as his flatulence soured the olfactory sense. On that same jaunt, a woman from Germany threw out the comment "Take me to a shopping mall" as we disembarked from the bus. Apparently, she did not enjoy nature.

After the conference, Frances and I saw some of Australia. We spent a day or two in Melbourne and then took a train to Sydney. In Sydney we saw the sights, the opera house, the bridge, the zoo, King's Cross, and so on. From Sydney we traveled north to Armidale where I was to give a talk at the University of New England. The trip to Armidale took us through a place called Tammworth, the "Country Music Capital of Australia." In Armidale, we stayed with Geoff and Adrian Gunther, who also took us to their vacation place on the coast right at the mouth of a river. Frances and I went canoeing on this river and discovered that tides can be formidable. As for my talk at the University in Armidale, it was fine, although some of the audience was round a corner and out of sight. Strange. They videotaped the thing and I am curious to know whatever happened to that tape. The trip from Armidale to the coast took us through the Blue Mountains where we stopped for walks and encountered snakes and a goanna. The coastal beaches were extensive, empty, and magnificent. The sand was so fine that it squeaked under our feet. I also remember the blue and still jellyfish on the shore. We left Geoff and Adrian and traveled on to Byron Bay, a throwback to the days of hippies, drugs, and rock and roll. In Byron Bay, Frances found a huge cockroach in our luggage. I had to unpack everything, check it for bugs, and repack. I might add that we have never seen the Gunthers since that trip back in 1993.

From Byron Bay, we went to Brisbane to fly home. This first trip to Australia introduced us to many fascinating flora and fauna. Perhaps the highlight of the trip was our visit to Phillip Island to see the penguin parade. At dusk and into the dark, fairy penguins come ashore in groups and waddle up the beach to their nesting places in the grasses and ridges above the beach. As we sat waiting for the first penguins to appear, we chatted with the woman next to us and learned she was from Bowness, part of Calgary. Small world. In any case, the penguins were a delight. Also, on the way to Phillip Island, the bus stopped in order to allow passengers to disembark and see a koala way up in a eucalyptus tree. Another highlight was seeing wombats and other creatures at a farm where they took care of wounded animals. All in all, Australia has to be the most marvelous land I have visited. As for Blackie, we had left him way back in Geelong.

As an addendum to this first trip, I note that we stopped in Fiji on the way home and spent several days in a resort. The trip from the airport to the resort was an adventure. The bus caught fire, flames flaring by the gearshift, and it took the persuasive power of an American on board to get the driver to stop. Stop he did by a field of burning cane. From the small buildings nearby came a number of people, including children in undress, who gawked at us impassively. Our luggage was piled on the side of the road and we waited, smiling at the onlookers, until another vehicle arrived to take us onward. At the resort, we were feted nicely, but such treatment was not our idea of a really good time. Feeling somewhat cramped, we took local transportation to nearby Nadi (pronounced Nandi) where we strolled the market and saw instances of racial discord. When it came time to leave Fiji, we were told to expect our bus to the airport at 7:00 p.m. It was important to leave by seven because the bridge connecting us to the airport road closed at eight. We packed and went to the resort lobby to wait. We were there shortly after six-thirty. Seven o'clock came without the arrival of the bus. At seven-fifteen, we were growing anxious. I called the travel people and they assured me that the bus would pick us up at seven. This news was not reassuring. The bus finally arrived at seven-forty. We boarded; it took off; we crossed the bridge where glaring lights and loud noises told us work was going on, and arrived in time to catch the flight home.

A further addendum: not long after we arrived back in Calgary, I acquired what seemed to be an exotic parasite. My doctor sent me to an internist for a sigmoidoscopy. This internist was Dr. Tom Lay, and he probably saved my life. But not by doing a sigmoidoscopy. Once he had completed the procedure, he looked at me and said he thought I might have the "bronze disease." I looked puzzled, and he explained that this disease was hemochromatosis, a genetic blood disorder that caused iron to build up to dangerous levels. He suggested I go for a liver biopsy. I did. The day of the biopsy, I entered hospital early in the morning. This was a hospital across the city from the one in which I had met Dr. Lay. Anyway, they told me I was to remain supine and still for eight hours after the procedure. Later that afternoon, not long before I was to be discharged, into my room walked Dr. Lay. He said he was passing and thought he would check on me. He also gave me his home phone number and said I could call if I had any questions. They told me that I might have cancer and he knew that such news was unsettling, and Dr. Lay said if I called him at work he would be called away, but if I called him at home, he could talk as long as I liked. I did not call his number, but one evening around eight a couple of days later the phone rang and when I answered, it was Dr. Lay. He asked me how I was doing. The long and the short of it was that I had hemochromatosis. My ferritin count was off the chart. More about this later.

That was the fall of 1993, and I became a volunteer patient for Dr. Lay, who was with the University of Calgary Medical School. I went for several years as a mock patient, but one year Dr. Lay did not call. I was perplexed, thinking perhaps I was not a very good pretend patient. However, sometime later I learned that Dr. Lay had left the practice of medicine because he had had a "breakdown." I felt terrible about this. Here was a physician who genuinely cared for his patients. The contrast with my hematologist could not have been greater. I first met the doctor who was to be my hematologist for over twenty years in January 1994. Our conversation on that occasion went like this:

"You know, your life is now shorter."

"Shorter than what?"

"Oh well, I can't say exactly."

"Then how am I to process this information?"

"Well, you have to decide whether to take the treatment or not."

"What happens if I choose not to take it?"

"You will die."

"Then I really have no choice."

"You might, if you were in your seventies, just let nature take its course."

"I am not in my seventies."

And so it went. Of course, I took the so-called treatment, and for the next thirteen months I went every week for a phlebotomy. After the year and a month, I began going at longer intervals. Once I asked my doctor if my blood could help the blood bank; he said yes, but that at the hospital they merely threw it away. I went to the blood bank and offered my blood. They turned me away because I had had liver damage caused by the hemochromatosis. I was livid.

In any case, my first trip to Australia had proven auspicious in more ways than one.

SECOND TRIP

In 2002, Professor Kerry Mallan wrote to invite me to her university, Queensland University of Technology in Brisbane, as a visiting scholar. I had met Kerry Mallan in passing at a conference in 1999, but I did not really know her. This was to change. I eagerly accepted the kind invitation, and in the summer of 2002 (the Australian winter), I traveled to Brisbane and took up residence in a grand house just off campus. On campus, I had an office and even some secretarial assistance. I felt pampered. The people who owned the house even provided me with a bicycle (and helmet). I did ride this bicycle, but the hills of Brisbane proved rather difficult for me; I had not yet become a serious cyclist. During the first month, I began to collaborate with Kerry; we wrote an experimental essay on the Australian verse novel. The essay appeared in the online journal, *The Looking Glass* (2003). A second collaboration, this one on camp aesthetics, appeared in *Canadian Review of American Studies* (2005). I wrote the foreword to one of Kerry's books, and I also contributed chapters to a couple of her other books. We have remained friends since then, and she was instrumental in my third trip to Australia in 2011. She also introduced me to several other good people: Raylee, Geraldine, John, Ross, Fitz, and of course her family, husband Mick and children Kim and Chris.

I enjoyed my time in Brisbane immensely. Australians are industrious, very hard workers, and they also know how to relax and have a good time. I recall one weekend when a small group of us went to Geraldine's vacation home in the country for a meeting. When we arrived, Geraldine told me to make sure the car window where I was sitting was closed; she added that I should not reach down to any plants I might see on the ground. I asked why and she replied, "Snakes." I passed this off as some silliness for a foreigner, but she assured me that snakes were a problem. Australian snakes are poisonous, she said, and they had to make sure windows and doors to the house were closed so none of the dangerous creatures could slither inside. She told of her husband sweeping off their deck one day when he came across a brown snake, the second-most venomous snake anywhere. The snake struck at him, and he scooted inside the French doors, only to hear the snake strike and hit the glass. Again, I thought she was having me on, but the others assured me that Australia was populated with snakes and I ought to be careful. Later that evening, we decided to have fish and chips, and Geraldine said she was going into town to get these. I offered to accompany her. We left the house after dark and Geraldine carried a flashlight (torch!) and she suggested I come closer to the light. I said I could see all right, and she promptly replied that the light was to detect snakes, not necessarily to light a path. Yeah right, I countered. We got to the car and just as I was about to open the door, I noticed something slither between my legs. Startled, I jumped and made a whooping sound. Geraldine quickly came round the car with her flashlight and asked me what was the matter. I told her I saw something slide along the ground. She said, "Snake, what colour was it?" I thought it was brown. She said I was lucky. And from that moment, I associate Australia with snakes, deadly snakes. Paradise always has a snake in it.

That summer/winter in Brisbane was productive. I worked diligently, and I also made close friends. As I noted, Kerry Mallan became a collaborator and family friend. Over the years, I collaborated with Kerry on three articles and one book. She and Mick exchanged visits a few times over the years with Frances and me. During my stay, I also told stories at a one-room schoolhouse, and gave a talk at the university, and also at a book launch for John Stephens's *Ways of Being Male*. I had known John for some ten years, but after this trip we became closer, at least for a while. When I approached retirement, I lost touch with John. Other people I met that time include Clare Bradford and Peter Mountney. I later became an examiner of Peter's Ph.D. dissertation.

I spent the first month in Brisbane by myself, but then Frances joined me for the second month. We rented a car and drove north to Cairns for a holiday. On this trip, we went snorkeling on the Great Barrier Reef. The experience was exhilarating. The small boat went far out until we could no longer see the shore. Then we donned wet suits and plunged into the sea. The coral is spectacular, and the fish that dart or slide here and there are equally colourful. This underwater world is stunning in its beauty, and it hurts to think that this living colour suffers from human pollution and exploration. As we swam beneath the surface, a huge sea turtle made its slow way past the gawking eyes of our group. The fantasy world becomes reality in this special place. After some time, I could hear as I came to the surface someone hailing me. It was time to depart, and I was the only one of the group still in the water. I was not ready to leave. Anyway, leave we did and almost everyone on board suffered from seasickness; neither Frances nor I suffered in this way.

The time came to return to Canada, but we did so with some reluctance. Australia truly is a fascinating and comfortable place (once one gets over the fact that snakes form a plethora). We could envisage ourselves living there, enjoying a life without the cold northern winters. I owe a debt to Kerry Mallan for having me to her home and university.

THIRD TRIP

And that debt only multiplied when in 2011, I once again visited Brisbane, this time for the IRSCL conference held on the QUT campus in downtown Brisbane. This was a short trip, but intense nevertheless. After the conference, I spent a few days with Kerry and Mick Mallan. They took me on short day trips to various places not far from Brisbane. One of these trips was to a hilly rainforest area where their daughter and her partner were intending to build a home. The three of us, myself, Mick, and Kerry, tramped through a dense forest on a precarious trail. Mick advised me to try and avoid the foliage lining the thin trail because the place was infested with leeches. This put me on my guard, but not on guard enough because I slipped and tumbled down an embankment, coming to rest in a soft thicket of rain forest foliage. A flurry of activity took place while Mick helped me back to the trail where a thorough investigation found no leeches clinging to the Canadian's soft flesh. What is life if not a series of such simple adventures?

And so I left Australia.

h. New Zealand

It seems appropriate to come to New Zealand here, both because of its proximity to Australia and because it is so different from Australia. Where Australia has many and varied animals that are unique to that continent, New Zealand has no indigenous mammals, unless one counts the seals that occupy some coastal areas. Where Australia has a population that dates back to long long ago, New Zealand's population comes from away and its arrival dates back to around 1250 CE. Where Australia has mostly a warm climate, the climate in New Zealand is on the cool side.

Frances and I went to New Zealand in 2008. I was invited to speak at a conference in Wellington, at the bottom of the North Island. My host was Anna Jackson, who later collaborated with me and Karen Coats on the book *The Gothic in Children's Literature*. The conference was fine and we spent some time with John Stephens, a friend from Australia. Wellington is a comfortable city, and interesting. Frances and I found bootlegged CDs of both Neil Young and Bob Dylan, so how could the trip not have been successful? We also learned that earthquakes are a daily occurrence in this island country. Aside from Wellington, we saw nothing of the North Island.

We did, however, travel across the channel to the South Island where we rented a car and drove perhaps halfway along and down that island. Memorable was the potter from Canada we met along the road, the aborted hike we went on, the fog that cut our hike short, the baby seals we encountered off the road and through a secluded forest walk to a small pond where the baby seals gathered, leaving their parents behind on the seashore, and the town of Nelson that reminded us so much of the Nelson we know in the West Kootenays at home. Those baby seals, by the way, gathered and frolicked around us, seemingly unconcerned by the visitors who had invaded their forest day care.

Although we enjoyed our time in New Zealand, I must say the experience was curious. We both found it strangely eerie to be walking in the woods and not have any animals around us, not even a squirrel. New Zealand does have a great variety of birds, but the only animals evident are imported sheep. The land is big and wild and the weather damp and grey. The place feels far away. It also looks, at times, like the Shire in Hobbiton. I think we ought to have explored more of this beautiful and unusual land.

i. China

Frances and I went to China in 2007. I was invited to speak at a conference in Ningbo, a city not too far from Shanghai. We flew to Shanghai, where two young men met us; they were to drive us to Ningbo. The journey took a couple of hours, as I recall. It was dark, but the traffic was heavy. I remember a huge truck filled with pigs passing us at one point. Anyway, we arrived in Ningbo and settled in a hotel on the university campus. This was a small conference consisting of scholars from China, Australia, and Canada. From Australia came Kerry Mallan, Clare Bradford, and John Stephens, all of whom I knew well. From Canada came Benjamin Lefebvre, David Staines, and myself and Frances. The seven of us formed a goodly company for the days of the conference. The young man assigned to us as a translator called himself "Smith." Among the Chinese scholars was Wang Quangen, a professor I had met previously in Canada; he gave me a fat book he had written on children's literature with a friendly inscription. The book I could not read, and as we continued the journey, I found it heavy enough to leave behind in a hotel room, like some strange gift from a non-Gideon. The days were long, with many talks. The meals were lavish; the local people were especially proud of their seafood, and Frances and I discreetly turned the lazy Susan so the food with eyes did not stare at us. Food was an adventure on this trip. We learned that the Chinese people eat just about anything that flies, walks, crawls, or swims. One delicacy was a pig's nose on a stick. On a day trip from Ningbo, Frances and I ate at a restaurant where the food had been pre-ordered. We really had no idea what we were eating. One plate had something on it akin to fried multi-legged crustaceans. Frances did not eat more than a wee bite, but I liked the zippy taste and ate nearly the entire plate of these things. That evening, back in the hotel I was, for about two hours, virulently ill. After two hours, the illness passed. That was my only tangle with food that trip. Once, however, after eating at a restaurant with our group—this was in Beijing, I believe—our guide, "Hannah," took us aside to show us something of what we had been served. She wanted us to see the large black slowly slithering snake behind the counter.

I fear that for at least the second time in my life I broke a cultural code. After dinner one evening, our host and a few of his colleagues sang a song. After the song, he announced that what we had heard was a Chinese song, and now the Australians and Canadians had to sing a national song each. The Australians heartily complied with a rousing rendition of "Waltzing Matilda." Then it was the Canadians' turn, but only two of us were present, myself and Frances. I declined, begging off because the others were absent. A short exchange ensued, during which I continued to decline. Some bond was broken, and our host treated us coolly after that. I had made a *faux pas*. Despite this *faux pas*, our time in Ningbo and at the conference was enjoyable. Once the conference ended, people parted ways. Frances and I decided to take the train back to Shanghai, and "Smith" took us to the station to get our tickets. All the signs were in Chinese, but we were prepared to sort things out for ourselves. "Smith," however, proved to be a loyal friend. He not only helped us purchase the tickets, but he then sat with us until the train arrived. As if this was not enough, he accompanied us aboard and got us seated comfortably. His kindness proved typical of the people we met in China.

Sitting across from us on the train was a woman and her two

children. During the journey, they had lots of things to eat, and at one point, the woman looked over at us and offered to share her food. In exchange for this kind gesture, I offered her a granola bar. She took it, set it aside, and later discreetly took it, opened the wrapper, and nibbled a bit. Then she quietly folded the wrapper over the end and put the granola bar away. Another instance of kindness to strangers took place a day or so later in Shanghai. Frances and I decided to find a travel place and inquire about a trip to Beijing. We found an address and phone number, looked at a transit map, and set out. Of course, we could not read signs and phoning the travel place was futile because no one spoke English. There we were on the underground gawking at the map of various stations. As we stared at the map, someone tapped my shoulder. It was a tall man in a suit, carrying a briefcase. He indicated that we should follow him off the train when it stopped. We did. The three of us stood on the busy platform and he gestured for me to give him the paper I was carrying that both Frances and I had consulted as we looked at the transit map on the train. He took the paper, pulled out his cell phone, and called the number we had recorded on the paper. He spoke for a few minutes. He put his phone away and returned the paper to us. Then he took us over to a large transit map on the wall. Without speaking, he showed us where we had to get off the train and where we would find the street we were looking for. Once we had the street, we could simply follow the numbers until we found the travel agency. Off we went, and we found the man's instructions as helpful as we could wish for; we found the agency and made plans to go to Beijing. While we were in China, we found everyone we met to be accommodating, patient, and warm. It is informative to visit historical and cultural sites, but travel really works when the food and the people prove powerfully attractive.

Speaking of historical sites, we did visit some of these. We went to Wenchang Pavilion, the summer palace of Chiang Kai-shek where a sign informed us that "Celebrities of Republic of China such as General Zhangxue shacked up here." Another sign assured us that what we were experiencing was wondrous: "The Wuling Mountain is like the land of Peach Blossoms with its natural landscape. You will be carefree and joyous in there." And I think we were. Since I am mentioning signs and crumbled translation, I might add that I later published an article in a Chinese journal that had its title only in English; in the title the word "postcolonial" came out as "post colon." We went several places that I can no longer identify, but the terrain was mountainous and wild despite the evidence of humans everywhere. This is truly a stunning land. The highlights of the trip were Tiananmen Square, the Forbidden City, and, greatest of all, the Great Wall. China is a contradiction: stunning beauty competes with pollution and sweltering humanity. City streets teem with traffic, including bicycles piled teeteringly high with various items. I recall standing almost ankle deep in urine inside a public washroom, and I recall the beauty of architecture and lake in Beijing's parks. Swarms of people were everywhere, sometimes slowing to graceful morning dance in a Beijing park, or performing tai chi. We saw a white-clothed man doing martial arts exercises with a sword and beside him a young man dressed in western garb attempted to emulate his moves. An evening at the theatre gave us evidence of sparkling and impossible feats of athleticism. We saw a demonstration of bicycling that tested belief. The same is true of plate spinning and acrobatics. The entertainment was colourful, daring, and beautiful. Still and all, it is the small things that register, the sharing of tea in a small open-air teashop in the back streets of Shanghai, for example.

China is huge and we saw such a small part of it that any comment I make must be tempered by the fact that we really don't know China at all. It would be good to return and see more of this wondrous place. The feeling that this place we saw shows itself in the many Chinese movies we have seen is strong. Chinese movies have a sensibility different from anything else we know, and it is a sensibility that welcomes myth and fantasy and magic and wondrous possibilities. Perhaps nothing indicates this sense of the marvelous more than the flying fighters shown in so many martial arts films. Although many of the films are products of Hong Kong prior to its attachment to the mainland, these films do contain the strange sense of an exotic place removed from what we are used to. Take for example just one film, *Fantasy Mission Force* (1983); it combines the absurd, the magical, history, and myth, all in a concoction so zany, so mad, that it is well-nigh impossible to either understand or dislike.

j. Germany and the Czech Republic

I have been to Germany several times. The first time was with Suzanne way back when I was a student in England. We went on a walking tour/hike of the Moselle Valley, staying in hostels. One day we passed a family hiking in the opposite direction; we had stopped by a thicket of wild raspberry. The German family spoke no English and we spoke no German, but we managed to communicate the word "raspberry" to them and in return we learned the German, "himbeere." I like this. On that trip, we visited Frankfurt, Bonn, and Cologne. We stayed in youth hostels and traveled by hitchhiking, as well as by train. I remember hitching a ride on the autobahn and watching with trepidation as the speedometer needle rose over one hundred miles per hour. I was glad to get out of that car.

SECOND TRIP

In 1985, I went to a small conference just outside of Frankfurt. The conference brought together some seven academics from Germany with another seven from North America. I was the only Canadian. This is where I first met Jack Zipes. We were secluded in a mountain resort, and met for long hours each day. The subject of Germany's past surfaced several times and it was fascinating to experience the reaction of the older and younger members of the German group to this past. The older members were guarded and hesitant; the younger people were more forthright in confronting a troubled past. As the days passed, I sensed a growing tension, and on the final morning this tension found an outlet. The two women from America began to express their unhappy reaction to what they perceived as sexism. This opened the proverbial can of worms and differences that had remained hidden became evident. Several expressed distaste for the manner in which proceedings had been controlled by the chair, a venerable elderly German scholar.

Other than this unpleasantness at the end of proceedings, the trip was fine. I recall having a lesson in wine tasting at a place associated with Heinrich von Kleist, and going for a walk in the hills and coming across a nudist-bathing place. On this same trip, accompanied by Anita Moss, I explored the Romantic Road from Würzburg to Füssen. Some years later, I returned to this region with Frances.

THIRD TRIP

Ten years later, I returned. Frances and I attended a conference organized by the group, the Inklings. This is where I met John Docherty and Stephen Prickett, both of whom I would see and work with again. We also met with Dieter and Renate Petzold who were and remain good friends. With Dieter and Renate, we traveled on the Rhine for a day or two, and then drove to the region known as *Fränkische Schweiz*. Dieter and Renate live in a small village called Heroldsbach in Bavaria. The village has some notoriety as a place of pilgrimage because in 1949 and through the early 1950s the Virgin Mary appeared several times, and so too did Jesus, a band of angels, and sundry saints. I even remember being told of a bunch of Russian soldiers appearing in the sky! The church built a chapel and shrine to commemorate the sightings, and Heroldsbach became a pilgrimage site. We spent some time in the village with the Petzolds, but I must report that we saw neither the Virgin nor Jesus. We did see a couple of pilgrims hauling small crosses toward the shrine. We did not see Russian soldiers. We did find Heroldsbach charming.

On this same trip, we traveled by bus to the Czech Republic. This bus trip is noteworthy for the fact that we were the only

North Americans and speakers of English on the bus. Before we left, we had purchased visas for the Czech Republic, but when we got to the border, an armed guard entered the bus to ask for passports, and in our case visas. He took a look at our visas and began to shout at us. We finally got the message that he wanted us to follow him off the bus. We did. His behaviour was formidable and even threatening. He led us into a small compound where we were stationed in front of a glass partition. The person behind the partition began shouting and pointing at my visa. This person passed me a new visa form and I began to fill it out. More shouting ensued, and the incomplete form was pulled away from me. I was beside myself. It took a long time, but eventually Frances figured out that I was the culprit because I had not filled out the visa application in uppercase letters. I completed the form for the third time, paid them some money (we had already paid for visas before we left Heroldsbach), and rejoined the people on the bus who gazed at us as if we were aliens, and I guess we were. After some two hours, the bus went on its way to Prague.

In Prague, we stayed in a concrete slab of a place somewhere beyond the old city. Where we stayed smacked of the Cold War and Eastern European starkness under communist rule, or at least what passed for communist rule in those heady days of Cold War politics. The contrast with the old city could not have been greater. Old Prague is amazingly beautiful. This is a city of music, as much as anything else. We went to concerts pretty much any time of the day in an assortment of churches and civic buildings. The city itself is dark, the city of Kafka. Streets and building are the colour of soot, but inside we found splendour. We also found friendly people. During our very short stay, it rained constantly and vigorously. At first, we did not have an umbrella, and we took refuge inside a shop. We did not purchase anything, but Frances exchanged cigarettes with the proprietor and had a chuckle despite not being able to communicate with words. Our stay in Prague was too short. The same is true of our visit to the spa towns Marienbad and Carlsbad. At Marienbad, I could not but be reminded of Alain

Resnais's *Last Year at Marienbad*. The real place is equally as beautiful as the place Resnais filmed back in 1961.

We returned to Heroldsbach and spent some time with Dieter and Renate. I gave a talk at the university in Erlangen. We met another Dieter and his wife Ute. Dieter and Ute Barnikel later visited us in Canada. I remember taking a drive with these people and Dieter Barnikel telling us of his relationship with his father. The two had quarreled over the Germany of the war years, and Dieter was sad that he and his father had never mended their differences. The war years loom over this country, or at least did the times I visited.

k. Switzerland

This section will be short. I have twice visited Switzerland, but neither trip was specifically for academic purposes. I first visited Switzerland in the company of Anita Moss, and we drove through the Alps. The experience of driving the Grimsel Pass is one of the most harrowing experiences I have had. The road is extremely winding with constant switchbacks and fearful drops close to the road's edge. What made this trip so stressful was the snow. The snow came down harder and harder until it was a whiteout. I could see nothing ahead except the white wall of snow. We crawled through this at a snail's pace and I was just about to stop and wait out the storm when the air cleared enough for us to see a lodge at the side of the road. I stopped. We went in, and the person who first spoke to us spoke in English. My relief was palpable. We stayed there overnight, and in the morning we woke to a glorious vista, a vision of the sublime suitable for any poem by Shelley or Byron or Coleridge or Wordsworth. I was agog.

On another occasion, I was in Switzerland with Frances and our daughter Kyla. We were in Lausanne for a night in a posh hotel. Next day we were back in France when I noticed that I had left my credit card back in Lausanne. Needless to say, I was once again beside myself. We had the phone number of the hotel where we had last stayed, and I called. But in my state of mind, what French I had ceased to function. Our daughter Kyla came to the rescue. She is bilingual, and she took the phone, talked with the hotel person, and sorted things out. They had my card, and offered either to send it to my home or destroy it. To be honest, I cannot remember what we decided to do. I do know that it was an American Express card, and the American Express people proved useless when we reached out to them.

And finally, I cannot forbear mentioning my first experience in Switzerland. Suzanne and I were returning by train from Rome to Paris. The journey took place at night, and we each had a berth. In the middle of the night, someone pounded on the door and then entered and shone a flashlight in my bleary eyes. The person who had so rudely entered was a customs official, and he wanted an entry fee for our arrival in Switzerland. I said that we were not getting off the train and therefore would not set foot on Switzerland's soil, and therefore I did not see why we had to pay a fee. He said we did. We exchanged words, mine unfriendly, harsh, and uncomplimentary. But he was adamant. He was not going to leave until we had paid the requisite fee. I said we did not have Swiss currency. He was willing to take British currency, and he gave us change in Swiss money. I told him that we had no use for the Swiss money. He shrugged. In any case, that was my first experience of Switzerland, a country I think is both beautiful and overly expensive.

Before departing Switzerland, I have to mention Villa Diodati, not far from Zurich. This was Lord Byron's place in the fateful June of 1816 when Byron, Polidori, and the Shelleys stayed there for three days during a storm. The results of that time are well known. I think visits are possible to the Villa Diodati, but I only managed to see the outside. Still and all, it made an impression on me.

l. France

Not only have I been to France several times, but Frances and I also have very good friends who live just ten minutes from the

Gare du Nord in Eaubonne. Jean Perrot founded the Charles Perreault Institute in Eaubonne, a research centre for children's literature. Jean and Annie Perrot are people we have met both in their home, in our home, and in several places where we were all travelers. Jean is perhaps the most scholarly person I know, and conversations with him are always intense. His knowledge of literature, history, and languages is prodigious. My respect for Jean and Annie is great, and I hardly know how to recount our times together. And so, I won't. Suffice to say that we have had intimate times together over the years, and I value this friendship as much as any friendship I have had. Jean's name has already appeared in this narrative of my adventures.

As I say, I do not know how to proceed. I can just ramble over my various trips. One trip took me to the Loire valley where Suzanne and I saw more chateaux than you can shake a stick at. We also moved through the French Riviera at one time, visiting Nice and the Chagall Museum. Twice I have been to Chamonix and from there driven to look over the Simplon Pass, made famous by Wordsworth. One visit to Chamonix was with Frances and Kyla, the same trip during which I lost my credit card. We did a bit of hiking on and around Mont Blanc, and I recall one hike when we were high on the mountain and a storm came with thunder and lightning. Within minutes, the trail down the mountain was filled with people reminding me of a department store escalator just before Christmas. I cannot neglect to mention Mont St. Michel. The swiftness of the tide here is justly famous. Other places of note are Chartres, Reims, Amiens, Versailles, and Orleans.

Frances and I and Kyla were in France the summer after Kyla completed high school. Among other things, we visited the wine district of Burgundy. The three of us enjoyed tasting wines in various wineries, and in one place we found ourselves alone in a room with brandy ready for tasting. So, without permission, we tasted. The three of us left that place happy and flushed, and feeling a bit naughty because, as it turned out, we were not supposed to sample that brandy.

But, of course, Paris is the dream city. Cluny, Notre Dame, Shakespeare and Co, St. Chapelle, the Sorbonne, Sacre Coeur, Montmartre, the Louvre, Musée d'Orsay, Gustave Moreau Museum, Espace Dali, the Pompidou Centre, Place de la Concorde, Avenue des Champs-Élysées, Arc de Triomphe de l'Étoile, the Opera House, Les Invalides, Jardin du Luxembourg, a late evening ride on the Seine, and just the grand feel of the place. I like sitting outside a café on the rue St. Germaine, with coffee, a croque monsieur, and a notebook. I have spent quite some time there on a number of visits. But I can remember my first visit when I approached a *parisien* on the street to ask for directions. I walked up, got ready, and said briskly, "Est-ce qu'il y a un metro pres d'ici?" The reply came even more briskly, and the person turned away. I had no idea what he had said. My French is schoolboy French, hardly good enough to function easily. Outside of Paris, however, I found the people patient and helpful. If they saw that I was prepared to try and speak French, they would not condescend and speak English. They spoke to me in French and if I did not comprehend, they would simply say what they had to say more slowly and in easier diction.

My theme here is education, what I learned from my travels, as well as the connections I made. Seeing the great buildings of this city, experiencing the great works of art—I saw a tremendous exhibition of the work of Francis Bacon at the Pompidou Centre that taught me more about modernist art than I could learn from many articles and books. I also recall being taken on a walk by Sonia Landes; she took us to a restaurant in order to show us the basement gothic catacomb. Sonia, who died in 2013, was the author, along with her daughter, of *Pariswalks*, a book for the peripatetic tourist. Sonia is someone I lost contact with long ago, but her kindness in showing a few of us the byways of her beloved city is invaluable. I have no doubt that such experiences are formative in ways I cannot explain. Sharing a meal with Jean and Annie Perrot was itself an education. I remember one year seeing the fireworks on Bastille Day in the town of Eaubonne with Jean and Annie.

I recall a concert at Versailles when I heard the music of Charpentier for the first time, walks by the river, back yard hijinks, and relaxed times over meals both home cooked and in restaurants.

m. England and (briefly) Ireland

Of course, you already know that I spent three years studying in England (in Reading), and then another year on sabbatical (in Bournemouth). I also taught summer school at the University of Roehampton (2001, 2003, 2007). Over the years, I was in England for conferences in 1997 and 2000, and in 1989 I traveled to London to prepare a scholarly edition of two books by George MacDonald. In other words, I have spent considerable time in the UK. As a student at the University of Reading, I worked in the British Museum and at the Senate House Library in London, and in the Bodleian Library in Oxford. In order to acquire a library card at the Bodleian I had to raise my right hand and recite a short statement swearing not to eat or smoke or otherwise do unwanted things while studying in this ancient and august library.

I suspect my exposure to England and Scotland and Wales did much to educate me. Learning about Medieval and Renaissance architecture, viewing paintings in the National Gallery and elsewhere, traveling the countryside, visiting the homes of writers such as Samuel Johnson, Wordsworth, Dickens, Johnson, Coleridge, George MacDonald, Dylan Thomas, Frances Hodgson Burnett, Ruskin, Carlyle, William Morris, Shakespeare, Dante Gabriel Rossetti, and wandering the streets of Oxford and London did much to shape my sense of history, literature, and the world.

I remember attending a conference in London with Victor Ramraj and Sam Selvon. This was an early introduction to the literature of the Caribbean. I also recall a gathering of Oxford illuminati where I was introduced to Owen Barfield and Barbara Reynolds. Such occasions taught me both a certain mode of behaviour and what I did not like about the academic life, its sense of privilege and self-importance. Seeing Grasmere Cottage where Wordsworth lived with his sister Dorothy and where he composed many of the famous poems that formed the two editions of *Lyrical Ballads* was salutary. The small cottage with its newspaper-lined walls and tiny fireplaces was a reminder of the humble nature of genius. Something durable survives in those ancient buildings, something that educates in a manner mysterious and deep. I will say the same of the places that serve as our study environment. From the beginning at the ivy-covered walls of Burwash Hall in Toronto, I have found strength and knowledge in the surroundings with long histories. The universities where I have felt most comfortable and where I have found stimulation include Oxford and London and Toronto, and also Yale, Princeton, the Sorbonne, and Aberdeen. These universities educate through their stones, their green quadrangles, and sometimes their walls of green. Simply taking the time to savour these surroundings nourishes the mind.

If I do not have a lot to say about England, this is perhaps because I know it so well. I have often remarked that the most beautiful landscapes I have seen are in the English Lake District; I have been to sublime places such as Mont Blanc and the Simplon Pass, Grimsel Pass, and of course the Canadian Rockies (as I write this in 2022, I can include the Andes too), and these are examples of Mountain Glory, but the English Lakes are special, their beauty combines the wild and the tamed. Indeed, England is a land of special corners, the Cotswolds, Snowdonia National Park, the Peak District, Dorset, Cornwall, Alderly Edge, Wenlock Edge and the Wrekin, the Brecon Beacons are places I experienced with great pleasure. England is truly a green and pleasant land, a gem, an emerald isle, quaint and ordered and yet wild and haunted with history. The pastoral nudges against the gothic in this land of opposites.

Of course, the countryside is dotted with famous places from the church in Lechlade to Tintern Abbey to Ludlow Castle to Stokesay Castle to the White Horse in Berkshire to Mapledurham House to Ashdown House to Blenheim Palace to Kelmscott Manor and so on and so on. A visit to Hay-on-Wye is essential for anyone interested in books, especially antiquarian books. A place I liked to visit on each trip to London was the Institute of Contemporary Arts on the Mall. Here I first saw the work of Jenny Holzer. The United Kingdom has so much to offer beyond the obvious.

Although Eire is not part of the UK, it seems appropriate to mention my only visit there. This trip happened in 2005 when Frances and I went to Dublin for the IRSCL conference. We liked Dublin, but we were struck by the apparent national love affair with strong drink. One evening, while strolling the dark streets, we noticed several inebriated people along the streets, and one of these persons seemed to be deceased. We were not sure. We approached this person with the intention of helping him if we could, but before we could reach down to him someone interrupted our progress and told us to step away. This someone proceeded to bend down and do something that caused the drunken man to wretch. He returned to the land of the living. In fact, drink seemed so important in this city that we found it nearly impossible to find a restaurant that served a full dinner after 7:00 p.m. Once that happy hour arrived, drink was on the menu full bore. Amazing.

In any case, we liked Dublin. One day, we walked out along the Liffey until we came to Sandycove and the tower that appears in the opening pages of Joyce's *Ulysses*. I admire this book and standing in the tower I could imagine the young Stephen Dedalus beginning his day-long journey. On this walk to Sandycove, I was wearing a bright red scarf, the scarf of the Madrid football club. We approached a couple of young men walking toward us and as we came together, one young man stopped to admire my scarf, saying he was from Madrid. Coincidentally, he was wearing a T-shirt with the name Bob Dylan emblazoned on it. And so in return, I admired his T-shirt. We spoke for a minute or two and had a good laugh. I like this sort of interaction.

This trip to Ireland was short and sweet. I would like to return to that country and visit Galway where John Ford filmed *The Quiet Man*. The cottage, White o' Morn in the film, has recently been saved from demolition and preserved as a museum and tourist site.

n. Mexico

Earlier I recounted my trip to Mexico with Suzanne, my mother and Aunt Ann. In 2009, I received an invitation to give a talk at the VI Congreso Internacional de la Asociacion Nacional de Investigacion de Literatura Infantil y Juvenil en El Siglo XXI, in Guadalajara, Mexico. Another guest speaker was a young man from North Africa, a person of the Tuareg people. This was an interesting trip. I wandered Guadalajara by myself noting the armed guards in front of jewelry stores, banks, and large department stores. When I asked someone why there were armed guards outside these places, the answer I received was that robberies would take place. Jaime Martinez took me to the maze-like market. Kay Gentry showed me about the city and took me to meet friends of hers. The conference registrants also went on an excursion to Tequila, the place from whence that famous spirit derives. I like the southern air, the colour of people and places, the food. Guadalajara is a bright and busy city, with interesting walkways and sculptures.

I was about to say that I like southern places—Mexico, Puerto Rico, Australia, Greece, South Africa. I like the heat, the colour, and the pace of things. But then I hasten to add that I like northern places too—Norway and Sweden and Denmark. I like the moisture, the mountains, and the friendliness of the people. What to conclude? There is no place like home.

o. The American South

In the mid-1980s, I spent considerable time with Anita Moss who worked at the University of North Carolina in Charlotte. I traveled to Charlotte to give presentations, and from there I traveled the southern states with Anita. What follows are mixed memories of what I saw there. I will begin with Charleston, South Carolina. I went to Charleston for a conference, and found the city fascinating. As usual, I decided to wander about the city, but people advised me not to do this. And, of course, I did it anyway. Finding myself a long way from the conference venue, I noticed that streets had become quiet, the neighbourhood a trifle downtrodden and shopworn. Then I noticed a group of young men heading in my direction some distance up the street. These were Black youth, and I was not uninfluenced by the stereotypical version of black youth perpetrated by the media and popular culture. In short, I felt anxious as they approached. I thought of crossing the street, but then thought that this would be to give in to the popular stereotype. I kept on watching the group of young men closing the distance between us. As we came together, they jostled me and one man placed his hand on the back pocket of my jeans where we used to carry our wallets. They laughed and kibitzed and slowly moved on. I then crossed the street, and as I did, I heard the sound of a motorcycle pull up beside me. I turned to see a large policeman equipped with much iron. He slowed down and said to me, "Are you all right, boy?" "Yes, officer," I said, and he rode off. I walked on for a block or so, and then broke into a run. Rounding a corner, I saw a park filled with people, white people. They were gathering for a charity run. I went into the melee and thought, "I'm safe." At the same moment, I thought, "What an idiot; I am no more safe here than anywhere else I have been today."

Charleston is a beautiful city with its impressive antebellum homes, large trees, moss, and historical places such as the slave market. Yes, the slave market, a place that gives the lie to all those huge houses. Just how close to us those slave markets are came to me when I went to a local covered market. Here were several Black women weaving baskets to sell. I approached one of these women and asked her where she learned to make these baskets. She did not look at me, but she did reply. She said that her grandmother taught her to make the baskets. There was a pause. And then she said: "She was a slave person." I was knocked back. A slave person. This woman had known someone who had experienced life as a slave. And she referred to her as a slave person, a reminder of just how hideous slavery was (and is). Charleston boasts a slave market as one of its tourist sites, and slavery depended, in part, upon white people not accepting that the slaves were people. In order to perpetuate the Middle Passage, these people were considered "cargo," rather than passengers.

Just how short the distance is between the life this woman's grandmother lived and our own time came home to me when we visited people at a home in Mississippi. Here we sat in the living room with two young boys who were negotiating what they should do this day. On the coffee table in front of them was a newspaper with a picture of local people on the front page. As the two boys discussed where they ought to go, one suggested tossing a coin to see whether they should go where he wanted to go or where the other fellow wanted to go. Accordingly, he tossed a coin. It rose in the air turning from one side to the other until it reached its apex and then descended quickly to land squarely on the newspaper photograph. The young man who had tossed the coin remarked: "Oh, look, it landed on a n*****." Just like that. The word fell easily from his mouth suggesting it received frequent use here in this place. Such easy, thoughtless bigotry seemed hardwired in the places we visited. Down there, the distance between Selma, George Wallace, James Meredith, Medgar Evers, and the atrocities of racial hatred that accompanied the civil rights movement seemed very short indeed.

And now, of course, we have Trayvon Martin, Michael Brown, Tamir Rice, Lacquan McDonald, George Floyd, and others to remind us just how slowly things change. In fact, we are witnessing a surfacing of racial intolerance and bigotry and ugliness the like of which we have not seen for several decades.

The U. S. south did strike me as a region with distinct ways. On that trip I saw Faulkner's home and the house where he spent his childhood (after the age of five) in Oxford, Mississippi, the Peabody Hotel with its ducks in Memphis, Tennessee, Graceland, home of Elvis Presley, also in Memphis, Beal Street, Nashville and Music Row, Vicksburg and the National Military Park, Underground Atlanta, New Orleans and the French Quarter, and lots and lots of kudzu. Also, in Charlotte, I saw a man who stood day after day on the same overpass on the same freeway holding a sign that read: "The World Will End Today at 4:00." Either he was an irrepressible optimist or he had some information withheld from the rest of us.

I might say a word about Graceland, a place I found profoundly sad. Never having been a great Elvis Presley fan, I went to Graceland with no emotional investment in the place. What I saw there, most tellingly the framed and wall-mounted high school graduation certificate with 50 percent proudly displayed, was a house desperately trying to indicate refinement and intellect, but managing to display a baroque crudity, a lack of taste, tawdriness, and a failure of imagination. The Jungle Room, the room with a bank of television sets, the huge couch big enough for all of Elvis's minions, and the huge dining room table with a television placed strategically so Elvis could watch while dining—all this smacked of a desire to impress, to convince Elvis that he was an important person. Outside was a collection of large automobiles, and a Ski-Doo with the skis removed and wheels attached so Elvis could ride around his estate. The Ski-Doo reminded me of a child's tricycle. Then there were the guests, those who came to Graceland as the end to their pilgrimage. Tears were a common sight among these visitors. The experience was strange, something akin to being in the Twilight Zone.

p. Summation

The travels I remember above took place mostly because my work took me to those places. I take a moment to reflect on the notion of work. When we meet new people, we often hear the question, "What work do you do?" I heard this question many times, and every time I would think to myself, "Well, I don't work." I always thought of work as something that one did in order to place food on the table and provide a roof over one's head. Work for me is associated with drudgery, that which one does because one has to, not because one necessarily wants to. I have a brother-in-law who went to the same office for nearly forty years, and every time he went, he was miserable. I mentioned above a colleague of mine who was ill every morning when she had to leave for the office. People like these two went to work because they felt this was a responsibility, not a joy. Of course, there are people who do enjoy their work, they enjoy the daily challenge of whatever it is they do when they are active earning a living. And many of these people will tell you that their work is something they do to shore up things for the future. People work until a time comes when they retire and enjoy the fruits of their labour. Academics are often no different. I say "often," because academic life strikes me as less a job than a way of life, a métier, and that way of life need not cease once one leaves the classroom for the last time.

Finally, I note that over the years I have visited other countries—Austria, Belgium, Greece, for example—but not for purposes of academic performance. I owe the profession a lot for providing me with the opportunity to see and experience so much of the world. Education never ceases for the traveler. My friend Keath Fraser will, I suspect, attest to this. In the early 1990s, Frances, Kyla, and Kate, and I took a family trip to the American southwest, the Four Corners. This trip was educational, although we did not set out for educational purposes. The American Indian Art Institute in Santa Fe, Mesa Verde, Acoma, these places tutored us in Native history. The Grand Canyon somehow teaches us that nature is precious. Temple Square in Salt Lake City fascinates with its irrational creation of history as fantasy. And for me, the great place is Monument Valley, a place I have twice visited and imagined the great film director, John Ford, and company setting up for shoots on the valley floor with the magnificent mittens and other mesas scattered about. I have anecdotes from this trip, but what I write grows long and more than tries the patience. I will move along.

In retirement, I have traveled little. However, Frances and I have traveled to South America, to Chile and Argentina. We took a cruise to Cape Horn, saw the Magellanic penguins, the glacier alley, albatross and cormorant, the fabulous "Horns," the two mountain peaks that grace the Chilean currency. And the cities Santiago and Buenos Aires. We also had an adventure on the return trip, a trip that was supposed to take fourteen hours, but took forty hours. The traveler never returns without stories. For the second time in my travels, I was on a huge airplane, one with some ten seats across, that was almost empty; we were some eighteen passengers plus flight attendants.

Before leaving this topic, I have to mention an incident that caused me to fear flying for a while. Back in the 1990s, I was returning from Europe, flying from Heathrow to Calgary and not thinking much of anything when the disembodied voice of the captain sounded over the plane's intercom to say that some of us may have noticed the plane was flying rather low; they were having trouble with number-one engine, but we should not be alarmed. I leaned over and peered out the window, and shockingly, the tundra below looked close enough to jump onto! This perked up people, and I began to talk with the woman sitting next to me in the window seat. She was on her way to Edmonton, the stop after Calgary. Up and down the cabin voices sounded, nervous voices. Then about twenty minutes later, that disembodied voice sounded again: "This is the captain speaking. Some of you will have noticed the flames from number-one engine. Don't be alarmed; we are just flaming off the fuel. Also, we are rerouting to Dorval airport, Montreal." As if this was not stressful enough, the captain went on to say: "We'll be landing in a few minutes and when we hit the ground (sorry, poor choice of words), do not be alarmed when you hear sirens and see flashing lights." The cabin was now as silent as a tomb!

We landed in due course, and sure enough, we heard sirens and saw flashing lights as service vehicles surrounded the plane once it came to a stop. We were then informed that the customs people were on strike, and therefore we could not deplane. We sat there as men in long white coats with tall ladders looked, like proctologists, into the troublesome engine. We sat for some hours until the news came that the flight crew had passed the allotted time for flying and needed to be replaced. We waited. Finally, that voice returned to tell us they could not find a fresh flight crew in Montreal on this Sunday night, and the present crew would fly the plane to Toronto where a new crew would take over for the duration of the flight. This was not reassuring.

Accordingly, the plane began to move and took off, every shift and creak causing the passengers to hold their breath. But the plane did make the journey to Toronto successfully, and once on the ground, the flight crew that had taken us this far departed the plane with smiles and waves, as if to say "so long, suckers." The new crew entered without smiles or waves. The plane took off for Calgary and Edmonton. As we approached Calgary, the disembodied voice of the new captain came over the intercom to say we were about to land, and those passengers going on to Vancouver should just remain seated. There was a collective whoop from the cabin. The captain's voice returned to say, "Sorry folks. I should have said Edmonton, not Vancouver. This has not been a great night for Air Canada." Anyway, we arrived at eight in the morning. Frances picked me up and drove me to the university for my nine o'clock class. We should have landed at eight the evening before.

After this flight, I began to reflect on flights I had taken earlier, such as the one that was just about to land at LaGuardia airport when it suddenly aborted the landing and flew upwards again before circling and making a second approach. Or the time we had been on a plane waiting for takeoff when we were told to gather our things and leave the plane because we were going to have a change of planes. In short, I began to fear flying. I have a nephew who works in the airline business, and I was not reassured when he told me that every plane that leaves the ground has some problem, minor as the problem might be. So much for flying.

CHAPTER FOURTEEN

A Way of Life

Once the 1980s got into full swing, so too did my so-called career. As I say above, I did not really think of myself as having a career; I felt lucky to be doing something I enjoyed, something that seemed important to me, and something that was not the drudgery of a nine-to-five job. I worked at my own pace, much of the time at home since we did not have to have a five-day teaching schedule. I began to publish essays and book chapters, and always eagerly waited to see my name in print. By the end of the 1980s, I had become associate head of the department, and the discipline of this job helped me organize my time and produce at a rate I had not reached before. I found I could be in the office working on an article when someone came along—like the man from Porlock—and interrupted my writing. I might be otherwise occupied for an hour or two, but when I returned to my desk, I could pick up where I had left off, even if this was in mid-sentence. I learned how to compose creatively, if this is not too pretentious to say. Writing simply took over; while writing, I became someone else, a creature that merely took down words from the ticker tape that moved across my inner eye.

As for the administrative work, I did not mind this at the time. Mostly, I was responsible for preparing the department's teaching schedule, keeping everyone happy with their assignments, dealing with student complaints and appeals, organizing department meetings and keeping notes for the meetings and writing minutes, looking after transfer credits for courses taken elsewhere, keeping the calendar up to date, and advising students regarding their programs. Mostly things went smoothly, but I can relate a story from my early days in this job, a story that once again chronicles loss of innocence. It happened this way.

One day a student entered my office looking perplexed. He was a foreign student enrolled in our first-year composition course.

This course was mandatory for all students who could not pass an entrance test in the English language. In order for students to pass this entrance English-language requirement, they had either to pass a test or to gain at least a C in this course. Many students opted for the latter option. This student had received a D+ in the course and he wanted to know if I could raise the grade to C. I replied that I could not simply raise his grade, but that he had the right to appeal his grade in the course. He did so, and handed in his course assignments along with all other handouts he had received in the course. One of these handouts contained the instructor's grading scale. I noticed an anomaly on this handout; the grades went as expected, A, A–, B+, B, B– and so on until it came to the C and D range. Here the Instructor had C, D+, D, D–, and F. What to note is the absence of C–. In the student's mind, he was just one grade or level away from the magical C that would allow him to go forward in his studies.

I read through his work for the course, averaged his grades, and came to the conclusion that D+ was, if anything, a generous grade. He returned to my office after a week or so, but this time he brought his parents. They were eager to have him succeed and move on. I explained that I had read his work and concurred with his instructor's grade. The student and his parents were concerned that he had "failed" the course. I tried to tell them that he had, in fact, not failed the course. D+ was a passing grade in the course. They could not grasp why, if he had passed the course, he could not proceed in his studies. Again, I tried to explain that the university's writing requirement was one thing and that our course was another. It just so happened that the university had targeted this course as fulfilling the writing requirement as long as a student received C. C was important for the writing requirement, but D was sufficient for a minimal passing grade. They left disgruntled. Such are the ways of the institution.

Not long after, the head of department returned, and he received a visit from that student and his parents. The head came to see me and looked over the course documentation. When he noticed the anomaly in the grade system that the instructor used, he said that we had to change the student's grade. He argued that the anomaly in the grading system was wrong since it deviated from the university norm, and therefore the student had to be given the benefit of the doubt. I confess I did not, and do not, understand that argument. For me, what mattered was the student's ability to write, and I had concluded that this ability was sufficiently lacking that he ought not to be given false indication of his ability. He could not write well enough to pass the entrance requirement. Of course, I lost. The student received C for that course. This was my introduction to the ways of administration.

I held this job for four years. By the end of my tenure, the 1980s were coming to a close and I was approaching another stage in my university life. I can't remember when, but sometime in the early '80s, I had received promotion to associate professor. Now I was approaching the time when I had to think of the next stage, promotion to full professor. Wow. It also happened that I was thriving as a member of the Children's Literature Association, and they invited me to become the editor of their journal, *The Children's Literature Association Quarterly*. Before I made the decision whether to accept this invitation or not, I thought I would see the dean of our faculty and ask if I could get a reduction in my teaching assignment, a reduced course load. In short, the dean said no. But he did not stop there. He noted that I was approaching the time for promotion, and he said he could offer some advice. This was his advice: do not accept the editorship of the journal. This gave me pause, and I asked why he should advise this. He replied that in order to make the transition from associate professor to full professor, publication was all-important and I should think of producing a book before I did anything else. I asked what more indicated the respect an academic received from his or her colleagues than the offer of an editorship? An editor has the publication of many scholars in her or his hands, and people would not ask someone to serve as editor if they did not think that person could write and assess writing fairly and judiciously. Besides, the name of our university would end up in every number of the journal while I served as editor. The dean simply smiled and reiterated his point about publications and a book. He also noted that the journal I was considering was a "children's literature" journal. Need I say more?

Consequently, I accepted the editorship. I also managed to produce a couple of books during the four years I edited the journal. True, one of those books was an edition of two George MacDonald novels in the Oxford World's Classics series, and the other was a collection of essays by various hands dealing with MacDonald's fantasies and fairy tales. I would not publish a single-authored book until 1996, when I published two. But that's later in the story. Editing was hard work. And my tenure as editor did not begin auspiciously. One of the first submissions I received was from an established, indeed a venerable, scholar from Wisconsin. As was my practice, I read every submission to see whether it was worth sending to readers. This one brought me up short. It was terrible, badly written and feebly argued. But it was from someone who had many publications, publications I knew only slightly since this person was from a faculty of education and usually published in education journals. I did own a copy of his big textbook. Anyway, I decided to edit the article, to offer suggestions for revision and to suggest he resubmit the essay. The response I got threw me into a tizzy. He wrote back in a cheerful vein, telling me he would leave things in my hands; I could revise as I thought fit and then publish the results without sending the essay back for his approval. What the —, or as they say these days, wtf. I made the wrong decision. I revised the essay, and the result was an essay largely written by me, although it appeared in the journal under this other person's name. He never did contact me to express approval or disapproval of the essay as it appeared. Believe me, I never did anything remotely like this again. I grew ruthless, but in a pleasant way. I received more than one note from someone we had rejected, saying how nice a rejection letter they had received from me.

Editing takes patience and close attention, two things I had in short supply. This explains my relatively brief tenure as editor of that journal. I have, however, edited or co-edited ten books, and special numbers of two journals other than the *Quarterly*. As I write, I find myself co-editing yet another journal. I find this work frustrating, mostly because so much of what we, as editors, receive is poorly written. I guess you could chalk this up as yet another example of lost innocence. Having been nurtured on the prose of such scholars as Frye, Fiedler, Trilling, Bush, Bloom, Hartman, Fish, and others, I looked for a critical prose that was not only clear and grammatically correct, but stylish in some way, even if this is the plain way. Simplicity is a virtue. And wit is welcome; I think of James Kincaid's prose. What I have seen, however, is a profession that does not place value in a graceful voice. I have mentioned along the way examples of writing that was faulty in some way; what I saw as an editor was writing that not only routinely accepted certain grammar errors, most notably the dangling modifier, but also failed miserably at idiomatic expression and accepted the academic cliché as gospel. Good news apparently comes gift-wrapped in a lingo that reeks of conformity. Prolixity too seems to have won the day.

The subject of academic writing is more complicated than I suggest. So far, I have implied quite simplistically that standards of prose have deteriorated over the years. And they have, for whatever reason. What comes to mind is Orwell's 1946 essay, "Politics and the English Language." Orwell thought that writing in his day had become ugly and inaccurate; I wonder what he would say today. Whatever happened to a crisp and clear prose, a prose that Strunk and White could admire? Well, it went the way of all things—down the spout. I am speaking of academic prose. We still have writers whose prose aspires to the condition of poetry: Cormac McCarthy, Alan Garner, Toni Morrison, David Almond, Patrick deWitt, Paul Auster at his best, and so on. But academic writing in the humanities and social sciences has suffered from the plague of self-importance. The usual culprit when this topic surfaces in academic circles is Judith Butler, whose prose is famously tangled and circumlocutionary. And the usual argument for such difficult prose is that difficult ideas call for difficult expression. This may or may not be, but most of the submissions to your average journal in English studies do not contain deep philosophical arguments. The arguments are more often than not fairly mundane. And yes, we have a thicket of jargon words hurled together in an attempt to sound profound. I understand the desire and the need for the work academics do to be taken seriously, but really, does seriousness have to come wrapped in such drivel?

Recently, I read an article that takes an interesting tack in its reflection on what appears to be a lack of moral urgency and drive in academic writing. I refer to Lisa Ruddick's "When Nothing is Cool" (2015), published in *Point* (http://thepointmag.com/2015/criticism/when-nothing-is-cool#sthash.09OXsCT9.dpuf). Ruddick points out the postmodern notion of the empty self, the self that is constructed by various external forces. We used to call this behaviourism. Without an inner core, she suggests, the writer does not have the commitment to profess (she does not use this word). The writer is without agency, individuality, or even point of view beyond what is current. In short, academic writing emanates from the Borg we call the academy. Another way to put this is for me to call on Althusser's industrial state apparatus and its power to interpellate. Insecurity and desire for acceptance can draw one into the institutional arms; these arms fold about the shuddering young acolytes knocking at the doors of academe.

Drawing on another writer, Ann Rippin, Ruddick writes: "Recruits to professional organizations ... are trained in glossy but dehumanized ways of speaking and feeling. The work they learn to do 'is silver service done at arm's length, hygienically, through a polished, highly wrought intermediary instrument.' In time, many of those so socialized 'report feeling unable to bring their whole selves to work, [and] being obliged to dismember or disaggregate themselves, having to suspend feelings, ethics, values on occasion.' I think our profession has its own version of silver-handedness, exacerbated by theoretical orthodoxies that suggest we never had a "whole self" to lose in the first place. Nothing inherently makes the theories that dismiss the idea of integrated selfhood better than the alternatives; they are just preferred by this academic community." She goes on: "The poststructuralist critique of the self, though associated with progressive politics, has an unobserved, conservative effect on the lived world of the profession. It protects the institutional status quo by promoting the evacuation of selves into the group. In the story behind the story, the decentered subject is the practitioner who internalizes the distaste for the inner life and loses touch with the subjective reserves that could offset his or her merger with the profession. What is correspondingly strengthened is the cohesion of the collective. For our profession, alienated in various ways from the American mainstream, needs members who will band together. One way to get members to commit to the group and its ideology is to make them feel ashamed of the varied, private intuitions and desires that might diversify their interests."

I find this analysis illuminating. In short, what Ruddick gives us is a way of understanding the blandness of much academic writing. Academics want to succeed and to succeed means to find acceptance by following the lead of others, not by forging new paths. I think back to that Ph.D. thesis from Australia I mentioned earlier, the one in which the constant use of the passive construction enervates the writing and removes the speaking voice of the subject. What I now think we see in such writing is the effacement of self, the embarrassment of standing alone. I also think of a successful colleague who, quite a few years ago, remarked to me in the interlude between rallies on the squash court, that he did not enjoy reading. He was quick to say that he enjoyed his work, but that reading was work and he would not go home of an evening and take a book to read in order to relax. You might recall what I said about work earlier in this meditation. There is no success like failure, especially when failure becomes the only success.

Sometimes a way of life can be rough.

By the end of the 1980s, I was well ensconced in academia. I was serving on the boards of ChLA and IRSCL, I had done administrative work at my university, and I was beginning to publish at a fairly regular rate. I had been in the job for some seventeen years. I do not remember exactly when I received promotion to full professor or even who my evaluators were, but somehow, I got promoted. My academic contacts were mostly outside my own country, and I did not have strong friendships within my own department. I kept busy playing squash with colleagues from religious studies, classics, and even the upper administration. I sat on a few committees, and generally kept a low profile. Academia provided me with a comfortable life. And I was convinced that what the humanities offered was an important life skill, the ability to reason, to assess, and to create a world out of words. The one thing I retained from my first acquaintance with Northrop Frye was the certainty that what passed for reality in the cold world was but a façade, or if you prefer more fashionable terminology, a simulation, shadows on the wall of the cave. Reality was that which we imagined it to be and we could choose to imagine it to be where tolerance, justice, equality, fairness, and liberty were the order of the day. If we imagined this world and imagined it strongly enough, it would be just like Adam's dream; we would wake to find it real! This is what literature and the arts meant and mean to me.

I might note here that during this time, the humanities came under fire, or more specifically liberal humanism came under fire. As theory developed from structuralism through post-structuralism, we saw what Ruddick describes above, an assault on the notion of the centred self, the idea of identity. Just at the time when identity politics were becoming more important, theory was telling us that identity was nothing more than our socially constructed ways of behaving; the subject was de-centred and in actuality each person was not one identity but several depending on circumstances. Such a challenge to the notion of a core personality, a self that was stable, appeared to challenge the basis of liberal humanism, and liberal humanism was the expression of that generation of critics that took their sense of value from Matthew Arnold and his notion of the best that was thought and said. Well hell, a liberal humanist such as Frye did trace his lineage back to Arnold and to the tradition that sees literature as the great civilizing force. Literature in this view forms the self, the stable and centered self. But Frye's liberal humanism was sensible enough to know that the best that has been thought and said is not for the passing on by fiat; rather each of us comes to an understanding of the best that has been thought and said through immersion, as it were. The educated imagination is the imagination that has steeped itself in what the grand traditions of art have to offer, and then decided for itself what is best thought and best said. Despite the niceties of post-structuralist deconstruction of the self, the self does survive. Deconstruction, after all, knows that the centre exists even if it is de-centred. The fun is in the exploration, the tracings of this self. Witness this document.

CHAPTER FIFTEEN
Publications, Children's Literature, and Beyond

Throughout the 1990s and early 2000s, I steadily increased the number of my publications. Mostly these were in the area of children's literature. And now it behooves me to say something about this discipline that has made my so-called career. Way back in Reading, as I was completing my Ph.D., I received that job offer from the University of Calgary to teach children's literature. I had told the people in Calgary that I could teach in this area because the writer I researched for my Ph.D. had written several important books for children. Truth to tell, I really knew nothing about either the field at large or even MacDonald's books for the young. But then neither did nearly anyone else at that time. When I told my supervisors in Reading about the job offer, both D. J. Gordon and Ian Fletcher advised me not to take the job. They warned me I might get mired in a subject area that was really intellectually bankrupt. No one of any intellectual stature taught or studied children's books. We can find this attitude in one of the canonical writers, Henry James. James pointed out that Frances Hodgson Burnett was a successful writer, but her work was not for everyone. Those seriously engaged with literature and with life did not traffic in children's books. So, of course, I accepted the job.

In those first years, the commentary on children's books was rudimentary. We were all just finding footing. I began teaching children's literature in 1973, just at the time when Jon Stott, Francelia Butler, and a few others were organizing the Children's Literature Association. Francelia Butler put together the first issue of the Association's journal in 1972. This was *Children's Literature: The Great Excluded*. The subtitle explains that this body of literature had routinely been left off lists of canonical books. With the possible exception of a book or two by the likes of Lewis Carroll or Robert Louis Stevenson, none of the great books written and published for young readers were included on course syllabi in universities. A few children's books did appear as texts on some courses, but these books were not taught as children's books. The obvious example is Twain's *The Adventures of Huckleberry Finn*. Another book, Swift's *Gulliver's Travels*, was thought of as a children's book only when it was severely edited and then published in editions aimed at a younger readership. Mostly books for the young were simply ignored in academic circles. And in many cases, neglect went beyond ignoring. By this I mean that a few books for the young from the nineteenth century and early twentieth century were still in print: the "Alice" books, *Treasure Island*, *Black Beauty*, *The Wind in the Willows*, the "Pooh" books, and so on. However, many more worthy books had fallen out of print: most of MacDonald's books, *The Water Babies*, the books of E. Nesbit, and a whole host of books that, if remembered at all, were remembered as hopelessly didactic or old-fashioned: the work of so many women writers from Maria Edgeworth to Evelyn Sharp. What we saw here is the familiar nudging from history of women writers.

The notion was that children's books were too transparent, too simple for the workings of new critical analysis. Also, they were meant to teach the young, not throw them into the complexities of maturity. They offered blueprints for behaviour. Sophisticated reading practices called for sophisticated books. This attitude was also responsible for the neglect of other popular types of literature, science fiction, fantasy, and detective fiction, for example. Such literary snobbery meant that the poetry and the one utopian novel of a writer such as William Morris were worthy of study, but his prose romances were not. A similar winnowing of a writer's work could be seen in the case of H.G. Wells. *The History of Mr. Polly* might prove acceptable in a course that deals with Edwardian fiction, but who ever read *The Sea Lady*? Or I might cite George Meredith, whose novels of social realism maintained their reputation, whereas his wonderful *The Shaving of Shagpat* was forgotten. Much has changed since 1970, but this sense that certain books are less worthy of study than others remains. Teachers of children's literature often find themselves marginalized, or at least they did in my years of teaching.

Another feature of children's literature is that it finds itself presented and presented differently in faculties of education, humanities faculties, and schools of library science. At first blush, one might think this speaks to the importance of such literature, but in fact, such interdisciplinary interest in the subject has served to increase the marginalization of children's books within departments of English and departments of modern languages. I guess the idea is that if this body of work can appeal across such disciplines, then it must not contain a depth and profundity worthy of the great works that find themselves the object of study in serious departments of literature. That schools of education and library science take an interest in children's literature confirms some in their belief that this literature serves only a pedagogic and an entertainment function. This is nice because it suggests this literature offers nothing other than instruction and delight. It is properly put away once childish things are no longer necessary.

Looking back, we can see that books for the young began to find a place in the university for reasons that we might call political. The late 1960s and early 1970s saw calls for recognition by a number of groups: Black people, women, gay and lesbian people. This was the early days of the so-called "rights movement." Identity politics was on the rise. Children too had their rights. As early as 1959, the United Nations General Assembly enacted the United Nations Declaration of the Rights of the Child. Along with this acknowledgement of children's rights came an interest in the child as a concept, one that alters over time. We began to see studies of the "child" in Romantic literature and children in art and culture over time. The seminal book in this turn to children was Philippe Ariès's *Centuries of Childhood* (1962). But studies that analyzed books for the young were few and far between. Such studies did not begin to appear until well into the 1970s, although John Rowe Townsend's *Written for Children* appeared in 1965. Looking back, I can see the irony in the search for the "child" amid the growing consensus that such a category is problematic, if not downright impossible to pin down. Liberal humanism would have it that such a creature as the child exists, whereas the postmodern take on the question is that only children (whatever they are) exist, only difference or, better yet, *différance* is available to us.

It is interesting to reflect back to those early years and remember just how awkward and fumbling were those first attempts to discuss children's books. I can recall reading *Charlotte's Web* for class and wondering what the heck I could say about it. It seemed so transparent. Where was the seriousness in this story of a spider that befriends a pig? Big deal. Okay, so the spider dies and the pig is sad. Youngsters, I guess, have to learn about death. And herein lies the didactic content that we all took for granted formed that literature we called children's. But this approach seemed so limited and unsatisfying. We wanted the complexities of George Eliot or Virginia Woolf. And we could not find them. We could not find them because we were unprepared for the intricacies of simplicity. Once I looked at *Charlotte's Web* with a new critical eye, spotting the ironies and ambiguities and formal beauties of the language, the book became rich in interpretive possibility. Simplicity, as Wordsworth so eloquently noted, does not mean lacking seriousness.

What helped in this search for things to say about books that seemed so transparent was theory. Theory gave us an insight to the variety of ways we have to read books. Books now became texts, and texts were everywhere for us to read, or to decode. Language was a code, hiding its meaning and significances behind a surface of familiarity. Once we had this notion that the text was everything, and that it consisted of textures and tracings, firmly in mind, we were off to the races when it came to writing about children's books. Readings of *Charlotte's Web* began to proliferate. So too did readings of the corpus of children's literature.

First came the urge to construct a canon of this literature, an enterprise that came to fruition in the 1980s with the *Touchstones* series edited by Perry Nodelman. Children's literature was entering the mainstream, at least on the surface of that stream. Underneath, the current swiftly dragged women's literature and postcolonial literature, but nearer the surface things moved more slowly for children's literature and queer literature. It took longer for the study of children's literature and queer literatures to find respect. Strange bedfellows. All of this was somehow new, a challenge to dyed-in-the-wool attitudes that literature consisted of a great tradition that did not include such juvenile work as that labeled children's literature. This is complicated stuff, but some of us, I think, knew that the great tradition was a mug's game from the start. Some of us knew, for example, that reading comics was not a waste of time. Ah, comics. Let me throw in this anecdote. I started putting Frank Miller's *The Dark Knight Returns* (1986) on my course syllabi in the 1990s. This was about the time Art Spieglman's *MAUS* won the Pulitzer Prize in 1992, and so I guess my selection was not too revolutionary. However, comics or graphic material did not become common on course syllabi until well after the year 2000. Anyway, I can recall one student rushing into class one day flushed and excited. He said he had been sitting on the C-train reading Batman when an older couple sitting nearby noticed him. The lady commented that this was inappropriate reading material for someone his age, and he promptly replied that he was reading the comic for his university English class.

The point is that with the advent of theory in the 1970s, university departments of English, along with humanities and social sciences generally, began to change, to widen the scope of their critical eyes and to accept the inclusion of material on course syllabi that was not part of the accepted canon of literature. The canon itself morphed. One might have thought that such change would bring a true spirit of adventure into academic studies. But adventure is not something easily embraced by institutional attitudes. I recall having a graduate student who proposed a thesis on Bob Dylan, yes that same Bob Dylan who is now a Nobel laureate, and the department refused to accept this proposal because the subject was not sufficiently literary. At the same time, institutional attitudes were changing in less salutary ways, becoming more and more drawn into managerial and corporate ways of doing things. I can only guess that the right-wing politics of the 1980s and 1990s (the Reagan and Thatcher years gave impetus to the right) with their emphasis on the private sector and the free market convinced governments to cut back on university budgets, prompting universities to look for monies elsewhere. And they found it in the corporate sector. As the 1990s moved into the 2000s, units on the campus where I worked became the Haskayne School of Business, the Schulich School of Engineering, the Enbridge Centre for Corporate Sustainability, the Werklund School of Education, and the Cumming School of Medicine. Perhaps the first sign of this corporate presence on campus came when Scurfield Hall was opened in 1986, and many of its rooms have names reflecting the city's oil business: Shell, Esso, and so on. By the 1990s, the privatization of the universities was well on the way. I have spoken of this earlier.

And so just as changes within the disciplines were seemingly growing more democratic and less elitist, universities were growing more focused on corporate money and corporate accountability. Universities still offer a way of life that is not tied to the nine-to-five office routine, but they are moving in that direction. During this time, faculty received more pressure to provide more varied and methodical teaching. Now we had an array of workshops to improve teaching, just as we had an array of workshops to improve sensitivity in the workforce. Administrative positions grew in number as faculty numbers shrank. We always seemed to have money for new and state-of-the-art buildings (e.g., the Taylor Family Digital Library that has no books), while classrooms in existing buildings have broken desks or not enough chairs or no lecterns or no chalk or broken elevators or crumbling ceilings and walls that cry out for a splash of paint.

Much of this did not affect me beyond the fairly innocuous irritation derived from witnessing changes I did not think were either necessary or productive. More and more students grew less and less curious and more concerned that their education lead to gainful employment. I recall one evening class when I was professing the virtues of Shelley's *Prometheus Unbound* ("Empire is no more"); I noticed a decided ennui among the students. I stopped blabbing and asked outright: "Why doesn't this poetry appeal to you?" One young man looked at me and remarked that he was focused on getting himself a job, and he did not know how the fine-sounding words of Shelley would help him do this. In short, what Shelley had to say just did not seem relevant to this young man or these students. University life was changing from what it had been when I was a student, and even when I first began to teach. The old notion that an education in the humanities prepared one to live life critically no longer seemed either just or important. Urbanity was no longer a virtue. I am connecting this malaise with late capitalism because under the capitalist banner the private sector has managed to convince the general public, including those who earn their living in the universities, that what is real and functional and useful is life lived under the mandate of private enterprise and individual acceptance of a system that depends on compliance and uniformity. We will all be happy if we all think similarly and thrive under corporate initiatives. Everything becomes, under this system, a commodity, including a university education. *The Truman Show* (1998) passes through my mind.

Again, take children's literature. True, this subject has arrived and found acceptance. Some universities even foreground the subject. Rutgers has its Center for Childhood Studies, Roehampton has its National Centre for Research in Children's Literature, Newcastle has its Children's Literature Unit, and a number of universities boast a concentration on children's literature: Kansas State University, Illinois State University, and the University of Connecticut, for example. For the most part, however, this subject remains a poor sister at established universities, Ivy League institutions, and such august schools in Canada as Queen's in Kingston, McGill in Montreal, and Toronto in, well, Toronto. If the university with which I am associated can serve as an example, I can give clear evidence of how unimportant children's literature is. During the period of growth in the 1980s and 1990s, funding of departments depended upon hefty enrollment numbers. Our department went to great lengths to make it look as if we had large enrollments. I recall one year that I had a large first-year class with an enrollment of about one hundred students. The department, in its quest for numbers, broke this class into sections of some twenty-five people so that it would appear as if we had more sections of the course than we actually had. When classes began and I began to call the roll the first day, some two-thirds of the students found they were not on the enrollment sheets. This administrative glitch did not please me. Once I calmed the students down, I proceeded to march across campus to the registrar's office, stomp inside where I was not supposed to be, and start shouting at whoever happened to be at the desk at the end of the room. Needless to say, the staff was not impressed, and soon they were threatening to call security. My irritation stemmed from the fact that numbers came before students in the university's thinking; to put this another way, I note that to the university administration, students were nothing more than numbers.

Anyway, how does what I say above link to children's literature? Here's the thing: the one course in children's literature in the English department began as a "service" to the Faculty of Education, and each year that course was guaranteed to have some forty to fifty students who were enrolled in the Division One and Division Two streams in the education faculty. In other words, the course looked good on the English department's rolls; it had a guaranteed clientele, a group, mostly female, who were going to become elementary school teachers. Right away, this situation set the course apart from the other offerings in the English department. When I arrived in 1973, no one wanted to teach the course because it was thought to be intellectually inferior to the department's traditional offerings. I was hired to teach this course. And I did, for nearly forty years. But, as I note above, the university experienced terrific growth in the 1980s, and demand for the children's literature course expanded. We went from one section in the first years I was teaching it to five in the 1980s. By then, we had six people in the department who regularly taught this course. Not only this, but we also added a second half-course in Literature for Younger Children. Of the six people who taught children's literature, three were active in research and publication in the area. In fact, as the years went on two of us became president of the Children's Literature Association. Our department was on the verge of becoming a force in the teaching of and research into children's literature. It seemed to me sensible to take advantage of what we were doing and create a Centre for Children's Literature Studies, or better yet, an interdisciplinary Unit of Childhood Studies. We could draw on the faculties of humanities, social sciences, fine art, and education, and create something to benefit students, faculty, and the general public. We could take advantage of the latest buzz: interdisciplinary studies.

This did not happen. Instead, as we rolled into the first decade of the twenty-first century, the department lost any interest it had in children's literature, largely because the education faculty no longer sought English as a service department. Slowly the number of sections of the two courses dwindled, slowly the number of people teaching the courses dwindled, and slowly the research into the subject dwindled. By the time we reached the end of that first decade, the department was back to offering just one course in children's literature, and offering this course intermittently. The two of us who were left teaching this course did so only now and then, not every semester. When department meetings took up the question of the department's strengths, its areas of concentration, children's literature did not come into play, despite the fact that an external review of the department back around the turn of the century cited children's literature as one of our strengths. The subject was, and remains, a poor sister, Cinderella waiting for the ball. The odd thing about this is that over the years publication in the subject has blossomed. When I began to teach children's literature, the first journal devoted to the subject began to appear: *Children's*

Literature: The Great Excluded. In the 1980s a few more journals appeared: *Signal* (from Great Britain), *The Lion and the Unicorn* (the U.S.), and *Canadian Children's Literature* (Canada). These were mostly produced cheaply. Fast forward to today and we see *Children's Literature* and *Children's Literature Association Quarterly*, along with the *Lion and the Unicorn* appear with the prestigious Johns Hopkins University Press. *Canadian Children's Literature*, now named *Jeunesse: Young People, Texts, Cultures*, first appearing from the University of Guelph, now has its home at the University of Winnipeg and looks more professional than it once did. More journals have appeared, such as the *Children's Literature Journal* (England) and *Papers* (Australia), and mainstream journals such as *PMLA* will now accept articles on the subject. At one time, they did not. The number of books appearing on children's literature has increased immeasurably. Reputable presses such as Palgrave Macmillan and Routledge have children's literature series. In short, children's literature has arrived as a scholarly subject. At the same time, it remains suspect among traditionalists. Such is academia.

If one were cynical, one might conclude that the increase in publishing in the area of children's literature has less to do with the intellectual acceptability of the subject and more to do with lucre. The market for children's literature is both large and international. Publishers seek to publish that which will sell and children's literature sells. We see this both commercially and academically. Books for young readers are popular with adults; in 2012 a British survey showed that adults made up 55 percent of readers of young adult books. According to the Association of American Publishers, in 2014, "Children and young adult fiction surpassed the adult fiction market with 843 million units and 746 million units sold respectively" (http://publishers.org/news/us-publishing-industry's-annual-survey-reveals-28-billion-reven). My guess is that this strength also appears in the academic sector. Children's literature both as a primary reading experience and as an area for scholarship and research is popular. Why, then, does the subject remain on the margins?

The answer to this question eludes me when I think of the importance of literature for the young. Very early, children, or at least many children, encounter the world through books, and these books not only begin to teach them to read both verbally and visually, but they also begin to educate them in the ways of the imagination. Books for the very young can and do deal with subjects as crucial as human relationships, the interaction of human and non-human animals, the ecosystem, the call of the marketplace, the variety of human beings, questions of race and culture, the history that shapes us, the threats to the planet, and other such serious and even grave matters. The same is true, only at an even more intense level, in young adult books. What could be more meaningful than a focus on this writing that sets out to present a picture of the traps and pitfalls that wrap and trip young people, or attempt to do so, in a confining cloth of conformity? This is a literature that prepares its readers for inevitable loss of innocence, for the poison tree watered both day and night with tears.

I might add that the popularity of children's literature has something to do with the rise of cultural studies in the 1980s and 1990s. Stuart Hall and others began to theorize forms of cultural production. The study of science fiction and fantasy emerged from the obscurity of fandom, and an accompanying focus on forgotten women's writing helped bring what was once dismissed as "popular" into view. Theory helped us render just about anything intellectually stimulating. And so we found ourselves with "childist" reading, queer reading, feminist reading, and so on. At the root here was a challenge to conservative thinking in the arts. Marxist-influenced critics such as Frederic Jameson, Perry Anderson, Raymond Williams, and Terry Eagleton demonstrated the artificiality of separation. What amounted to class divisions in literary study was no longer quite so *de rigeur* as they used to be. This fluidity of literary types was familiar to me from the work of Frye, who valued Romance as much or more than Tragedy, Comedy, or Satire. Indeed, Frye could find the Romance in any of these other modes. All literature shared the drive to create reality and not just to philosophize. We arrived at a time when criticism will examine any type of cultural production. Having noted this, I also notice that the urge to valorize some things over others has not left the academic mind. Children's literature, for example, may have its researchers and its champions, but it remains a peripheral interest in the academy at large.

This section is about publications, and with the utmost immodesty, I scan my publications. I began slowly in the 1980s to publish journal articles. One of the first articles was on fantasy literature and it appeared in *The English Journal*. I mention this because when it appeared it was garbled, pages rearranged so that it made little or no sense. It was an embarrassment. Other early attempts to place articles resulted in rejections that indicated what I had written was intellectually light or was insufficiently original or was saying what was agreeable. I suspect these criticisms are as relevant to what I write today as they were back then. Perhaps an exception was one of my first articles. This was a daring exploration of *Alice's Adventures in Wonderland* that took as its starting point one of John Tenniel's illustrations, the one in which Alice confronts the Queen of Hearts. The two of them face each other near the prone "bodies" of the cards that had been painting the roses.

I digress here to note that when I was in my third year of undergraduate study at Toronto, Lois gave me a copy of this first *Alice* book. This would be late in 1966. I read it and flipped. It jived so well with everything that was in my head and in the air back then. "We're all mad here." "Oh, your're nothing but a pack of cards." Nonsense spiced the air of the 1960s; just have a listen to the *Basement Tapes*. Read a bit of Timothy Leary or R. D. Laing. Or what about Genghis Khan and his brother Don, could not keep on keepin' on, "Apple Suckin' Tree," "Tiny Montgomery," or remember "I Am the Walrus" and other John Lennon concoctions? It was a time of fine madness. Madness and lobotomy were the two approaches to the world, as we see in *One Flew Over the Cuckoo's Nest* (1962). Anyway, Lewis Carroll became an important figure for me right then, when I received that gift from Lois. To publish something about his work was a thrill.

And that daring exploration pleased me because I managed to argue something without divulging the argument. In short, what I had noticed was that in the illustration I identify above, Tenniel has placed the White Rabbit on the extreme right side of the illustration with his back turned to the rest of the cast. His posture makes him look as if he is urinating. I did not say this, but this is what I was writing about. In other words, I had noticed something transgressive. Tenniel was giving us something forbidden in Victorian culture, but he was also pointing out the rebellious nature of the characters in the book. The satire marked Victorian culture, royalty, the class system, justice, indeed just about anything we can imagine. I loved this. And apparently *English Studies in Canada* did not mind it either because they accepted the article with few emendations. I was on the way. Over the next few decades, I published fifty-three journal articles, twenty-two essays in reference works, thirty-four chapters in books, two co-authored articles, and sixteen editorials and columns. In addition, I published sixty-seven book reviews of various lengths, and fifteen other publications.

Then there are the books. I had worked at the university for about twenty-three years before I published my first authored book. And I worked there for about seventeen years before I published my first edited book. This first book was an Oxford World's Classics edition of George MacDonald's two "Princess" books, *The Princess and the Goblin* and *The Princess and Curdie*. To prepare this edition, I traveled to England in December of 1988. I have a memory of this visit that has nothing to do with research or publishing or anything academic. But I shall toss it in here just because I remember it so well. Somehow over the years I had acquired a taste and tolerance for very spicy food. In fact, I have a collection of hot sauce bottles with names such as Sir Fartalot, Peaches and Scream, Mad Dog Inferno, Colon Cleaner, Whoopin' Ass Hot Sauce, Original Death, Fire & Brimstone, Acid Rain, PMS Psycho Bitch, and the Hottest Fuckin' Sauce. Some have noteworthy messages. For example, the last one I list says this on the label:

> We warned you. This is a serious fuckin' hot sauce. That's right we said it—because we had to. There is no other way to describe just how hot this sauce is. I suppose we could have said "It's like the fiery depths of hell" or "That it's ass-burning" and even "Keep away from pets and small children and avoid contact with sensitive areas," but that just seems so wordy. The sauce is hot as fuck! Succinct, to the point—no beating around the bush! Honesty is always the best policy, isn't it? If this sauce burns intensely, don't be afraid to let it out. Scream fuck at the top of your lungs. You'll feel better. There is no better verbal therapy.

Anyway, I like hot sauces.

Back to that trip to London in December of 1988. I was working in the British Museum, and in the evening, I looked for places to eat nearby. One evening I came across an Indian restaurant just off Russell Square. I went in and, as I usually do, I ordered a lamb vindaloo. The waiter, a middle-aged Indian gentleman, looked concerned, and he advised me that this dish was very hot. I replied that hot was okay. Away he went to place my order. In a while, he was back and placed before me the vindaloo. Having lived in England before, I was familiar with what they think of as hot. Once I had tasted the dish, with the waiter standing by with a worried look on his face, I asked if I could have some hot pickle or sauce. My request discombobulated the waiter, but he went off. When he returned, the kitchen staff came with him. Three of them stood by as I applied the hot pickle and began to eat. I smiled, and they all gave sighs of relief. After the meal and when I had paid the bill, the waiter asked for my name and address. We exchanged addresses. For the next couple of years, at Christmas, I received a card from the people in this restaurant.

I managed to finish that research and publish the World's

Classics edition. It stayed in print for half-a-dozen years and then disappeared. Too bad. The early '90s also saw another book publication, the first of a number of collections of essays by various hands that I have published. This was *For the Childlike*, essays on George MacDonald's children's fiction and fantasy. By the time I retired, I had edited six more collections and one other edition. Some of these I co-edited with the following colleagues: John Pennington, Karen Coats and Anna Jackson, and Kerry Mallan.

Not until 1996 did I publish an authored book. That year, I published two, *The Nimble Reader: Literary Theory and Children's Literature*, and *A Little Princess: Gender and Empire*, both with Twayne Publishers. The first of these books has long since gone out of print, but when it appeared in the mid-'90s, it was pretty much alone in its attempt to see children's literature in the light of various theories of literature. I assume that this is the reason the IRSCL chose the book as the best book on children's literature for its year. It won Best Book Award for 1996. My second book that year, was a short study of Frances Hodgson Burnett's *A Little Princess* from the perspectives of feminist and colonial discourses. This little book is, I think, still in print.

I had to wait another ten years to see two more authored books of mine in print. One of these is academic and the other is a fiction. The more interesting story is how the fiction found life, and so I shall begin with the academic book. By this time, I was working on material that was of personal, as well as academic, interest. Growing up with western movies and cowboy heroes, I had never lost my fascination with the west and its itinerant cowboys. Since I was teaching women's writing and thinking about gender, I thought it would be interesting to study the cowboy stars of my youth in light of studies in masculinity. Accordingly, I set out to watch as many B westerns from the 1930s to the mid-1950s as I could, and think about the construction of masculinity in them. I wrote the book, and for a cover I sought permission to use a picture of the singing cowboy, Monte Hale. In the picture Monte is kneeling by a campfire, holding a frying pan in one hand and a pistol in the other. He is wearing a white hat (of course) and white shirt with large Indian head insignia. This was perfect for what I wanted to convey in the book. When I contacted Mr. Hale, he was elderly and infirm; his wife undertook the correspondence. The Hales agreed to have me use the picture as long as they received twenty-five copies of the book gratis. I think I negotiated a smaller number, but in any case the press agreed to send books to Mr. Hale. By the time the book appeared, Monte Hale had passed away. However, his wife did send me a short note congratulating me on the publication of the book. Her tone was measured and I could tell that the contents of the book did not entirely please her. I don't know that the book sold in great numbers, but it did garner some positive reaction. It was shortlisted for *Fore/word* magazine's award for best book of the year in popular culture. I also received a few emails from readers, one of whom, Tim Bazzett, wrote in praise of the book on amazon.com.

But, as I say, the more interesting story pertains to my fiction. After my mother died and throughout the 1990s, I worked in a desultory way at a fiction. By the late '90s, this was unfinished and stagnating on my computer. One day my daughter Kate saw the file, read what was there and asked me if I was ever going to finish the narrative. Her interest prompted me to sit down and bring the relatively short narrative to a conclusion. I printed the document and sent it to a publisher in Vancouver. The publisher rejected it and I shelved the thing thinking that was the end of that. By chance, however, I met the French author Laurent Chabin. I had invited Laurent to be a speaker at the conference I was organizing for July 1999. Over lunch one day, he asked me if I wrote anything. Knowing a bit about creative writers and a bit about Laurent, I knew he was not thinking of academic writing, and so I said in an offhand way that I had written a novel. He asked who had published it, and I replied that it was unpublished. He pursued the topic, asking if he could read it. I said sure and told him I would email him a copy. I did.

Some months passed. Then one morning I checked my emails

to find one from Laurent. He said he had read my novel and he was "astonished." He went on to speak of my wee fiction as similar to work by the likes of Celine, Paul Auster, and William Faulkner. My head was getting larger by the second. As he closed his message, he said he hoped I wouldn't mind, but he had already shared my fiction with his publisher and she had expressed great interest in publishing it—but, wait a minute, in French. I was somewhat puzzled, but I wrote back and said of course I was flattered by his response to what I had written, and as far as I was concerned, he could do whatever he wanted with it. When his reply came, it came with the caution that he would not translate my book without getting paid because he made his living by writing. I was chastened, and I thought that would be the end of any chance my book would appear in French—or English for that matter.

But this is Canada! After a long interval, I received an email from the publisher, Andrée Yanacopoulo, enquiring whether I would agree with her wish to apply for a Canada Council grant to translate and publish my book. As I say, only in Canada! I replied in the affirmative and the next thing I knew I was receiving reader's reports saying how intricate and sophisticated and original my book was. One reader actually said the book's sensibility was more French than English. Go figure. Anyway, the publisher received a grant of some $10,000, and Laurent began to translate what I had written. Only in Canada would the government give a grant to translate and publish an unpublished book so that a book written in English would appear under the author's name in a language he cannot write. The process of translation was fascinating and I have a large file of questions and answers that chronicle the translation process. The book finally was prepared by 2006, and it appeared in 2007. It received a positive review in *Le Devoir*, and a very positive review in an online blog where the reviewer called it "un roman d'un originalite extraordinaire." Laurent encouraged me for years to find an English publisher for the book, but this has never happened.

However, Laurent was strong in his belief in my ability to

write fiction, and he invited me to write a short story for a special number of a magazine he was putting together. I did write a story, Laurent translated it, and it appeared as "Le Locataire Revisite," in *Moebius* 125 (Mai 2010). The story has as its main character, someone who first turns up in my novel, and who then makes many appearances in Laurent's fiction. I like the way this character has resonated with Laurent and has a life beyond my first attempt at fiction. And by the way, Laurent is a writer of distinction. His fiction is experimental, absorbing, intellectual, and clever. He has a wicked wit. His detective or suspense novels for both young readers and adults are intricate experiments with genre. His prose is difficult and resonant. I owe him much for his belief in me as a writer and in his hours of conversational excellence.

In total, thirteen books have my name on their covers. Thirteen is not a good number to end with, just as a preposition is not a good part of speech to end a sentence with. (Since I wrote this a fourteenth book has appeared, *Around the Block; or the Tricks of Memory* (2021); this one I self-published.) Who knows if there will be any more? I do have a few works in progress, but whether I actually publish any of these remains uncertain. One is a memoir of sorts, setting out my development as an academic. It has grown quite lengthy, and I may or may not ever finish it. (Those last two sentences are something of a joke here.) I also have an internet blog that no one reads and various other bits and pieces. Writing is an exercise, a craft, a game, a way of life. To write is to make things happen, if only for oneself. Writing is the only skill I have; I will not say the only skill I have mastered because language refuses to succumb to a master. Language always and ever stretches before us like the universe itself. And like that universe, language has its black holes and its galaxies and its star clusters and its zodiacs and its myriad combinations.

CHAPTER SIXTEEN

Accolades

My friend and colleague, John Pennington, mentioned my modesty in his introductory remarks to our co-edited edition of George MacDonald's *At the Back of the North Wind*. I appreciate John's comment, but as you can see, I am anything but modest. Already I have noted that two of my books received nominations for prizes, and one of them won. Now I offer a short chapter on other recognition I have received.

In 1991, I was awarded a Humanities Institute fellowship. This meant I was relieved of teaching duties for the year and given an office in the institute across campus. The institute had six fellows that year and we got along well. I was to carry out research for a book on literary theory and children's literature. The book did not appear until 1996, but the year in the institute provided impetus to my work, and I am grateful to have been selected as a fellow. In fact, some years later I applied for the position of director of the Institute. When the hiring committee made their final list of two, I was one of these two. So near. My colleague Richard Davis got the job, and I got thanks for applying. A year later Richard was out of that job and I was glad that I had not been in his place. Those were the years when the institution was divesting itself of any and all financial drain that it could, and the Humanities Institute was faced with having to find outside funding. I suspect I would have been terrible at doing this kind of work.

Coming in second was something I should have got used to. Twice I was shortlisted for the International Grimm Brothers Award, given annually by the Children's Literature Institute in Osaka, Japan, for distinguished work in children's literature. This happened in 2007 and again in 2008. Always a bridesmaid, never a bride. To be honest, I would have liked to receive this honour and traveled to Japan to receive the award. I have never visited that county. I add here that I have never visited India either, and just a couple of years ago I had to decline an invitation to India for health reasons.

Not receiving the Grimm Brothers Award was disappointing. On the other hand, as early as 1997 I did receive the Anne Deveraux Jordan Award for distinguished service to children's literature. Anne Jordan was one of the founding members of the Children's Literature Association; she had died young and this award was meant to commemorate her work in establishing the Association and promoting the study of children's literature. I say I received this award "as early as" 1997 because this was relatively early in my years of service. I was the seventh or eighth recipient of that award, receiving it two years before Jack Zipes received it. This just goes to show how illogical the profession can be. Anyway, I had edited the association's journal and I had served as the association's president, and so I can only conclude that the award was a sort of compensation for my service. I certainly did not deserve to receive this award ahead of someone like Jack Zipes.

Speaking of Jack Zipes, I have him to thank for another honour. In 2002, I received the Distinguished Scholarship Award from the International Association for the Fantastic in the Arts, and I know Jack was instrumental in making this happen. The phone rang in the office one day and when I answered, I heard a person on the other end say that I had won the Distinguished Scholarship Award for the Fantastic in the Arts. I said that they must have the wrong person and hung up. I certainly had not done any distinguished work on fantasy literature, as far as I knew. Anyway, a few minutes later the phone rang again. When I answered the person on the other end asked if I was Roderick McGillis. I said yes. Then they asked me if I wrote this and that article and I said yes. Then they said I had won this award for my work on fantasy. That was that. I went to the association's annual conference in Florida and delivered myself of a luncheon speech, a speech that has entered the lore of that association because in the middle of it the fire alarm went off and I found myself acting as fire marshal, directing people out the doors. My speech was, I assure you, much less memorable than my stint as fire marshal. Anyway, I also received a T-shirt with my name listed among the names of other honourees.

Speaking of T-shirts, I have another story. In that same year, 2002, I received the University of Calgary's President's Circle Award for Excellence in Research and Creativity. Crazy, eh. The university put on an evening's event to dole out its awards; I can't remember how many people received awards, but I was assured that the President's Circle Award was prestigious. Right. On the evening of the gala event, Frances and I went to the appointed place. In the crowd milling about, having a drink, I saw the Vice-President, Academic. I had known this person since graduate school back in Hamilton. He approached me with a smile and a T-shirt in his hand. He gave me the shirt and told me I was going to receive one like it later in the evening. I held it up to see "Excellent U" emblazoned on the front in bold red letters on a black background. Just as I was admiring the T-shirt, a woman came rushing up to tell the VP that he should put the T-shirt away because the president and board of governors had decided not to give out the shirts at this time. It seems they did not think the university had achieved its goal of excellence just yet. Excellence was a buzzword on campus and around the academic world in those days. The VP reached to take the T-shirt back from me, but I snatched it from his outstretched hand, saying there was no way I was giving this up. An awkward moment or two followed as the woman and the VP realized I was serious. I still have that T-shirt! I also have a photograph of myself shaking hands with the president in which I look like a deer caught in the headlights.

In 2003, I received a Killam Residence Fellowship. Killam Awards are highly sought after and I was pleased to receive the honour. I do not recall applying for the fellowship, but I may have. Anyhow, it came my way, and I had time away from the classroom to do research on the cowboy book I was working on, the one that appeared in 2007. This award was for six months.

I consider a couple of other items to be noteworthy. In 2004, I was appointed first ever scholar-in-residence at Hollins University in Roanoke, Virginia. They flew me down to Roanoke, and settled me in a wonderful little house right in the middle of campus, one of those pastoral, tree-filled campuses with what are old buildings here in North America. My duties were few. Actually, my duties seemed to be nothing more than sitting on the porch of my little house and chatting with students who happened to drop by. I did attend a few lectures, and I may have talked in one or two of these. And I delivered the Francelia Butler Lecture at a student conference that took place while I was there. But mostly, this was a week of leisure. As a result of this sojourn at Hollins, I agreed to participate in Hollins's study abroad program the following summer. However, things did not work out. Frances and I did go to England to meet the Hollins group, but not long after arriving Frances became ill and we returned to Canada. I am, however, indebted to Hollins for the honour of staying there in the summer of 2004, and to Karen Sands-O'Connor for inviting me to work with her on the Hollins study abroad program.

I am also indebted to Norchilit, the Nordic network for Ph.D. students, for allowing me to participate in workshops in Copenhagen, Denmark and in Kristiansand, Norway, both in 2003. The network's mission was to encourage young scholars by gathering them together and sharing ideas. At each workshop, students would present papers and then discuss these with the so-called "senior scholars." The latter also gave papers at these workshops. The one in Copenhagen is memorable for a couple of reasons not related directly to the workshop. First, this was still early days in the Iraq War, and, as I mentioned earlier, I remember attending an evening protest against the war. A large crowd gathered in the city centre, many carrying candles. The speakers I do not clearly remember, mostly because of the language, but I do clearly remember the sense of solidarity and peace that moved through the crowd. Second, this was the conference at which I was given the picture book about the small boy who refuses to defecate. He willfully constipates himself (have I just coined a verb?). Nina Christensen, director of the Children's Book Centre, assured me that the book was not really a gift; rather, the people at the Centre hated this book but did not want to throw it in the garbage. Then I arrived and they thought I would be the perfect person to have this book.

I know what you are thinking. But honestly, it was not really like that. You see, at that time I was experiencing fifteen minutes of fame because of a couple of articles I had published that dealt with the recurring presence of scatological material in books for the young. One of these essays is a chapter in a book that has the title "Coprophilia For Kids." The book this chapter appears in is *Youth Cultures*, and my chapter is nicely tucked away at the end where only the discerning or persevering few will find it. The other essay is on the Captain Underpants books and this one got some notice because it was first delivered as a conference plenary talk and then appeared in the *Children's Literature Association Quarterly*. Somehow Reuters got wind of this and a small notice of my work appeared on the internet. Next thing I know, I am receiving phone calls from around the world asking for interviews. For example, I got calls from Dublin, Vienna, Melbourne, Seattle, Winnipeg, London (England). Then *Parents Today* magazine called and asked for a face-to-face interview. When the interviewer showed up at my office, she was accompanied by a photographer who had spectacular equipment (in the context, I know how this sounds). When the interview appeared in the magazine, my picture occupied two-thirds of the page and one-third contained the "interview." The point in all this is twofold: fame is fleeting, and I received the gift from the Children's Book Centre in Copenhagen because they wished to get rid of an offensive book without having to destroy it.

While I am writing about workshops and residences, I should mention the three summers I spent as a visiting lecturer at Roehampton University in London. Those summers in Roehampton were gratifying. Twice I was by myself and once Frances came with me. The summer Frances came, the two of us saw a fox outside our window, right there in central London. These were summers when

I could spend time with good friends such as Liz Thiel, Kerry Mallan, John Stephens, Maria Nikolajeva, Irene Wise, and others. I also remember a wacky talk that Aidan Chambers gave, during which he schooled some Japanese women in the audience on their Japanese culture. The Roehampton experience is precious and I am grateful to have had the opportunity to work there. Other visiting professorships I held, briefly, were at the University of Puerto Rico, the University of Winnipeg, and of course Queensland University of Technology. These sojourns at universities were invaluable, especially in a time when most scholars spent their entire working life in just one institution. It is good to get the perspective of other places. I also spent a short time at the University of North Carolina, Charlotte.

I said this would be a short chapter, and it is. I might have mentioned the seventeen invited and plenary talks over the years that took me to such places as Cardiff, Princeton, Ciudad Real, Waco, Ningbo, Wellington, Guadalajara, and Aberdeen. It was a privilege to receive these invitations, and I just wish I could have done a better job at delivering myself of talks in these various places.

And while I am mentioning invited talks, I want to acknowledge the two invitations to Princeton University. On one of the occasions at Princeton, I was introduced by the venerable scholar, U. C. Knoepflmacher. This introduction has to be a highlight of my career. For one thing, Uli went on for what seemed to me a very long time, and he had obviously reviewed my vita assiduously. He mentioned not only my main publications, but also obscure items such as my short article on Marlene Dietrich and my foray into writing on music (Duane Eddy). But what floored me was the moment when Professor Knoepflmacher said he had walked in my footsteps for some years. In all honesty, this was an impossibly generous statement. Professor Knoepflmacher was, and will always be, a far more distinguished writer and critic than I am or will be. However, this introduction remains the closest I will ever be to hearing a eulogy after I am gone. Too bad I did not record it!

CHAPTER SEVENTEEN

Teaching

I have always said that the most important thing we do as academics is teach. We may get paid and promoted to publish and publish furiously, but most of what we publish reaches very few readers. Most of what we publish languishes in the pages of periodicals or gathers dust on the shelves of libraries. We reach far more people in our teaching. Just think of it. We teach roughly two hundred or more students every academic year (some academics teach twice this number each year). Multiply this two hundred by, say, thirty-five years of teaching and you get seven thousand students. This number constitutes a conservative estimate, and it may look small. But I can assure you that 95 percent of what we publish will never reach seven thousand readers. Perhaps that should be 100 percent. Seven hundred might be possible, but not seven thousand. Oh, yes, the top-line academics such as Frye or Bloom or Fish or Zipes may reach large numbers of people, but the great majority of academics are not top of the line. I certainly was not. And so teaching is crucial to what we do, especially if we believe what we do is of central importance to our polity. And not only is teaching crucial, but teaching undergraduates, and first-year undergraduates, is most crucial of all. I say this because over the years fewer and fewer senior professors chose to teach undergraduates. The emphasis is on graduate teaching, in promoting the profession through the manufacture of more Ph.D. people. Something narcissistic is happening when what matters is replication and replication only. But it's all right, Ma, its literature and literature only.

The reason undergraduate teaching is important is simple: we will not reach the majority of these students more than once or twice. If we are committed to our subject as a life-forming, as well as a life-enhancing, discipline, then we should want to carry this subject to those who will only briefly encounter it academically. The goal is to make what the current jargon likes to call lifelong learners. I give you an example. Years ago I had a student doing his honours thesis with me. This was a student who had genuine curiosity and an eagerness to gather in experiences books could offer. He went on to become a medical doctor. He now practises medicine in Calgary. He also writes at length about the books he reads and puts what he writes on the social network Goodreads, and has organized a local cinema group that screens films and then discusses them. This student evidences what we hope for when we teach our subject.

Do not misunderstand me. I am not suggesting that literature (or film, for that matter) makes people better than people who do not read. Urbanity is not assured by the reading of books, or even of good books, whatever these may be. However, I have been sufficiently immersed in what is sometimes called the "great books" tradition, what Matthew Arnold meant when he referred to the best that has been thought and said, to think that reading can be a civilizing activity, can lead to urbanity. I say "can be civilizing" because reading alone is no guarantee of civility or good manners. Just look at the profession I have worked in for many years. The professoriate contains bullies, boors, and downright bad people, just like any other group of people. But we cling to the notion that at least the possibility is there for refinement through books and through art. The creative gene seems somehow connected to the sensitivity gene; the two work in tandem much of the time. Why is this? For one thing, the great books tend to be life affirming and democratic in spirit. Yes, we have examples, plenty of examples, of writers in the canon who sit on the right in the political bleachers: Dante, Pope, Edmund Burke, Disraeli, Ezra Pound, T. S. Eliot, perhaps even the likes of Dickens and John Stuart Mill, Joyce, and Yeats. But some alchemy is at work that transforms most writers' work into something humanly positive. Take Eliot, for example. No writer has presented the human connection to time, place, past and present with more intensity and more vision than Eliot. His *Four Quartets* are as deeply visionary as anything by the avowedly leftist writers such as Blake or Shelley. I take the word "visionary" from Blake who used the word to identify his own work. By "vision" Blake seems to mean a comprehensive understanding of the importance of human imaginative activity, its enterprise in building (creating) the magnificent city of humanity, the place where each and every human being finds celebration, beauty, freedom, and equity. We can find such vision even in a short imagistic poem by the fascist, Ezra Pound:

> The apparition of these faces in the crowd;
> Petals on a wet, black bough.
> ("In a Station of the Metro," 1913)

The darkness of the underground filled with a crowd, with a number of faces flashing as if they were ghosts, or as if they are special, as indeed they are simply because they are human, representatives of the nameless gathering of people on this planet. This may be an underground, in more than one sense, filled with its ghostly presences, but the very delicacy, simplicity, and starkness of the language elevates both the place and the people. These are parts of a flower, a flowering humanity. They exist on the tree of life.

For another thing, the great books challenge readers; they elicit thought. I read, therefore I think. Reading without thinking is well-nigh impossible. I hesitate here because of course I can think of students who appeared to read and appeared also not to think. But this is harsh. Such students did not read. Reading is something we must learn to do; it does not come like the leaves on the trees. And by learn, I do not mean the activity of learning letters, of learning how to decode so that one can fill out a tax form or apply for a passport. Reading with attention to detail and with an eye for the idea, with a desire to grasp the implications of the word, with a sense of the rhythms possible in language—this constitutes reading. Reading carefully can affect our speech patterns in a positive manner. A good reader is unlikely to sprinkle her or his speech with "uh," "like," and "you know." Such speech stutters or crutches for a paucity of vocabulary recede the more comfortable we become with language.

And so I reiterate: getting them early is important. Undergraduate teaching is central to our mission as professors. I mean, what else is it that we profess but a love of language, and a love of the impetus graceful language gives to our thinking? We often use the word imagination when we speak of the benefits of reading, and imagination is nothing if not a constructive faculty. It allows us to build structures of words, and structures of words are what humanity relies on for its sense of purpose and meaning. Of course language is a communicative device, but it is more than simply that. In a similar vein, reading is communicative, but it is more than simply that. We communicate to fulfill mundane tasks such as to acquire goods and services, but we also communicate to create understanding and to provide fulfillment beyond daily needs such as food and shelter. Our reality depends upon structures of words.

As I write this, I think of the many who read scriptures of one kind or another and then call on these scriptures to sanctify certain behaviours and beliefs. I hope my sense of reading differs from this one-dimensional, self-serving, hopelessly deluded manner of reading. Reading in such a manner reminds me of Humpty Dumpty in Lewis Carroll's book. Humpty asks who is to be the master, the speaker or the words he or she speaks. Clearly, in Humpty's case, the speaker is or sets out to be the master, making words mean whatever he desires them to mean. This is how religious zealots approach the language of scripture, making it mean whatever they desire it to mean, or whatever serves their purposes. I like to think the other way of approaching language is preferable. Language is the master and submitting to its mastery is the only way to render us authoritative. Authoring means mastering the master. The author gains authority through submission to the rich heritage and grand possibility of language. I guess humility is one result. And humility ought to remind us that we are small and meek, like Dorothy and her three friends in *The Wizard of Oz*. That foursome gives us diversity in all its generous proportions. When we think the meek shall inherit the earth, our reading should remind us that all are meek. Even the great and powerful Oz is meek, lowly, humble. Reading ought to remind us that we are all in this together. Comfits for everyone after the race.

And so I taught mostly undergraduates during my time in the classroom. In the early years, we taught three courses per term, and one of these for me was invariably Children's Literature. A second course was a first-year course, most often over the years the first-year course in fiction, although for a while I taught composition until the department, in its wisdom or lack thereof, dropped the course from its offerings. For my third course I taught a variety of courses, mostly the course on Romantic literature. But over the years I also taught science fiction, fantasy, eighteenth-century literature, Victorian literature, poetry, literary theory, and film. My publications reflect this range of teaching; I have published articles on just about everything listed in my teaching, plus a few things not mentioned in my teaching.

A side note: late in my teaching career I began to teach film. I taught a course called Introduction to Film Studies and another on the history of popular cinema. Film has always been a passion of mine. When I arrived in Calgary in 1973, I met another young fellow who had just been hired as a sessional. This was Fred Shegda, who had come to Calgary from Yale University. Fred was working on the poet John Milton, but he had a deep interest in popular culture, comic books, and movies. He had organized the first comic book exhibition at the Beineke Library at Yale. Anyway, Fred and I struck up a friendship, largely based on our mutual interests in comics and film. We decided to make use of the extensive film library that the university had; it held a large number of historically crucial films, even though the university did not have a film course on offer in any department. We asked if we could screen a film every Thursday evening in our department lounge, but the film librarian said no, we could not, because the films could only be used for courses, not for personal interest. We reacted to this news by concocting a film course that did not exist; we gave it a number and a name. The librarian accepted this, no questions asked. We also sent a memo each week to members of the department. The memo came from what we called Snappy Productions, and it described each week's film. The idea was that anyone could attend the screening. Each week we showed up at the department lounge—four of us, Fred and I and our wives. We watched many films by Chaplin and Keaton. We also watched such classic films as *Greed, Intolerance, Battleship Potempkin, The Cabinet of Dr. Caligari, The Last Laugh, Nosferatu, Tabu, Nanook of the North, L'Age d'Or, Metropolis*, and *The Nibelungen*. We did watch sound films as well, films such as *Freaks, Coconuts*, and the Universal horror films of the early 1930s. This was an immersion in silent film and early sound film that has served me well.

Snappy Productions was shortlived. Many years passed and the university did not have courses on films. Only in the early 2000s did film become a part of the curriculum in the Faculty of General Studies. Then I found myself seconded by general studies to teach film. The Introduction to Film Studies has one class of about two hundred students per academic year. The technician who set things up for me was William Hageman; William later became a friend, one of the few I still had once I left the university. As for the students, they were different from students I was familiar with in literature classes. Teaching literature, I often had students who grumbled when they found a book or two on the reading list that they had read before (or at least had had on another course syllabus). Film students, on the other hand, tended to be eager to view a film they had seen before, especially if they had enjoyed the film the first time. In general, film students demonstrated enthusiasm more visibly than literature students. In other words, I enjoyed the experience teaching film.

I did not enjoy having to have student teaching evaluations. In fact, I object to the manner in which student evaluations are carried out; I think the institution encourages unethical behaviour in the matter of evaluation. We tell students that they have the opportunity to say whatever they want to say about their instructors, without being held responsible for what they say. Their evaluations are anonymous. And believe me, they take advantage of this anonymity to say cruel things. Of course some students praise their instructors, others say inconsequential things (e.g., he or she wears colourful clothes), a few are constructive, and then there are the ones who say things such as "a case for Alcoholics Anonymous," or "this person should be shucking peas." More often than not, comments correspond to grades students receive. How do I know this? Well, some students actually admit to this. Others one can identify or used to be able to identify when essays were handwritten, by their handwriting. In any case, the message the university gives students is that they can say whatever they wish without being accountable. As far as I am concerned, this is irresponsible on the part of the university.

Besides, these evaluations do not do what they, ostensibly, set out to do: improve teaching. Over the years, I have seen the diminishment of the traditional lecture, replaced by group work and other sorts of projects. Nowadays we see the attempt to incorporate the latest technology into classrooms, instructors going so far as to employ the cell phone for taking questions from the students. For all the so-called innovation, class attendance continues to decline. Aside from the stand-up routine, nothing seems to work to catch students' attention or interest. Ideas and a love of language no longer cut it as a means to classroom attendance and participation. I say participation because the Socratic method remains the best method for learning. Question-and-answer and discussion are what work, at least in my subject, but these will only work when students are engaged and when they come to class prepared. Too often, in my experience, students come to class without having read the material.

I need to pause here because I was a student who cut classes many times and I also came to class unprepared many times. The difference, I think, between myself and students like me and the students I faced has to do with genuine hunger for learning.

Today's students are eager to get on with life, to get a job, and to enjoy the consumerist life beyond academe. Many have jobs while they are at university and find themselves stretched for time. They come to class tired and anxious for rest. They see their studies as a means to an end rather than an end in themselves. I do not recall spending much energy thinking about what I would do with my life when I was a student. And I did not work in term time. Things now are immediate; students look for immediate gratification. For the most part, they show little curiosity about the past or the connection between the past and the present, especially in popular culture. And students have influence in a way they once did not. One example of this is grade inflation. When I began to teach, grades were distributed across the spectrum from A to F. Over the years, for a variety of reasons, this distribution has shrunk towards the middle and upper letters. My university, in its annual calendar, has a graphic listing the grades and what they signify. In this graphic, a C grade has the word "Satisfactory" beside it. B has the words "Clearly above average" as its descriptor. As for A, this grade is deemed "Superior." Now to my mind, if a C is satisfactory and a B clearly above average, then this means that the average grade will be in the range of C to B–. However, it is clear that this is not the case. B has become the default grade, the grade handed to the majority of students. And more students will receive a grade in the A range than receive a grade below B–.

One reason for this upward shift in grades has to do with the emphasis on grades over and above reference letters. I would never have made it into graduate school on the strength of my grades; had I been applying to graduate school in the past twenty years or so, I would not have found acceptance. My grades were insufficient. But I had referees who believed in me and this made all the difference. Nowadays, grades are the most important part of an applicant's file. This usually means anything less than a B+ will not be good enough. Consequently, students are fixated on their grades; it is quite common for a student to state that he or she has failed when they receive a C grade. It is also quite common for students to come to the office and ask that you raise their grade, and they give you the grade they want. It is as if they think: I paid for this education, and I want to get rewarded for paying. They might wish to get acceptance into law school or medical school and they need A–; they boldly—no, blithely—say they want the instructor to raise whatever grade they have to an A–. This request for a raise in grades happens too often for the request not to be successful some of the time. A student will say that she needs a grade of A– to be accepted into law school. Since she has a B, why not simply raise this to A– and let her get on with her life. To this student, the letters are meaningless in themselves; what matters is whether she has passed and if she has then she ought to be allowed to continue on the path she has chosen. Dealing with this sort of pressure on a regular basis is enervating. I am sure some instructors simply give up. After all, the institution looks with suspicion on the instructor who gives grades that conform to the C-is-average dictum. What the institution wants is student success and success is measured in As and Bs, not Cs and Ds. In other words, the institution is complicit in grade inflation.

The education system right from elementary school lets students believe that they can succeed whether or not they have the ability to succeed. I note the case of the Edmonton high school teacher who was fired for giving a student zero on an assignment the student did not submit; the teacher's name is Lyndon Dorval, and he was suspended in 2012. This is crazy, yet this is where we are in the education system. Mr. Dorval was later reinstated, but what happened to him is a sign of the times. (See for example: https://edmontonsun.com/2014/12/12/lynden-dorval-teacher-who-was-fired-for-giving-out-zeros-cleared-for-charges-of-unprofessional-conduct.) Remember that graduate student who proudly said, "And I still don't know what a dangling modifier is." We seem to value failure: there is no success like failure because failure is actually success after all, to rephrase Bob Dylan again. As I write, we are in the throes of an election campaign in the United States, and one of the leading candidates has recently remarked that he "loves the poorly educated." Yes, everyone loves the idiot. Just look at the success of the film, *Forrest Gump* (1994). The present generation of students, for the most part, appear to value money and position over knowledge and curiosity.

And what about graduate teaching? Over the years I did teach graduate classes, and I can note that one of the most gratifying classes I ever taught was a graduate class, and I taught it the year before I retired from teaching. On the whole, however, teaching graduate students did not thrill me. For one thing, these students find their way into graduate school because they are already interpellated, or, as the academy prefers to say, they are already professionalized. They are guarded in the way undergraduates are not. They have assimilated assumptions and therefore are more difficult to challenge and to move out of their comfort zone in what they think. I have written earlier about the sense of privilege many academics possess, and this sense of privilege, this notion of entitlement begins as early as graduate school (if not before).

Mind you, the young students are not the root of the problem; we need to look to the institution and its manner of doing business (a word I use deliberately here). When I applied for a job in the university, I had a c.v. (curriculum vita) that was half a page long. It listed my education, the focus of my Ph.D. research, and the names of my referees. That was it. Today, a c.v. like mine would receive nothing but ridicule. Students graduating with a Ph.D. now regularly have conference papers, articles in journals, book reviews, and not uncommonly a book or two to grace their vitae. Does this mean that today's graduates are somehow better than those of my generation and earlier? I don't think so. More often than not, the work these students publish is hasty and unpolished. Critical and scholarly writing takes time to percolate. Writing should not be rushed. It needs time and long and deep thought. A minority of students can produce valuable contributions early in their academic lives, the majority cannot.

CHAPTER EIGHTEEN
Storytelling

In 1984, I attended a conference in Charlotte, North Carolina. One evening we had a storytelling concert with renowned storyteller Donald Davis. I vividly recall that evening and the thrill I felt listening to Davis's stories. He was one person standing on a wide stage, no props, no costume, and no special effects. I was entranced for just about two hours, and I am usually not a good listener. He was not a stand-up comic and he did not rely on racy or profane language. He simply told stories, a mixture of family stories and folk tales. Leaving the theatre, I looked at a woman next to me, someone I did not know, and said to her: "I can do that." The moment I said this was the moment I began my ten years or so as a storyteller. I returned home and offered to tell a story at my daughter Kyla's summer day care. If not a triumph, this was at least successful enough for me to think of continuing to tell stories, and I called the public school board and offered my services as a storyteller. That fall I began to receive phone calls from various schools asking if I would come and tell stories. At the beginning, I was more than a bit naïve. I thought I could offer my services gratis; this was something I could do and I thought the activity was important. But I had a good day job and so I thought of my storytelling as a sort of volunteer work. It was fun for me (most of the time). I felt a commitment to the oral tradition, thinking this was important for both family and community solidarity. Storytelling was a way of passing on an enthusiasm for both language and narrative that did not require the skill of reading. Consequently, when I was asked, as I always was, how much I charged, I invariably said nothing. Well, nothing will come of nothing, and I learned to speak again.

More often than not, when I arrived at a school I would go to the office and announce my arrival. Again more often than not, I was met with puzzlement. Once I was even asked what I was selling (those were the days when anyone could enter a school unannounced). When I explained who I was and why I was at the school, I would be told to go to such and such a room where the teacher who had invited me was. I would find the room and quietly indicate I was there. The teacher would instruct me to wait in the hall until she (I cannot recall many male teachers) was ready for me. I would wait. Finally the teacher would come out to the hall and say I could go in; then she would walk away down the hall leaving the class to me. She took the opportunity for a break. I experienced this treatment for a year or maybe two before I became disgruntled. Aretha Franklin sang my theme song.

Then one morning the phone rang in my office. I answered and heard the usual invitation: could I come to a certain school (it was, in fact, King Edward Elementary School) for the morning and tell stories to two or three classes. I said yes. Next came the question: how much did I charge? I replied: "Three hundred dollars." What surprised me was the response: "Fine." That was it. I was going to get $300 for two or three hours work—well, hardly work, just telling stories. What happened next was the kicker. When I arrived at the school, the teacher who had invited me was waiting on the school steps. She took me in and introduced me to the office staff before taking me into the teacher's lounge where she made more introductions and offered me coffee and a muffin. Suddenly I had become important. When we went to see the students, we went to the library. Students filed in and sat politely. Then the teacher introduced me, and she stayed for the performance. On my way out, she handed me an envelope with a cheque for $300. My days as a professional storyteller had begun.

And herein lies the problem with our society. No one seems to value that which they do not have to pay for. From that time forward, I received money for storytelling performances. Soon I was asked to do workshops, and I did, but very poorly. I tried giving a course on storytelling at a local senior's centre, but this too did not go well. I could perform stories, but I could not instruct others in how to do this activity. But I kept on performing at schools, seniors' homes, festivals, and conferences. It was not long before people asked for a card, then a brochure, and then a tape. I had none of this stuff. What I had envisaged at the beginning was simply offering myself freely as a storyteller in order to help perpetuate what I thought was a valuable communal and familial activity. I did not wish to have this activity caught up in the whole celebrity mindset of our culture. I winced when kids would ask for my autograph after a school session and I cringed when teachers asked if I had a book they could access. The thinking was that the storyteller was somehow special, and my whole idea was that the storyteller was not special; he or she was anyone with a story to share freely. This was a way of bringing people together in a sharing and comfortable atmosphere. Story was a way of strengthening the language and of passing on traditions. Over time, I grew weary of the emphasis on money and dramatics. I realized that many storytellers used props and costumes and even musical instruments to make their stories flashy and entertaining. As for me, I wanted just a group of people seated comfortably; nothing else other than a willingness to share. Early on, I did try to use props. My friend Victor Ramraj made a few things for me: a Styrofoam hand with removable fingers and a great Bristol board catfish. I much appreciated Victor's interest and help. But I soon found that children could take or leave such things, and I stopped using them. What mattered most was my interaction with the audience.

This meant that I did not mind interruption, as long as it was participatory interruption and not disruptive. Teachers often fretted and interfered when a student would interrupt a story with a question or an assertion, but questions did not bother me. In fact, such interaction struck me as crucial to the experience of story. Storytelling is not a one-person show. It is communal, participatory, and spontaneous. At least this is how I thought of it. And I learned that audience reaction was not always self-evident. I recall one time when I was in a junior high classroom telling stories. I could not help but notice a kid at the back of the room who was constantly stretching and writhing and generally looking as if he wanted to be anywhere but here. He was not disruptive because the other kids could not see him at the back and he did not make noise; he simply writhed. But I could see him and he was not a little disturbing to my sense of success. I assumed he was bored. Then, after I finished with stories and the teacher asked the students if they had any questions, this kid's hand shot up. He had a question, and although I no longer remember what this question was, I do remember that it indicated he had heard and taken in everything I had said. In other words, despite appearances, he was attentive and receptive.

Experiences such as the one I have just recounted were useful to me. Here is another one. Again the phone rang in my office. I answered and on the other end was a Mrs. Smart from Catherine Nichols Gunn School in east Calgary. Mrs. Smart (this was, in fact, her name) asked if I would come to her kindergarten class for an afternoon. Now the younger the audience, the less comfortable I was. My preference was for a mature audience or an audience that contained both young and old together. The thought of a whole afternoon with a room full of five-year-old children scared me. I said I would not come for the afternoon, but I would come for twenty or thirty minutes. Mrs. Smart said she hoped I would stay longer, but we could see how things went once I got there. And so I went with not a little trepidation. Mrs. Smart taught her class of some fifteen kids in a portable classroom. So we were sequestered away from other school distractions. The kids were attentive and I found the time flying by. After about an hour, we stopped for a snack. After the snack I told a few more stories and before I knew it the afternoon was over. School was out. The real lesson came about ten days or two weeks later when a packet came in the mail from Mrs. Smart. She had had the students make drawings of the stories they remembered me telling, and then she transcribed their comments. I still have this packet. Among the comments, I read such things as, "Mr. McGillis tells good stories. My father does not tell stories, he gets drunk and kicks the TV," and "I like Mr. McGillis's stories. My mother does not tell stories because she works all the time," and "My father does not tell stories, he is in jail." And so on. What I was hearing was that my stories, even ones that contained decapitated ghosts and a cat that carried its head in its mouth (!), served a purpose; they were safe and they created a community in which the kids could feel comfortable and welcome. This was a profoundly important lesson for me.

As years passed, I began to write some of the stories I told, and what transpired fascinated me. Once I had written a story, I found difficulty telling it. I could not remember the words, and the words were now more important than they had appeared to be previously. Before writing the story, it had existed as a series of pictures I would see in my mind and describe. The words, although obviously important, were not fixed; they could change from telling to telling. Of course, certain phrases remained stable because they were a mnemonic, but much of the narrative was *extempore*. The spontaneity went out of the telling once the words were on paper.

I tried to read manuals, guides to telling stories, but these, with the exception of one by Jack Zipes, proved less than helpful to me. And I began to find it more difficult to prepare new stories. For a variety of reasons I began to lose contact with storytelling. I realized that when I went to a school or any other venue, I was taking the place of someone who was trying to make a living telling stories. As I said, I did not need the money and I did not want to make the effort at self-promotion that the activity called for—the cards, brochures, and tapes. Perhaps I simply did not have what it takes to become a real storyteller. My time as a performer lasted about ten years, and during this time I told stories on the radio and in various countries and for audiences of all ages. At its peak, my storytelling performances numbered just about once a week for a year. Then it came to a halt. Since about 1996, I have told stories only once in a while.

CHAPTER NINETEEN
Retirement

In 2011, at the age of sixty-six, I retired from the university. You might remember my leaving Port Hope High School way back in the early summer of 1970. I left without fanfare. So too did I leave the university where I taught for thirty-eight years—without fanfare. Once I had made the decision to retire, the head of my department contacted Frances to ask what I might like for a retirement gift. This was supposed to be secret, but Frances asked me and I said they could use any money for a get-together. The other person retiring at the same time indicated that she did not wish to have a retirement party, and so the decision was made not to hold a party. So Frances asked me again what I might like as a parting gift from the department. I responded with precision. I wanted a brand new silver watch and chain, and I wanted a sentiment on the back. The sentiment was to read: "Professor McGillis, from C Troop. Lest We Forget." Anyone who has seen the John Ford/John Wayne film *She Wore a Yellow Ribbon* will know what I was alluding to.

That was in the spring of 2011. In the fall of that year, I was asked to vacate my office. One day, as I was packing boxes, the head of department appeared at my door. This was a person who had assumed the headship only a couple of months earlier. Anyway, he appeared at my door carrying a small gift bag. I looked and he began a conversation.

"I've got something for you."

"Oh. What's in the bag?"

"I have no idea. I didn't buy it."

"Okay, put it on the desk please."

And so, he placed the gift bag on the desk, and left. Curiosity got the better of me and I peeked in the bag. I found a card signed by about ten of my colleagues in the department, at least one of whom was unfamiliar to me. The bag also contained a box. In the box was a book on Swiss watches and some other promotional material and a silver watch and chain. I checked the back of the watch to see the sentiment. What I found was the engraving of a train, a replica of a train that travels up the Jungfrau in Switzerland. I knew what was implied. For many years I had taught the Romantic poets, and one of these was famous for his connection with the Jungfrau. John Martin had painted one of Byron's characters, Manfred, on the Jungfrau. In the first place, Byron was the Romantic poet I had the least enthusiasm for. In the second place, the head of department who had purchased this gift had known me long enough, I think, to know of the relationship I had had with my father. And my father was a railroader. As long as I knew him, he worked for the CPR. He was connected with trains. And so my reaction on receiving this gift for serving the department and university for thirty-eight years was mixed. Sure, it is a lovely watch and probably worth much money, but it also resonates with my past in a manner I do not appreciate.

That was over ten years ago. In those years, we have lived mainly in British Columbia. And writing and reading continue to be a way of life. I have done a lot of bike riding, and both Frances and myself have experienced reminders of our mortality. In my case, this reminder came in form of a pulmonary embolism I experienced in April of 2014. In Frances's case, this reminder came in the form of a blockage in an artery to the heart; she had a stent implanted in the summer of 2015. Later that same year, we traveled to Chile and Argentina and took a cruise to Cape Horn, following in the wake of Charles Darwin. We continue to travel towards the next hill. Growing old ain't for the faint of heart, but as I said at the outset, for the most part we have been in fat city living the life of Riley. Ha, anyone reading this is unlikely to catch the drift here. Suffice to say, the ride has been comfortable.

I will end, if I may, with one more story. This deals with life in the small village of Nakusp, B.C. We have had a place here since 1997, but we moved there permanently after we both retired (2011–2012). Nakusp is an old logging community, or was in the heyday of the lumber industry, and owning a chainsaw was common, if not obligatory. Frances suggested I would be better off without a chainsaw; she feared I would sever an arm or leg. However, on a trip to the city, I happened to see an electric chainsaw on sale in Canadian Tire. I couldn't resist and I bought the thing and took it back to our place in the woods. Once there I got ready to try my new chainsaw. As I opened the box, I noticed in small letters on the side of the box the words, "Battery Not Included." I hopped in the truck and drove to Marvin's Small Motors just off the main street of Nakusp. This place sold chainsaws and lawn mowers, and other such items. I walked in. Off to one side a couple of men were in deep conversation. Behind the counter was a formidable woman who asked if she could help.

"I hope so," I said. "I would like to purchase a battery for my chainsaw."

"Chainsaws don't take batteries," she replied.

The two men off to one side stopped talking, and one of them moved closer to me and asked if there was some trouble.

"No," I said. "I'm just looking for a battery for my chainsaw."

"Chainsaws don't take batteries," he said, echoing the woman behind the counter.

"Mine does," I offered.

"Okay," he said, "if you go out the door and turn right and go to main street, you will find just a block to the west a store called Lester's Hobbies. I suggest you try there."

In other words, he was telling me that I had a chainsaw toy. Nonplussed, I did manage to find a battery for the thing on a trip to the Canadian Tire store in Castlegar.

At that time, I was a member of the village Rotary club, and about a week after my experience in Marvin's Small Motors, I went early one morning to the weekly Rotary breakfast meeting. I entered the room and took a seat beside an older fellow known as Diamond Jim. As soon as I was seated, Jim gave me a friendly knock with his elbow, and said, "I hear you got yourself a chainsaw." He had a mischievous glint in his eye.

Somehow, this story takes me back to my beginnings in Smiths Falls and the clothesline that finally got fixed.

CHAPTER TWENTY

Wrapping Up, or an Endless Ending

If you have made it this far, you deserve an addendum in which I readjust the title. Wordsworth may have outlined the "growth" of a poet's mind, but I confess I have not done the same for an academic's mind. What I have done is try to pass on some of my experiences of academia and how I got there. In doing so, I have neglected to mention many people important in my time as a university professor. I would like to mention the neglected here: Norma Bagnall, Marilyn Olsen, Lois Kuznets, Alethia Helbig, David Russell, Elaine Showalter, Roberta Trites, Joseph Thomas, Nancy Huse, Michael Joseph, Jan Alberghene, and Mia Österlund. No doubt I have forgotten others. To offer anecdotes about those I list would take many more pages, and I have tried your patience enough. Suffice to say that some of these good persons are no longer with us, while the others remain; all are with me in thought.

I suppose all things must end. I know, the old saying is that "all good things must end," but it behooves me to drop the "good." It also behooves me to say that nothing ever ends, as Dr. Manhattan informs Adrian Veidt. Everything passes, everything changes, and we do what think we should do. Someday baby, well who knows what comes next?

FINIS—for now

Endnote

Bill Readings published *The University in Ruins* in 1996, and he examined the changes that were taking place in universities including the shift of a university education to a jobs-oriented focus. In what I write in this memoir, I make silent reference to *The University in Ruins* and to other similar examinations of the university that chronicle the changes within the institution over the years. Yes, I am critical of the institution in several ways. And yet a university education remains crucial for an enlightened citizenry. There is little that can equal a liberal education in preparing a person for the slings and arrows that one must dodge getting through this earthly life. As much as I found things to unsettle me during my working life, I also found a way of life unique in its satisfactions, satisfactions that include a schedule largely self-plotted, an ability to interact with stimulating people both students and colleagues, a solitude and refuge from the cold world. Light shines from the Ivory Tower, a light that just might reach the world beyond in salutary and bracing ways—if we keep striving, striving, striving.

About the Author

Roderick McGillis grew up in a small town in the Ottawa Valley. He is now a retired Professor of English, having taught at the University of Calgary for thirty-eight years. He is the author of five books: the novel, *Les Pieds Devant* (2007), the award-winning *The Nimble Reader: Literary Theory and Children's Literature* (1996), *A Little Princess: Gender and Empire* (1996), *He Was Some Kind of a Man: Masculinities in the B Western* (2009), and *Around the Block; or the Tricks of Memory* (2021). He has edited or co-edited another ten books. In 1997, he received the Anne Devereaux Jordan Award for distinguished service to children's literature, and in 2002 he received the Distinguished Scholarship Award from the International Association for the Fantastic in the Arts. That same year, 2002, he received the President's Circle Award for Excellence in Research and Creativity from the University of Calgary. He has been president of the Children's Literature Association, and he served as editor of that association's journal (*ChLA Quarterly*) for four years.

www.ingramcontent.com/pod-product-compliance
Lightning Source LLC
Chambersburg PA
CBHW022203090526
44583CB00012BA/255